D1570387

A Way of Work and a Way of Life

NUMBER NINE
Texas A&M Southwestern Studies
Robert A. Calvert and Larry D. Hill,
General Editors

A Way of Work and a Way of Life

Coal Mining in Thurber, Texas, 1888–1926

Marilyn D. Rhinehart

Texas A&M University Press
College Station

The paper used in this book meets the minimum requirements
of the American National Standard for Permanence
of Paper for Printed Library Materials, Z39.48-1984.
Binding materials have been chosen for durability.

Library of Congress Cataloging-in-Publication Data
Rhinehart, Marilyn D., 1948–
    A way of work and a way of life : coal mining
in Thurber, Texas, 1888–1926 / Marilyn D.
Rhinehart. — 1st ed.
        p.   cm. — (Texas A&M southwestern
studies ; no. 9)
    Includes bibliographical references and index.
    ISBN 0-89096-499-8 (alk. paper)
    1. Coal miners—Texas—Thurber—History.
    2. Coal mines and mining—Texas—Thurber—
History. I. Title. II. Series.
HD8039.M615R47   1992
338.2'724'09764551—dc20   91-35907
                                            CIP

FOR MY PARENTS
Emmett O. Dubberly and the late Rebekah Lane Dubberly,
who taught me that honest work
is honorable work.

Contents

Illustrations

Tables

Acknowledgments

The encouragement and assistance of many persons made this work possible. James C. Maroney suggested the topic, generously shared some of his own research and ideas on the subject, and critiqued the manuscript. John O. King assumed the responsibility, under unexpected circumstances, for overseeing the project out of which this book developed and smoothly guided that effort to completion. Profs. Stanley E. Siegel, Bailey S. Stone, and Joseph Pratt at the University of Houston agreed to read the manuscript and, in conjunction with Professor King, made numerous valuable suggestions. Ron Brown at Southwest Texas State University and George N. Green at the University of Texas at Arlington likewise evaluated the manuscript and offered advice that made the work publishable.

The interlibrary loan staffs at the University of Houston and North Harris College facilitated research in material to which I otherwise would not have had easy or any access. David Murrah and his staff at the Southwest Collection at Texas Tech University took every opportunity to make my research on Thurber in the voluminous Texas & Pacific Coal Company records a lot easier, including microfilming ledgers, seeking and reproducing photographs, photocopying material, and allowing me to work in a "user-friendly" environment. Janet Neugebauer and former Southwest Collection staff members Richard Mason and Michael Q. Hooks were particularly helpful. Trudy Carlson, education librarian at the Dick Smith Library, Tarleton State University, helped me wade through volumes of Erath County records and uncovered original copies of the coal company's newspaper (printed in Thurber) that I did not know still existed. Staff members at the University of Texas at Austin Barker Texas History Center and the Oklahoma Historical Society Archives Division also lent special assistance during the project, as did Jane Boley at the Texas Labor Archives at the University of Texas at Arlington. Tony Black at the Texas State Archives facilitated my research in the massive Adjutant General Records there, and Jan Hart, formerly at the University of Texas at Arlington, made it possible for Jim Maroney and me to meet and interview William K. Gordon, Jr., whose father played such an important part in Thurber's history. I am especially thankful to Mr. Gordon for his generous willingness to share some of his father's business correspondence with Jim, Jan, and me, so that the story of Thurber's miners might be told more completely. His efforts to encourage public interest in the community's history have helped keep alive the memory of the town and those who lived there.

I am fortunate that over the years both professional and amateur historians have interviewed many who worked and lived in Thurber and have preserved these oral histories, most of which are in the Southwest Collection. Their stories give life to this study and have enabled me to understand the unique camaraderie that they shared. Almost anyone who knows anything about Thurber can still sense, on viewing the landscape around what was once a thriving community, what life must have been like in the days when the train carried hundreds of miners speaking a multitude of languages to and from the mines.

I owe a special debt to friend and former colleague Vernon L. Williams, now at Abilene Christian University, who took many hours from his own busy schedule to teach me the language of computers and to run almost 150 statistical analyses of census data for this study. I appreciate the effort of George B. Ward and the staff at the *Southwestern Historical Quarterly* to make possible my first published work on Thurber, "'Underground Patriots': Thurber Coal Miners and the Struggle for Individual Freedom, 1888–1903," which appeared in volume 92 (April, 1989), pp. 509–42. I further appreciate their granting permission for me to use portions of the article throughout the first four chapters but most particularly in chapter 4, where I discuss labor difficulties in Thurber.

Direct quotes are used throughout this book. In an attempt to preserve their authenticity, I retained misspellings and variations of names as they appear in the original sources.

To my fellow historians and friends at North Harris College I must say a special thank you for their encouragement and interest. The members of my family, Kenny, Rachel, and Brooks, also deserve a word of gratitude for their sacrifices in my behalf and for never asking why I was writing about coal miners. Finally, I am indebted to the late George T. Morgan, Jr., with whom I began this study and whose own work served as an inspiration to me.

Introduction

In his study of iron- and cotton-worker protest in nineteenth-century New York, Daniel J. Walkowitz argues that "to begin to understand workingclass behavior we must be city-specific, industry-specific and skill-specific."[1] At the local level, David Montgomery correspondingly states in his own evaluation of labor studies, "working-class life flourished."[2] Since the pioneer work in the 1960s of Herbert Gutman and other North American labor scholars (whom English writers such as Edward P. Thompson and Eric Hobsbawm heavily influenced), an increasing number of labor historians have chosen the local scene and specific industries for intensive examination. In contrast to the "old school" of labor history associated with John R. Commons's Wisconsin school of labor economists, these more recent studies treat the labor union movement as only one component of the workers' experience. The "new" labor history focuses on all aspects of working-class life, both on and off the job, to understand better the context of worker behavior.[3] The result has been an outpouring of illuminating studies that tell us more about the demographic makeup of worker communities and the importance of the culture of an occupation, family and social life, and the habits that shaped everyday events and patterns of protest. At center stage throughout is the worker.

The work that follows attempts to synthesize the old and the new labor history while analyzing and narrating the story of a coal-mining, company-owned town in turn-of-the-century North Central Texas. Located about halfway between Fort Worth and Abilene, Thurber rose up from the dusty, brush-covered hills where Erath, Palo Pinto, and Eastland counties met. The town itself sat in Erath County, just twenty miles or so from the county seat at Stephenville. The Texas and Pacific Railroad, the primary market for the bituminous coal that lay beneath the surface on which Thurber developed, ran east and west about three miles to the north of the original village. For many years after the town's appearance there in the 1880s, travelers regarded the growing industrial community as one of the few outposts of civilization on the Texas frontier that spread west from Fort Worth to El Paso. Owned by a corporation financed largely by New Yorkers, the town of Thurber, Texas, housed a large immigrant population and experienced many of the same growing pains in its forty years of operation as did more well known mining communities in other parts of the country. At the same time, it displayed a certain uniqueness, not just in Texas, but among other mining communities nationwide; by the 1910s, that uniqueness afforded it the status of a model unionized company town.

One of the most articulate members of Thurber's mining community was Welsh immigrant Gomer Gower. In 1945, Gower, then an elder statesman in the United Mine Workers' Union in Oklahoma, reminisced about his turn-of-the-century experiences in the coal-mining town. Alluding to wartime resistance fighters in Europe, Gower wrote: "We, too, had our underground forces [in Thurber]." And, he said, "it was due to the silent and patient activity of this band of underground patriots that Thurber was transformed from a 'Bull-Pen' in its early history, into one of the most pleasant mining communities in the entire country."[4]

At the time Gower wrote his recollections, little physical evidence remained to indicate that in its heyday over a thousand miners had lived and toiled in Thurber. Yet the memories of life there ran deep, and in the more than forty years since Gower's statement, interest in Thurber has hardly waned. Gower himself spent some thirty-five years in or around the town, working as a miner, labor agitator, local union officer, weighmaster, mine foreman, and mine superintendent. He also reared a family and, with a keen eye, observed the vicissitudes of life and labor in a community owned solely by one company.[5]

Gower typified the first coal diggers who sought work in the rural North Central Texas site, where a narrow bituminous coal vein cut through the terrain. Born in South Wales in 1869, he emigrated to the United States at age eleven with his parents, Thomas and Eliza. Thomas Gower, a coal miner by occupation, first settled his family in Illinois in 1880, but in pursuit of more steady work moved them to Indian Territory and then to northern Texas, where a son-in-law dug coal. The younger Gower learned the mining trade and the power of union organization at his father's side.[6]

His memories of Thurber in its infancy as a "Bull-Pen" (the town probably reminded him of a cattle pen where people were treated like animals) and of the protest activity of "underground patriots" indicate in the simplest of terms that adverse working and living conditions there produced a protest movement with far-reaching consequences. Indeed, the 1903 United Mine Workers' organization of the miners employed by the Texas & Pacific Coal Company, after fifteen years of periodic labor unrest, is certainly the most dramatic and recounted episode in the community's history.[7] It was not, however, the only indicator of workers' response to life in a company town. Every day they adapted to company rules, and the company likewise adapted to their patterns of life and particular needs.

This study of Thurber cannot and does not presume to tell the complete story of industrial life and protest in late nineteenth- and early twentieth-century America or Texas; however, the careful and discriminating utilization of available sources and the placement of one mining community in the context of a nation and state in the throes of industrialization can offer the reader, as did Walkowitz's study of Cohoes and Troy, New York, a "window into the complex world of local particularities that influence protest patterns."[8] It can also provide a better and more complete view of who unionized or nonunionized industrial workers were, particularly the often-overlooked industrial employees in the Southwest, what mundane and spectacular events filled their lives, and the manner in which they controlled and shaped their existence both on and off the job. In this way, the study that follows endeavors to complement and expand previous accounts of Thurber, Texas, and its colorful coal-mining population.

A Way of Work and a Way of Life

I

Laying the Foundation

*On the surface, there is nothing in the region of the Palo
Pinto Mountains to invite human activities. The winding,
barren hills have stood for centuries as frowning sentinels
over waste places where the wolf and the cougar could
scarce make shift for a living. The stunted post oak and
black jack that fringed the red colored ridges were the
only evidences it gave of even scant fertility. He would
have been a bold dreamer who . . . would have dared to
predict that in the heart of such a scene would arise the
most important and most successful industrial enterprise
now in operation in Texas.*
— E. G. Senter

In 1888, the United States Geological
cal Survey (USGS) first reported the potential for commercial production of bituminous coal in the carboniferous coal beds running through
the isolated and desolate western fringe of North Central Texas. "Probably the most important enterprise which has been organized in the
State for mining coal," the USGS prophetically noted, "is that of the
Texas and Pacific Coal Company, which owns about 25,000 acres of coal
land in Palo Pinto and Erath counties." In the fall of that survey year,
the Texas & Pacific Coal Company had purchased the financially insol-
vent Johnson Coal Mining Company to tap the market created by the
burgeoning railroad industry. Ten years later *Texas Farm and Ranch*
enthusiastically concluded that "the establishment and successful operation of the coal mines and collateral industries . . . of Thurber is,
undoubtedly, the greatest industrial achievement ever witnessed in Texas
[and] proof indisputable . . . of the industrial possibilities of Texas."[1]
In the process, the company also spawned the community of Thurber,
which in terms of population, economic significance, and ethnic diversity rivaled coal-mining centers in other parts of the country by the
early twentieth century.

As exaggerated as the article's evaluation of Thurber's importance to the industrialization process in Texas appeared, the author made a valid point. Coal mining literally fueled America's industrial transformation. In Texas as elsewhere coal production did represent potential, because it made other industrial growth possible. Thus, a study of a coal town provides a special vantage point from which to view the industrialization process and its far-reaching effects on a society and those who lived in it. Entrepreneurs in Texas early appreciated the significance of coal deposits to the state's, the region's, and the investor's economic future. Workers likewise recognized the stake they held in the success of such enterprises and aggressively asserted their notions of what constituted good work and fair pay.

Although the Johnson effort first attracted the attention of state and national geologists and large investors hoping to seize the commercial opportunity created by the railroad's fuel demands, coal mining was not unknown in Erath County and nearby Palo Pinto County before the mid-1880s. Texas state geologist Dr. B. F. Shumard described the state's coal formations in 1860, and for years local residents extracted coal from the coal veins for personal use. As early as 1882, the USGS announced that promising fields existed in both Palo Pinto and Erath counties, but because the state had conducted no geological survey of its own, the full extent of the coal formation remained unclear. Future prospects, the survey concluded, were good, however, because "the railroads are now penetrating the [known] coal formations . . . , and this great source of wealth will soon doubtless be rapidly developed." Considering that the closest commercial coal resources were 625 miles away in Indian Territory, the existence of those reserves assumed an even greater significance.[2]

The railroads, so anxious to see the development of the state's coal reserves, apparently even offered rewards for the discovery of coal along their lines. Jay Gould's Texas and Pacific Railroad demonstrated a particular interest in coal resources in Erath, Palo Pinto, and surrounding counties by 1880, when management extended the line west of Fort Worth into the sparsely populated Texas frontier. For several years, the railroad even operated its own mines near Gordon at Coalville in Palo Pinto County, approximately eight miles from the site where the Johnson Company sank its first shaft in 1886. The poor quality of the coal and labor problems in the area, however, posed too great a handicap for continued operation of the mines, resulting in their closing in 1886.[3]

The existence of labor unions and reports of labor unrest in Erath

4

and Palo Pinto counties further indicated the extent of mining operations in the area by mid-decade. Coal miners established a local assembly of the Knights of Labor as early as 1882, and within three years
claimed a membership of over 200. The United States commissioner
of labor included in his summary of labor difficulties in the nation for
1884 a 186-day-long strike at Gordon by 450 coal miners and laborers.[4]

If the latter is accurate, particularly in the number of miners employed in Gordon, considerable mining activity must have preceded
the Johnson enterprise. The report also suggests that a significant number of skilled and union-organized miners already populated Palo Pinto
County when the Johnson company began operations, and that they
played a central role in the industrial development and shaping of
employee-employer relations there throughout the last decade of the
nineteenth century.

Although complete coal production figures for Erath County in the
1880s are not available, the yearly USGS reports indicate the growing
importance of coal removal in Texas by the end of that ten-year period.
The USGS listed no coal production (outside of local and colliery consumption) for Texas before 1883, but for that and the following year
the agency estimated production at 100,000 tons. By 1885, this amount
had risen 30 percent.[5]

Production levels temporarily fell in 1887, but by then the Texas
legislature, reflecting the growing interest in exploitation of the raw
material, had instructed every county collector to submit complete
reports on all mining and minerals in their counties to the next legisla-
tive session. By 1889, the survey listed a total of 4,031 coal mine employees in nine Texas counties; only four of those counties, including
Erath County, produced coal for commercial purposes. Texas' total coal
production in 1889 amounted to 128,216 tons. More than half, nearly
75,000 tons, came from coal mines operated by the Texas & Pacific
Coal Company.[6]

The Texas & Pacific Coal Company had its beginnings at the village
of Johnson Mines in Erath County, a small company town that William
Whipple and Harvey E. Johnson founded in 1886. Hoping to avoid
unpaid business debts and to recoup financial losses suffered in their
native Michigan, the brothers, who had settled in nearby Palo Pinto
County in 1880, sought their fortune in the coal-mining business. Encouraged by geological and engineering reports, the Johnsons purchased
the Pedro Herrera survey tract in far northwest Erath County for twenty-

five hundred dollars in October, 1886, and incorporated themselves as the Johnson Coal Mining Company in 1887.[7]

The "pencil" vein of bituminous coal into which they sank their first shaft averaged a thickness of eighteen to twenty-eight inches and extended some sixty-five miles. The vein's width varied from five to ten miles. The Johnsons recruited miners from the railroad's failed mining operation in nearby Gordon and Coalville and, to assure a steady market, signed an agreement with the Texas and Pacific Railroad to sell the company all the coal it needed. In return the railroad laid a spur to the mine shaft.[8]

Despite the potential for profit, financial difficulties plagued the brothers from the start, the result of their failure to raise sufficient capital to run a cost-efficient operation. As the Johnson brothers struggled to earn a profit, bonds issued to provide necessary financial strength sold poorly. Unfortunately, the brothers avoided public stock sales until they found themselves in a desperate situation. Labor difficulties, prompted by the company's unsuccessful attempt to operate the mine at a lower wage than that which had been paid at Coalville, slowed the first shaft's start-up, delaying production and, hence, company earnings. Poor roof conditions in both Shafts Number One and Number Two, the latter opened only shortly before the company sold its assets in 1888, also periodically caused costly collapses, which further complicated the Johnsons' effort to turn a profit.[9]

In addition, complaints from the company's chief customer also threatened financial stability. Railroad officials groused about low production levels, poor-quality coal, and high prices and even threatened in March, 1888, to remove the spur to the mine and to terminate the exclusive contract. The company, lacking capital, could not introduce improvements to deliver a higher-quality coal and reduce the costs of operation. The diversion of profits to the sinking and equipping of a second shaft and the untimely death of the more employee-oriented Harvey Johnson compounded problems already starting to overwhelm the enterprise by 1888. A twenty-five-thousand-dollar loan from a local bank in the spring of that year apparently did little to ease the financial crunch. At that moment, Robert Dickey Hunter entered the scene to salvage or, as William Johnson later contended, to sabotage the Johnson Coal Mining Company.[10]

One of Texas' early captains of industry, Robert Hunter quickly earned a reputation as an opportunistic entrepreneur, fierce competitor, and autocratic employer. In his lifetime, he built an estimated $750,000 to $1,000,000 personal fortune as a cattle broker, mining investor, and investment banker. A native of Ayrshire, Scotland, Hunter emigrated to Illinois with his parents in 1842. As a young man he failed at his first mining investment enterprise in Colorado on the eve of the Civil War, but the invaluable experience he gained there served him well thirty years later in Texas.

In the interim, Hunter turned to the cattle business, where he attracted considerable attention across the Southwest during and after the war as a cattle raiser, trader, and commissioner/broker. In 1873, "the Colonel," as his friends honorifically tagged him, joined with Capt. Albert G. Evans in forming Hunter, Evans & Company, which earned a reputation as one of the leading cattle commission firms in the country. The partners located one of their branches in Fort Worth, where they operated stockyards and sought buyers for clients' stock. In the wake of the decline of the cattle industry in the late 1880s, Hunter sold his interest in the company to Evans and directed his attention to coal prospects in Texas.[11]

Hunter's exact role in the Johnsons' two-year effort to mine coal is unclear. In November, 1886, Edgar L. Marston, a New York financier, Hunter's son-in-law, and a future major stockholder and officer in the Texas & Pacific Coal Company, received a copy of the assay report performed for the Johnsons on the coal reserves that the brothers had purchased the previous month. In August, 1887, Hunter himself inspected the mine shaft, apparently at the behest of a Johnson associate, to assess the value of the property and to assist the struggling entrepreneurs in their effort to obtain a fifty thousand–dollar loan. He reported the property as being "very valuable" and the coal of "superior" quality for both domestic and commercial use. Within a year, he bought controlling interest in the company and then purchased it outright in the midst of a labor dispute over unpaid wages.[12]

In late September, 1888, the Johnson miners walked out of the mines when William Johnson defaulted on the August payroll. At stake were seven weeks' wages, since the company remunerated its employees on the twentieth of each month for earnings from the preceding month. Miners, thus, had to wait one month and twenty days before they received their first compensation. If Johnson could not meet the August payroll, little hope existed that he could pay the miners for their work in September. Nevertheless, at a mass meeting the miners awarded

Johnson a vote of confidence and continued to work, at Johnson's request, until the twenty-fifth. When the company did not distribute earnings on that date, the miners abandoned the shafts. While the mines stood empty, financial negotiations between Johnson and Hunter continued, culminating in a sale. The newly incorporated Texas & Pacific Coal Company quickly prepared to assume control of the properties and the workers, whom Hunter blamed for the Johnsons' financial difficulties. [13]

In his first annual report to stockholders, Hunter labeled the striking Johnson employees as "refugees from Justice and Mollie MacGuires [Molly Maguires]" who had wrested control of the mines from the Johnson brothers. Gomer Gower, who with his father and four brothers-in-law worked for the Johnsons, and Robert Spoede, William Whipple Johnson's biographer, challenged Colonel Hunter's explanation for the Johnsons' collapse. Although Gower admitted that a "strong" local assembly of the Knights of Labor had won recognition from the Johnsons and successfully struck the company in the first months of operation to forestall a wage reduction, he attributed the company's demise to mismanagement and the Colonel's early difficulties to an "antiunion attitude." [14]

Gower recalled that when a union committee attempted to reach an understanding on wages with the Colonel, who had announced he would pay a lower mining rate than the Johnson brothers, Hunter refused to consider any proposals from the miners. In return, no one applied for the work, resulting in zero production the last two months of the year and only small production levels for the first few months of the following year. Gower believed that the Colonel had to save face before his investors: "It was squarely up to [him] . . . to make some kind of a showing in his report to the stockholders of the Texas Pacific Coal Company for the fourteen month period following the purchase of the property." Having no coal to show for two of those months, Gower argued, "what better alibi could be devised than hurling a charge of 'refugees from justice and Mollie McGuires' against the men whom he had rendered homeless, jobless and penniless. Surely," Gower concluded, "the miners could not be held responsible for any mismanagement of the property by its previous owners." [15]

Spoede, likewise, questioned Hunter's explanation of the Johnsons' problems. He identified undercapitalization and the untimely death of Harvey Johnson as the culprits. He even speculated that Hunter may

Gomer Gower, circa 1908–11. *Reprinted by permission of Sara Gower Cooney and Eileen Cooney*

have tricked the miners into leaving the mines. By allowing the payroll default to occur before the new company assumed control, Spoede theorized, Hunter could legitimately declare the previous company's commitments null and void, devise new ones, and deny any responsibility to the striking miners, who technically had never worked for him.[16]

There is some evidence to support that theory. Time and time again, Hunter based his refusal to cooperate with the striking miners on the argument that they had never been in his employ and therefore that no strike existed against the Texas & Pacific Coal Company. It is more likely, however, that Hunter simply seized the advantage when the Johnson employees left the mines. A letter to Hunter from a Johnson associate apprised the Colonel on October 1, 1888, that the miners "came out" and that he regarded it "best not to start the mine again" on the same basis. A "more opportune time," he counseled, "to make . . . changes in prices, as will be fair and equitable, and enable the mine to run without absolute loss, will perhaps not offer again soon if ever."[17]

Whatever machinations characterized the transfer of Johnson's properties to the Texas & Pacific Coal Company, the Johnson enterprise, like others in the area before it, seemed doomed to failure without substantial outside financial assistance. That Hunter succeeded is a testament to his aggressive entrepreneurial ability, his background in the mining business, his contacts with northeastern financiers, including his own son-in-law, farsighted opportunism, and, perhaps as Gower contended, "the greed for the dollar and utter disregard for human rights and needs." The Colonel's authoritarian style, assumption that he owned the right to control the lives of those employees living and working in "his" town, and total opposition to labor organizations no doubt did little to disprove the latter assessment.[18]

As president and general manager of the newly incorporated company, Hunter moved quickly to invigorate the enterprise. The small camp was renamed Thurber in honor of New York grocer H. K. Thurber, Hunter's friend and a major investor. In November, the Texas & Pacific Coal Company assumed legal control of the Johnson properties, which included the almost twenty-five-hundred-acre Pedro Herrera survey, all improvements on that land, including machinery, mining tools, and a store and its stock, as well as more than twenty thousand adjacent acres in Erath, Palo Pinto, and Eastland counties.[19]

The investment lacked much value without a labor force, a resource that Hunter found in short supply as the legal transfer of property was completed. He resorted to hiring people from nearby farms to build houses, clear streets, paint, haul rock, build water tanks, improve the mine shafts and guard them, build a wire fence around the mining property, and load dirt. The company's time book listed 127 employees in December, 1988, including 25 with Spanish surnames and 2 among them designated as interpreters. By the following February, the total number of employees had grown to 173, and much more of their labor centered around the two mine shafts.[20]

By this time, Hunter had sent half a dozen agents to mining centers all over the country to recruit skilled coal diggers. "Our miners," Hunter later testified, "had to be hunted up because we had none out here." Agent Thomas Lawson claimed to have traveled, between December and May, to fifty or sixty camps in Indiana, Pennsylvania, Missouri, Kansas, Illinois, Kentucky, and Tennessee on Hunter's orders; he shipped 450 to 500 miners to Thurber. The largest group, almost half of whom were black, migrated from Brazil, Indiana. Company agents successfully transported over 300 miners and family members to Texas from this location alone.[21]

The job of recruiting had its difficulties. Lawson found the work "very disagreeable and very dangerous" because "of the antagonism of the Johnson men," who had distributed circulars all over the large mining districts warning workers that a strike was in progress. The company also used correspondence in newspapers such as the *National Labor Tribune* (e.g., December 8 and 15, 1888), a union-sponsored newspaper, to draw miners to local hotels. Company agents then talked with prospective employees, signed agreements with the interested ones, and made preparations to transport them to Texas on special trains to prevent their interception by union lieutenants. Production figures for 1889 reflected the success of these trips. In January, the company posted its first coal output — less than two hundred tons. By December, however, production had reached almost ten thousand tons.[22]

As the Texas & Pacific Coal Company continued to expand its investment in the coal deposits by opening nine new mines by 1901, Thurber's population increased correspondingly. The federal census of 1890 reported the population of Thurber Village as 978. The 1900 federal census recorded 2,559 residents in Thurber, of which 828 of the males who listed occupations (75 percent) identified themselves as coal diggers or coal miners. Two-thirds of these 828 miners, representing sixteen nationalities, claimed a foreign birth (see table 1).[23]

That the importation and migration of immigrants to work the mines in Thurber played a significant part in the town's population growth in the late nineteenth century can be seen in countywide figures compiled in 1890 and 1900. The *Compendium of the Eleventh Census* for 1890 reported only 351 (less than 2 percent of a total population of 21,594) foreign-born residents in Erath County. By 1900, the number of immigrants had nearly tripled, to 955 (and doubled in percentage of the county population of 29,966).[24]

In ledger books that the Johnsons maintained before sale of the coal property and in Texas & Pacific Coal Company payroll records for 1890,

TABLE 1

Ethnicity and Assimilation Components in the Coal-Mining Population, Thurber, Texas, 1900

Nationality	Ethnicity of Coal Miners			Citizenship			Residency in U.S.	
	Number	% All Coal Miners	% English-Speaking	% Alien	% Natural-ized	% Pending	% Less than 10 Years	% Less than 1 Year
Italian	341	41.0	71	71	15	14	82	55
Polish	47	6.0	19	22	41	37	45	11
Mexican	32	4.0	6	54	42	4	56	25
English	28	3.0	100	0	100	0	0	0
Austrian	24	3.0	13	43	38	19	63	25
German	15	2.0	53	21	79	0	27	7
Scots	13	2.0	100	0	100	0	8	8
Irish	11	1.0	100	0	91	9	0	0
French	8	1.0	13	33	33	34	50	13
Belgian	7	0.8	0	0	66	34	71	0
Russian	5	0.6	20	50	25	25	60	40
Welsh	4	0.5	100	0	100	0	50	0
Hungarian	4	0.5	0	0	50	50	25	0
Bohemian	2	0.2	0	0	100	0	0	0
Swedish	2	0.2	100	0	100	0	0	0
Swiss	1	0.1	100	0	100	0	0	0
Total Foreign-born Miners	544	65.9	16	54	31	15	65	39

SOURCES: Twelfth Census, 1900, MS; computer analysis of data base for Thurber, Texas, 1900.

English, Irish, Scots, and Welsh names predominated. By 1900, however, 41 percent of Thurber's coal miners listed Italy as place of birth,
making the Italians the most numerous of the alien population. The
forty-seven Poles in the mining population in 1900 constituted the
second-most-numerous alien group. Other immigrant groups represented in Thurber included Mexicans, Germans, Austrians, Hungarians,
Russians, Belgians, French, Bohemians, Swedes, and Swiss (table 1).[25]

The transition in the area around Thurber from miners of primarily
British heritage to those of southern and eastern European extraction
paralleled population changes in bituminous coal–mining communities throughout the United States in the last decade of the nineteenth
century. In the 1870s and 1880s, native whites and northern and western Europeans, most of them highly skilled and familiar with union
organizations, filled the industry. The steady infiltration of the coal-
mining industry by less-skilled southern and eastern Europeans began
in the 1890s, first with the Poles and then the Italians.[26]

In the Southwest, mining companies transported the first mine workers by special train from Pennsylvania and the Midwest. From 1895
through the turn of the century, however, southern and eastern European immigrants, whose numbers entering the United States reached
high tide by 1900, poured into southwestern coal mining centers like
Thurber. Operators, who expected these "new" immigrants to work
for cheaper wages and to behave in a more docile manner than their
U.S. and northern European counterparts, actively recruited them abroad
and in coal-mining camps across the United States. As a consequence,
throughout the Southwest, southern and eastern Europeans comprised
a majority in the mines and mine villages by the turn of the century.[27]

As Hunter consolidated his financial undertaking in Thurber, therefore, the mining population took on a much more obviously diverse
ethnic quality. In 1900, more than half of all miners in the community
could not speak English; 95 percent of the coal miners who emigrated
from non-English-speaking nations lacked fluency in the English language. In fact, on any one day a mine superintendent might hear as
many as ten foreign languages spoken in the coal pits (see table 1).
Furthermore, on the whole, the miners who arrived in Thurber in the
1890s showed little interest in establishing permanent residence in the
United States. This was particularly true of the Italians, less than one-
third of whom were naturalized or awaiting citizenship by 1900. This
stood in sharp contrast to the old Johnson miners of English, Scots,

Welsh, or Irish background, none of whom still retained alien status
in 1900 (see table 1). Although all workers sought financial security,
the nation's newest immigrants generally preferred to return periodically to their homelands with the benefits their work had reaped. As
a result, a palpable sense of impermanence, always a feature of an industry dependent on unpredictable environmental factors, permeated
mining communities like Thurber.[28]

Coal mining and ethnic diversity went hand in hand in the coal town,
for the foreign born dominated no other major enterprise as they did
coal digging. The second-largest industry in Thurber, the brickmak-
ing plant, which opened in 1894, employed fifty-four workers in 1900,
only two of whom were foreign born, one, English, the other, Ger-
man. Only one salesman and one manager employed by the Texas &
Pacific Coal Company in Thurber listed themselves in the 1900 census
as foreign born. Neither represented the "new" immigration. No store
clerks, mine or shop foremen, or company executives—Thurber's white-
collar population—claimed a foreign birth for themselves or their fa-
thers or lacked the ability to speak English (see table 2).[29] Country

TABLE 2

Occupations by Ethnicity and Race, Thurber, Texas, 1900

Occupation	Foreign Born in Occupation		Blacks in Occupation	
	Number	% of Total	Number	% of Total
Coal miner	544	66	107	13
(see table 1 for				
nationalities)				
Saloonkeeper	3	60	0	0
Italian (2)				
Scots (1)				
Seamstress	1	50	0	0
Scots (1)				
Cook	2	66	0	0
Italian (1)				
Chinese (1)				
Preacher	2	50	1	25
Italian (1)				
Dutch (1)				
Boardinghouse keeper	3	27	5	45
Scots (1)				
Mexican (1)				
Irish (1)				

TABLE 2—*continued*

Occupation	Foreign Born in Occupation		Blacks in Occupation	
	Number	% of Total	Number	% of Total
Salesman	1	7	0	0
German (1)				
Carpenter	4	19	0	0
German (1)				
Irish (1)				
Polish (1)				
English (1)				
Blacksmith	3	27	0	0
Scots (2)				
Polish (1)				
Day laborer	2	5	2	5
English (1)				
French (1)				
Launderer	2	66	1	34
Chinese (2)				
Lawman	1	25	0	0
Irish (1)				
Servant	1	20	2	40
German (1)				
Waiter	2	100	0	0
Chinese (2)				
Hotel proprietor	2	100	0	0
Chinese (2)				
Brick plant worker	2	4	2	4
English (1)				
German (1)				
Manager	1	17	0	0
Canadian (1)				
Railroad worker	1	17	0	0
English (1)				
Teacher	1	20	0	0
German (1)				
Barber	1	100	0	0
Italian (1)				
Machinist	1	17	0	0
Scots (1)				
Meat cutter	1	25	0	0
German (1)				
Justice of the peace	1	100	0	0
Russian (1)				
Teamster	0	0	3	20

SOURCES: Twelfth Census, 1900, MS; computer analysis of data base for Thurber, Texas, 1900.

of origin (or ethnicity) and related language capabilities, thus, shaped the mining population as they did few other occupational groups in the community.

Racial diversity similarly characterized the mining population. During the company's early labor difficulties, from late 1888 to the middle of 1889, Hunter recruited an estimated 100 to 150 black miners. In 1900, the mining company still employed 107 black miners, the largest group of black workers in the community. Almost 90 percent of black adult males in Thurber mined coal (table 2).[30]

Approximately two-thirds of the miners employed by the Texas & Pacific Coal Company in 1900 fell between the ages of twenty-one and forty. The average age was thirty-one; the census reported the youngest "miner" as seven, the oldest as seventy-two. Although 70 percent of these miners were unmarried, widowed, or married but not living with a spouse, a group-living experience prevailed. Almost one-third of households headed by coal miners included nonrelatives, usually boarders, in addition to family members (see tables 3 and 4). These workers, then, tended to reside in close proximity to one another, surrounded by members of their own ethnic or racial group. Such living arrangements afforded them the opportunity to share their common work experiences and to establish the "bonds of companionship" so critical to the development of group consciousness.[31]

Thus, at the same time that Colonel Hunter was establishing the town that he proprietarily viewed as his own, miners of many different backgrounds built their own communities underground and above-

TABLE 3
Marital Status of Coal Miners,
Thurber, Texas, 1900

Marital Status	% of Total Reported
Single	56
Married	37
Living with spouse	30
Not living with spouse	7
Widowed	7

SOURCES: Twelfth Census, 1900, MS; computer analysis of data base, Thurber, Texas, 1900.

TABLE 4
Household and Family Structure of Coal Miners,
Thurber, Texas, 1900

Type of Household	% of Coal Miner Households
Nuclear — 2 parents	41
Nuclear — 1 parent	2
Extended — 2 parents	5
Extended — 1 parent	1
Augmented — 2 parents	28
Augmented — 1 parent	3
Mixed adult group, including married couples with no children	20

NOTES: A nuclear family is defined as parent(s) and child(ren); an extended household as parent(s), child(ren), and other relatives; an augmented household as parent(s), child(ren), and nonrelatives (Walkowitz, *Worker City, Company Town,* p. 113).
SOURCES: Twelfth Census, 1900, MS; computer analysis of data base, Thurber, Texas, 1900.

ground. Ultimately, this sense of occupational community proved to be the primary link between them that enabled a diverse population successfully to challenge the company's control over their at-work and after-work lives.

II

The Subterranean Community

*The bituminous coal mine was a city buried deep in the
earth, where work was carried on in a perpetual blackout.*
— GEORGE KORSON

The uninitiated visitor to a bituminous coal mine in the 1880s would see this subterranean city as a black "inextricable labyrinth" chaotic in its layout and haunting in the darkness of an interior that was broken only by the flickering of carbide lamps mounted on miners' caps.[1] For the seasoned miner, however, the shaft, the cage, the entry, the face, the gob or refuse piles, and the rooms were all parts of a systematically planned underground community. There the skilled worker commanded respect and retained an autonomy and independence unique among industrial workers in Gilded Age America. The old miners of English, Scots, Welsh, and Irish stock recognized the need for regulations, but they bristled at the prospect of "being told what to do." Challenges to their notion of the value of their own labor, which was rewarded not at an hourly rate but according to individual production, raised their ire quickly.

Even as the increase in southern and eastern European immigration transformed the racial and ethnic makeup of the mining population in the United States, the traditions in the pits remained surprisingly constant. The old craft miners transmitted not only their skill to the newcomers but also their attitudes toward the operator and the industry in general. Whatever competitive impulses, racial, ethnic, or religious prejudices, or individualistic behavior separated miners by the turn of the century, they all emerged from the mines so blackened by coal dust that even the obvious distinctions among them disappeared. Thus, within the busy metropolis that coal miners populated underground, occupational bonds based on shared knowledge, experiences, fears, and traditions quickly developed.[2]

This special occupational community quickly appeared in shaft mines that both the Johnson Coal Mining Company and its successor, the

Texas & Pacific Coal Company, developed in the Thurber Field. Sunk from the surface to the coal bed below, these mines operated on the longwall method, with diggers working along an extended coal face. Once a good site was selected and a shaft sunk to the bottom of the coal seam, workers cut four passages at right angles to the shaft, each ten to fourteen feet wide, for transportation and ventilation purposes. In rooms or chambers off lateral entries driven from the four main entrances, miners blasted and picked for coal in a dingy, colorless, cramped environment hardly suitable for human occupation.[3]

The narrowness of the seam at Thurber especially contributed to the hostile nature of this daily workplace, challenging even the best miner. According to the United States Coal Commission, that one factor — the height or thickness of a coal seam — determined more than any other how much coal a miner produced in a day. Thurber's coal diggers quickly learned, if they did not already know, the especially difficult task involved in mining the narrow "pencil streaks" of bituminous coal that crossed Erath and Palo Pinto counties. This thin or "low" coal averaged only twenty-seven inches in thickness, and its removal required twice as much labor as a vein two times its thickness.[4]

The trip to the seam below began in an elevator or cage at the mouth of the shaft from which the miners gained entry into their underground workshop. Once lowered into the pit, they approached a lateral tunnel, off one of the four main entries. From there the miners crawled into their rooms or chambers to work a "place" some thirty-six feet wide but perhaps less than a yard high. To open their rooms, they lay on their sides in almost complete darkness and undercut or undermined a horizontal channel 2½ to 3½ feet deep beneath the entire width of their assigned places. Digging inward with a needle-sharp pick or mandrel, striking the coal seam an average of forty times a minute, the coal diggers protected themselves from debris falling overhead by setting up short wood props as they moved along.[5]

After undercutting, the miners braced their backs against the roof or rib (the side) of the chamber. After calculating the points that would produce the best results, they drilled 2-inch holes to a depth of 4½ feet at the top of the seam with a churn drill or a hand auger braced against their bodies. All the way to the end of these holes, which they carefully cleaned out with a scraper, the miners tamped homemade black blasting powder cartridges and inserted long needles that pierced those cartridges. They then wet and packed the hole with clay, withdrew the needle in such a way as to leave a space to insert the squib, a pencil-sized type of firecracker, and lit the fuse on the squib to ignite the explosive. To protect miners nearby they shouted "fire" or "fire in a hole" and sought cover as the fuse sizzled and the charge finally exploded.[6]

When the coal had fallen and the smoke cleared, the miners reentered the crawl space to survey the results. They often repeated this "shooting" process as many as four more times to increase the chamber's length four or five feet before they removed the loose coal with a heavy pick. In a low coal vein they also performed the latter while lying on their sides or squatting on their knees. From a recumbent position they even kicked the coal lumps into waiting mine cars with their identification numbers on them after handpicking refuse such as rock, sulfur, and bone from the lumps. Miners risked being docked, at the least, or fired, at the worst, if too much trash consistently remained on the coal they sent to the surface for weighing. In the several months that miners usually spent in only one room they repeated the shooting and picking process hundreds of times.[7]

As arduous as this labor could be, mining involved much more than merely digging coal. Cleaning up the debris from even a small roof collapse in their chambers, for example, could consume a great deal of uncompensated time. Shallow mines, in particular, created this kind of problem. The Johnsons had located two shafts where the coal outcropped at the surface, but neither mine reached a depth of more than seventy-five feet. As a result, poor roof conditions, the bane of miners working underground, plagued both pits. The unstable shale that sat on top of the seam periodically caved in, to the profound annoyance of workers and operators alike. Fortunately, the coal seam to Thurber's west dipped deeper, so a more stable overburden, or roof, covered the mines opened by Hunter's company in the 1890s.[8]

Water rarely seeped into the mines at Thurber, but when it did, the miners had to bail it out on their own time. This, along with "cribbing," or propping the roof, removing fallen debris, lowering the floor or raising the roof to provide adequate head room in crawl spaces, and even assisting in the laying of track from the working area to the main entry constituted what the miners called "dead work," They usually received little or no compensation for such work, a fact that directly shaped their attitude toward the operating company and wage expectations for actual coal picking.[9]

Certain physical signs identified workers as coal miners. They often
looked pale because of so little exposure to the sun. They walked with
a stooped back caused by years of working under low mine roofs, and
streaks of coal dust had invaded their skin through scratches and cuts.
Low coal mining added other occupational marks. Narrow seams like
those in the Thurber Field demanded that the miners conduct virtually all their work on their sides or on their knees. "Second knees,"
large calluses caused by constant pressure on the kneecaps, and strained
necks from lying on the side and stretching to undercut, shoot, and
pull down the coal further distinguished the low-coal miner from other
workers. The thin-seam miner also suffered from "miner's nystagmus,"
a condition characterized by eye twitching, impaired vision, a light-
headed feeling, and the sensation of seeing lights and objects before
the eyes.[10]

The miners even smelled alike. Their clothes reeked of carbide or
other oil, powder and smoke, sulfurous fumes, and sweat. And, of course,
at the end of a day's work, they all resembled one another. They dressed
in overalls or ducking pants with a spare tin of carbide in the back
pocket, perhaps a flannel shirt, jacket, and heavy shoes or boots, all
splashed if not saturated with oil. A cap on which burned a tin oil
lamp with a long "snout" covered their heads, and coal dust blackened
their clothes, hands, and faces. Only a scrubbing with pumice could
completely remove all the black residue. Experienced miners even carried their picks in a similar fashion, sticking them in the crook of the
elbow. Transporting them any other way immediately labeled a miner
a novice.[11]

Attitudes toward their work also linked miners. The United States
Coal Commission described the coal miner as "more independent in
his work than . . . the worker in almost any other trade." The very nature
of the job, conducted in rooms as much as 265 feet apart, precluded
close supervision. Most miners worked alone or with a "buddy," usually a relative or partner of the same race or ethnic group, and operated as contractors of a sort who provided their own tools and other
necessities, including blasting powder. Coal diggers labored at a piece-
work rate and regulated the amount and pace of their work. In addition, miners often acted as unofficial employment agents, soliciting
family members and compatriots to work in the pits.[12]

This much freedom on the job distinguished underground workers
from other industrial laborers and poorly suited coal miners for factory

discipline. One writer explained: "His mining experience is no asset to him as an industrial worker. In fact, his work habits in the mine tend to be a definite handicap. He does not fit easily into this rigorous, lock-step, boss-controlled factory organization." Furthermore, the "indiscipline" of the mine was "contagious." It was one of the first principles of mining the apprentice learned. Thus, as operators introduced more mechanization and a factory-type discipline into the pit, they encountered considerable resistance from the miners, who were used to doing as they "'darn pleas[ed].'"13

Wage earners at the Thurber mines (like all bituminous coal mine workers) fell into two main groups—the inside workers and outside or surface employees. In 1890, at least 68 percent of those working underground in Thurber were actual coal diggers; the other 32 percent transported the coal to the surface and maintained the ventilating system. Outside, engineers, blacksmiths, firefighters, and carpenters, usually paid at a daily rate, composed the main working force. Some 62 percent of all coal mine employees in Thurber in 1890 worked for tonnage rates—that is, their earnings depended on the amount of coal mined. In such numbers, they left an important imprint on work attitudes both inside and outside the mines.14

Skilled miners were the elite among pit workers, and less-skilled laborers, who spent one to two months with the craft miners learning the trade, aspired to that prestigious position. Miners attached a great deal of importance to the rooms that the mine boss assigned them and rarely transferred out of a chamber once work began there. This place became almost a personal possession and served as a type of underground residence for as long as several months at a time. In these rooms, miners and their buddies labored with little supervision. A ratio of one hundred miners to one foreman kept supervisory visits to their rooms in one day brief, few, and far between. "Almost of necessity," Carter Goodrich wrote, "the working arrangements place[d] a quite old-fashioned reliance . . . on 'the skill, dexterity and judgment of the individual workman.'"15

Despite the relative independence miners enjoyed in their work, the underground workers found themselves increasingly dependent on other mine employees as greater job specialization invaded the pits by the turn of the century. They could not remove the coal and dispatch it to the surface without direction and assistance from the pit boss and his assistant, who coordinated the multitude of interrelated activities taking place underground. The miners also relied on a myriad of other employees, such as mule drivers, motormen, cagers, brakemen, trackmen, timbermen, electricians, machinists, pipemen, and trappers, who kept the pit in operation. The diggers' status as a type of contractor required their dependence on other mine employees for such necessities as empty mine cars, timber for shoring the roof, car haulage, and their own transportation to and from the mines and hoisting into and out of the pits. In turn, some of the miners' greatest frustrations in the workday emanated from delays caused by other employees' failure to fulfill their responsibilities.[16] Whatever the cause, when such delays occurred, miners usually blamed the company for unwanted free time.

Unwanted slack time consumed 20 to 40 percent of every workday in the six-day week. Too few mine cars for each miner's daily output caused much of the dead time. This situation alone, the United States Coal Commission estimated, reduced the miners' possible earnings by 20 to 33 percent. "Even if this failure occurs only occasionally," the commission's report concluded, "the depressing effect upon the men is inevitable." One mining expert claimed that the lack of cars was the single most important factor limiting a miner's output.[17] In Thurber, loading delays and even mine shutdowns because of an insufficient number of mine cars periodically disrupted production.

On February 3, 1894, for example, the *Texas Miner* (the company newspaper) reported that the railroad's inability to provide empty cars to the mines caused a "slight let-up" in pit work. Although by the end of the year the company apparently believed it had found a solution, within two years the resident manager, William K. Gordon, wrote Hunter: "You already know of the trouble and expense we are having on account of scarcity of empty coal cars. All pits are idle to day and we were only able to get in parts of days during the past week. As matters now stand," he concluded, "we are unable to keep the miners we now have steadily employed."[18]

Ongoing correspondence suggested that the problem remained a chronic one even after unionization, and as bold a response as refusing to work after a car shortage that continued too long reflected the miners' strong feelings on the issue. Since any reduction in a miner's individual output directly affected the company's total production as well, particularly in a period of high demand, management also complained about the delays caused by haulage inadequacies. It was not unusual, in fact, for a pit boss to apologize to the miners for car-related delays.[19]

When the lack of cars or other supplies cut the workday short, another problem developed about which the miners in Thurber constantly groused. The locomotive that transported the miners to the pits each day also pulled coal-loaded cars to nearby Thurber Junction, retrieved empty cars, and then distributed them at each mine before quitting time. Any disruption in either the train's or the miners' schedule meant more unproductive slack time. The miners had either to walk several miles in dirty clothes to get home or to wait for the evening train. Under the best of circumstances the train often ran late, lengthening a day that had begun with the ride or walk to the mines at 6:00 A.M. An announcement that the train would be a half hour to an hour late usually prompted "a cursing," according to one account, "in all the known languages of the earth."[20]

An occupation in which workers passed so much of their working time in the mine waiting left plenty of opportunity for discussing grievances and other common interests. Oratory abounded during dead time on the gob piles at the entries and strengthened bonds that naturally developed in the pits. A tradition of oral transmission of information in the mining community heightened the significance of such meetings as well as the time spent lined up for hoisting to the "bottom" (the surface) and riding in the train to and from the pits. The train ride actually served as a kind of "melting pot" where "men from all nations sat" and "strong friendships grew."[21]

The miners probably spent considerable time on the ride to and from work complaining about the company's policy of deducting one dollar from each miner's monthly earnings for transportation to the mines, whether an individual rode the train or walked. According to company correspondence, the transportation charge represented "a source of serious discontent with . . . employes." The company's resident town manager, William K. Gordon, even discussed the possibility of eliminating the charge; he thought this might reduce objections to the length of the workday. "They all claim," Gordon wrote, "that from six in the morning until six-thirty in the afternoon is entirely too long for a days work. Of course if they had free transportation this length of time could not be reduced, but it would be much more satisfactory to them."[22]

The means of weighing the miners' output served as yet another major source of complaint against the company. The Johnsons and their predecessors in the area had paid the miners on a "mine run basis," crediting them for all coal, large and small lumps alike, that they loaded into the mine car. When Hunter bought the company, he not only announced a reduction in the day wage rate from $2.50 to $2.25 but also lowered the mining rate from $1.75 to $1.15 a ton. In 1889, he initiated the screened coal weighing system at Mine Number Two, an act, Gordon recalled, "fought by the coal miners most strenuously."[23]

Under the screen system the miners received credit only for the coal that passed over a 6-foot-wide by 12-foot-long screen with 1¼-inch spaces between its bars. An article in the *United Mine Workers' Journal* described this screening process in detail: "When taken from the shaft the coal is dumped on to a large screen, between which are two more screens. The first screen has apertures which allow of coal falling through in lumps as large as a man's fist . . . ; beneath this screen," the writer continued, "is another with smaller apertures and through this goes what is known as 'slack,' the second screen giving the mine what is known as nut coal. Now," the journal pointed out, "all of the coal which passes through the first and second screens belongs to the company, the miners being paid only for that which slides over the first screen."[24] This alone, Gomer Gower contended, reduced a miner's potential earnings by 12 to 13 percent, a practice he and other miners deemed "iniquitous." The company argued that it actually "saved the coal industry of the state" by providing the railroads with the "clean coal" no Texas mine had produced previously.[25]

The operator's use of and profit from the coal that slipped through the screens especially incensed the miners. A former "check puller," who removed the miners' identification tags from the cars hoisted to the tipple for dumping, recalled that the company utilized the "nut" and "pea" coal that fell through the screen to fire boilers and to trade with a Fort Worth brewery for barrels of beer, which the company sold to the miners at the saloon. The *United Mine Workers' Journal* levied the same charge.[26]

The Texas & Pacific Coal Company held no particular distinction among coal-mining companies for irritating its miners on the issue of weighing. Arthur Suffern, who in 1915 traced the development of union organization among American coal miners, listed the question of mine-run versus screen-weighing procedures as one of the most "hotly disputed" issues in the coal industry. To this he also added abuse of the dockage system, lack of pay for deadwork, and "shortweighing."[27]

Miners in the bituminous coal industry generally assumed that the company's weigh boss cheated them. Mining folklore recognized it as "an old bituminous custom . . . so common . . . that even operators otherwise fair and honest accepted it as a trade condition." Although miners from Thurber seldom mentioned in their reminiscences any concern over shortweighing (Gomer Gower himself was working as a company weigh boss or weighmaster at Mine Number Two by 1894), they made the same demand, once they won union recognition, as countless other miners before and after them: they wanted a union checkweighman to work the tipple (the place where workers emptied coal cars raised from below to weigh the contents) to assure that miners received a fair weight for the coal they mined.[28]

Suffern also included the short working season on his list of miners' grievances. In theory, the tonnage rates that coal operators paid reflected the fact that the mining industry did not operate on a full-time basis all year. The United States Coal Commission defined a full-time year in a bituminous mine as 308 days, but the actual work year between 1890 and 1921 averaged 213 days. Nationwide, then, coal miners faced unemployment more than 3 months a year (or 4½ months if one includes Sundays and holidays).[29]

In Texas the average number of days worked in both bituminous and lignite mines between 1890 and 1902 was 236. For the period 1895–1902, the average days worked in counties where companies mined most of the bituminous coal was 233. The fact that between 1897 and 1902, the production of bituminous coal at the Thurber mines represented 50 percent of all bituminous mine output in the state suggests that this estimate of average days worked would be a fair approximation of the work year at Thurber. Hence, before they unionized, the Thurber miners were probably idle the equivalent of 72 days per year (or a total of 132 days if one counts Sundays and holidays) (see table 5). Few opportunities existed for underground workers to find collateral employment when work in the mines slowed or halted, so they either sought work at another camp or remained idle.[30]

A multitude of factors determined just how many days a mine operated during the year. Because of the location of coal seams and the high labor costs and great danger necessary for the mineral's extraction, labor expenses represented 70 percent of the cost of mining one ton of coal. As overproduction drove coal prices down or as demand diminished, operators reduced their overhead by cutting labor costs first. Working mines only part time or closing them temporarily, which

TABLE 5

Average Number of Days Worked in Texas Mines, 1890–1902

Year	Average Number of Days Worked	Number of Employed	Production in Tons, Texas	Production in Tons, Thurber Mines
1890	241	674	184,440	132,040
1891	225	787	172,100	159,635
1892	208	871	245,690	211,272
1893	251	996	302,206	243,948
1894	283	1,062	420,848	291,518
1895	*167	1,642	484,959	283,932
1896	*191	*1,173	544,015	255,263
1897	*201	*1,378	*422,727	260,490
1898	*249	*1,786	*490,315	284,998
1899	*260	*2,087	*687,411	312,768
1900	*247	*2,443	*715,461	323,537
1901	*267	*2,616	*804,798	353,391
1902	*278	*1,963	*696,005	385,234

Average, all Texas mines, 1890–1902 — 236 days
Average, all Texas bituminous mines, 1895–1902 — 233 days

*Bituminous mines only
SOURCES: USGS, *Mineral Resources of the United States, 1893, 1902; Seventeenth (1895–1896), Nineteenth (1897–1898), Twentieth (1898–1899) and Twenty-first (1899–1900) Annual Reports of the United States Geological Survey;* data submitted by W. K. Gordon, p. 29.

had the effect of lowering wages, provided a stopgap solution to the problem. In August, 1897, for example, Gordon reported an overstock of coal to Hunter, "orders [being] so light that our surplus has now reached 110 cars; and this," he added, "despite the fact that our pits are only working one day each per week."[31]

Cave-ins, accidents, fires, and bad weather also caused mine slowdowns and shutdowns. Gordon reported to Colonel Hunter in 1897 that workers were leaving Thurber and receiving the company's assistance in finding employment elsewhere because a fire in Mine Number Five had completely halted production there. The previous month the elevator in Mine Number Seven broke down, limiting operation in that shaft to one-fourth of the day before it became necessary to close it completely. Although on Hunter's suggestion Gordon had "arranged to run [the mines at] ¾ full time," the severe cold and snowy weather the same month prevented even that level of production, since few men turned out to work. On June 18 the following year only one mine of four was working.[32]

Sometimes miners simply chose not to work. It was not unusual for miners to slow their pace or to stop work and leave the pit before quitting time if they had worked steadily in the morning and earned what they considered a satisfactory wage. Self-awarded holidays and low turnout at the mines because of extreme heat or cold occurred frequently, and employers often complained about them when large coal orders and good conditions in the mines made full-time operation possible.[33]

On occasion, conditions that made working difficult and the miners' disinclination to work coincided. The "full halftime" operation of the mines in June, 1898, posed no labor problems as far as Gordon could tell, because it was "as much work as they [the miners] want at this season of the year." In July, 1900, when Gordon wrote Edgar Marston about the impact that the lack of railroad cars had on full-time operation in the mines, he added: "Our miners seem to be thoroughly satisfied with the work as they really do not care for full time during the hot weather."[34]

Each day that they worked the miners largely determined their own pace and individual output, often to the company's annoyance. Payroll books indicate how widely production varied in Thurber. In October, 1890, 366 tonnage workers produced over 9,500 tons of coal, digging an average of 26 tons each. On an individual basis, however, some miners extracted as much as 90 tons, whereas others dug fewer than 10. Many of the miners worked twenty-six days that month; others less than half that many.[35]

Coal operators encountered a natural resistance from their employees to standardization of output. Preindustrial values, especially among the large agrarian element within the immigrant population, contributed to this lack of discipline, but the individualistic traditions of mining, which experienced coal diggers transmitted to the new mining generation, also partially explained this feature of the workplace. Variable output, then, could be expected in an industry where the "miner's freedom" prevailed.[36]

The *Texas Miner* of January 20, 1894, addressed the implications of that fact of mine life. "The Texas & Pacific Coal Company has quite a number of men that every day they work will mine from four and one half to six tons of coal a day," the article stated, "earning from $5 to $6.75; others that mine from three to four tons per day, earning

$3.50 to $4.75 per day; others who mine from two to three tons per day, many who only mine from one and one-half to two and one-half tons per day." Experience and physical strength partially explained the disparity, the author conceded, but "steady, intelligent application" also determined output. "Some men never seem to learn how to take advantage of the situation and their surroundings. . . . One thing is . . . certain, the men that lay around the saloons a good portion of their time do not get to be the best miners, and consequently do not earn the money, even when they work, that good miners do."

To cope with the difference in output the company appealed to the miners' competitive instincts. The *Miner* publicized pit production figures, photographed miners at work, and applauded mine shaft crews who turned out the best results. "No. 5 shaft made another record breaker last Tuesday," the company announced on August 18, 1894. "She hoisted 702 tons of coal." Another shaft, the "Queen Bess" (Mine Number Seven), the paper bragged, "is a record breaker. Cages [are] now hoisting 100 tons daily" (December 15, 1894). Payroll records indicated that despite the company's effort, individual production and earnings still varied (October 1, 1898).

Since output fluctuated, so did yearly wages. In October, 1890, Hunter paid 11 percent of his tonnage workers, probably the most experienced or those who paid their own helpers, $1.40 a ton. The other 89 percent earned $1.15 a ton. He also paid them "yardage" at a flat rate for opening entries, building main haulage lines, "brush[ing]" the roof or floor, and moving slate. Day employees on the surface and underground worked for $1.00 to $3.00 a day, depending on what they did.[37]

The 251 tonnage workers who produced more than ten tons but fewer than eighty tons mined an average of thirty-five tons in the twenty-six-workday month. At $1.15 a ton a miner earned a monthly wage of approximately $40.25. Since the company was undertaking considerable yardage work at the time to improve the condition of the two shafts purchased from the Johnsons, the actual average earnings for those miners in that month was $50.51. Assuming miners worked eight months (see table 5) at that income level, they could earn about $400.00.[38]

By 1900, the company had lowered the tonnage rate to $1.00, since the average price for coal had fallen 34 percent, from $2.32 a ton in 1894, to $1.52 in 1897. Management also shifted to a one-inch screen for weighing purposes, which somewhat increased the miner's output. The average earnings in October for those producing more than ten but fewer than eighty tons was $47.00. The mine payroll ledgers for 1900 did not discriminate between the number of tons mined and yardage work, so it is impossible to determine how much of the miners' wages came from actually digging coal. The month's average wage, however, fell about $5.00 from the wage of ten years earlier. Based on the average number of days worked in Texas' bituminous mines in 1900 (table 5), the miner earned just over $360.[39]

A comparison of wages in Thurber with those in other parts of the country is practically meaningless, because mines differed so much in the height of the seam, the presence of impurities, and the type of roof and floor. In 1897, Texas mines paid almost three times the thirty-five to forty-cent wage rate paid by companies operating in such leading bituminous coal-producing states as Pennsylvania, West Virginia, Ohio, and Indiana. Miners in Texas, however, found the work much more difficult in shafts like those at Thurber because of the thin seam. A coal digger in Indiana, for example, working in a tall seam, could produce twice as much coal as a miner in Thurber—hence the lower tonnage rate. The United States Coal Commission report specifically described the impact that seam height alone could have on a miner's output and thus earnings. In 1917, the report stated, "the average output per man per day in seams 2 to 3 feet thick was 2.41 tons; in seams 5 to 6 feet, 4.18; [and,] in seams 6 to 7 feet, 4.27 tons."[40]

More useful in describing the income level of miners in Thurber is a comparison with other wage earners in the community. As shown in table 6, a Thurber miner's average salary in October, 1890, and Oc-

TABLE 6

Earnings Comparison, Tonnage Workers vs. Other Occupations,
October, 1890, and October, 1900, Thurber, Texas

Occupation	Average Wage, October, 1890 ($)		Average Wage, October, 1900 ($)	
Miner	52 (month)	416 (year)	47 (month)	376 (year)
Laborer	1.25 (day)	300 (year)	30 (month)	270 (year)
Driver	2.00 (day)	480 (year)	35 (month)	280 (year)
Track layer	2.00 (day)	480 (year)	70 (month)	560 (year)
Trapper	.75 (day)	181 (year)	22 (month)	176 (year)
Cager	2.00 (day)	480 (year)	45 (month)	360 (year)
Weighmaster*	60 (month)	600 (year)	54 (month)	540 (year)
Pit boss*	80 (month)	800 (year)	81 (month)	810 (year)

TABLE 6 — *continued*

Occupation	Average Wage, October, 1890 ($)		Average Wage, October, 1900 ($)	
Fire fighter	1.50 (day)	360 (year)	50 (month)	400 (year)
Blacksmith	2.00 (day)	480 (year)	50 (month)	400 (year)
Car inspector	NA	NA	55 (month)	440 (year)
Timberman	NA	NA	65 (month)	520 (year)
Electrician	NA	NA	70 (month)	560 (year)
Motorman	NA	NA	50 (month)	400 (year)
Shaft engineer*	NA	NA	54 (month)	540 (year)
Carpenter	NA	NA	60 (month)	480 (year)
Boss driver*	NA	NA	75 (month)	750 (year)
Manager — Hardware, saloon, drugstore, grocery	NA	NA	100–125 (month)	1,200–1,500 (year)
Bookkeeper	NA	NA	80–100 (month)	960–1,200 (year)
Butcher	NA	NA	75 (month)	780 (year)
Petty cashier	NA	NA	30–50 (month)	360–600 (year)
Bartender	NA	NA	60 (month)	720 (year)
Seller	NA	NA	35–60 (month)	420–720 (year)
Clerk	NA	NA	50–60 (month)	600–720 (year)
Physician	NA	NA	225 (month)	780–1,500 (year)
Constable	NA	NA	75–125 (month)	780–1,500 (year)
Paymaster	NA	NA	125 (month)	1,500 (year)
Superintendent	NA	NA	150 (month)	1,800 (year)
Printer	NA	NA	60 (month)	720 (year)
Dairy farmer	NA	NA	55 (month)	660 (year)
Watchman	NA	NA	45 (month)	540 (year)

NOTES:

NA = Not available

*Amount of income based on the assumption that these middle-management employees worked 308 days (the Coal Commission's definition of a full-time year), which equals 10 months. Other "white-collar" workers are calculated on a 12-month scale, since they were often paid a monthly salary. The income of all other inside and outside mineworkers was calculated on an 8-month year.

According to census reports, the average annual wage of Texas workers employed in some type of manufacturing in 1890 was $435 ($36 per month). In 1900, their wages averaged $427 ($36 a month). As indicated here, the short work year in the mining industry kept a miner's annual compensation below that of the average industrial worker in Texas, although the miner's monthly income when working was about $10.00 higher. The average annual income for Erath County residents involved in manufacturing (miners not included), $299, was considerably lower than the statewide mean in 1900.

Numbers have been rounded to nearest dollar. Miners included in the compilation of averages are those who mined more than ten tons of coal and fewer than eighty. Earnings of other employees are representative rather than averages.

SOURCE: Texas & Pacific Coal Company, Mine Payrolls, 1890, 1900; *Twelfth Census of the United States Taken in the Year 1900, Manufactures,* part 2, pp. 862, 868–69.

tober, 1900, compared favorably with that of other mine employees. In those two periods, even lower-level white-collar workers earned a wage only slightly higher than that of the "typical" miner. However, conditions in the individual shaft or in the industry in general rarely favored full production year round. Unlike tonnage workers and other mine employees whose wages directly depended on the mines' operation, clerks, butchers, cashiers, sellers, and printers received their pay on a steady hourly, daily, weekly, or monthly basis. Delays and slowdowns common in the pits affected them less directly. Annual differences in income, therefore, could be more striking. Company employees outside the shafts did not have to contend with the same kind of financial uncertainty that most mine workers perennially experienced.[41]

Other factors also affected the size of the miners' paychecks. They rarely received gross earnings in the envelope the payroll clerk distributed on the third Saturday of each month. The company deducted rent, electricity, blacksmithing, hospital, and train service charges as well as the amount of "checks" or credit forwarded to employees. The amount differed from one individual to another, but on a monthly basis the company charged every miner a flat one-dollar fee for the train ride to and from work and fifty cents for the services of a physician whom the company hired.[42]

A sampling of monthly deductions from miners' wages in 1890 for services reveals that deductions of twenty-six to thirty dollars left the individual tonnage worker with about one-half or less of gross earnings on payday. In 1900, deductions for these same services averaged a similar amount — about thirty dollars — leaving around seventeen dollars in net income. Approximately 10 percent of the miners owed the company money at the end of the month; their "credit" was thus extended on the books to the following payday.[43]

In 1894, the company chartered a new subsidiary, the Texas Pacific Mercantile & Manufacturing Company, to operate the company-owned stores and to issue scrip or credit coupons to workers who lacked cash between paydays. The company held the equivalent of two weeks' wages for each employee to guarantee rent, utilities, and other fixed charges. Before payday, however, a worker could draw in scrip any amount above those charges up to the monthly earnings to date. The company issued the coupon checkbooks in denominations of one dollar to ten dollars, with five-cent to fifty-cent coupons inside.

Although the scrip system assured employees ready credit, many of them still resented it, because they could spend scrip only at company stores. This, of course, worked to the company's financial advantage. Also, once indebted to the company, it seemed, always indebted to the company. The miners argued for years that a biweekly system of payment would reduce the necessity of their securing credit between paydays.[44]

The issue of wages, whether expressed in the debate over screen weighing, shortweighing, the scrip system, or the once-a-month payday, dominated employer/employee relations for years. This concern, along with shared work habits, attitudes, traditions, and working conditions, established important links between the diverse members of Thurber's mining population. The danger of working underground and exposure to frequent injury also encouraged a cohesive feeling among the miners.

The greatest number of accidents in bituminous coal mines occurred because of the special hazards underground: falls of roof and coal, accidents involving underground transportation, and gas and dust explosions — the first killing and injuring more workers than either of the other two. Even exercising the utmost care, miners suffered injuries, but a wage system dependent on volume of production created an extra incentive to take chances that left workers more vulnerable to accidents. The inexperience that the immigrants who were entering the mines at the turn of the century brought with them compounded the ever-present danger of accident and injury.[45]

No major disasters or great loss of life occurred in Thurber, but the threat of accidental injury loomed every day in the miners' work lives. In a community that lived by whistles that announced almost every work activity as well as lunchtime and the start and end of the school day, residents dreaded most the low whistle. It signaled that the train was bringing injured workers back to town.[46]

The most common accidents in Thurber among those recorded in the 1890s involved cave-ins and partial roof collapses, although almost every imaginable injury occurred: Joe Kubiak stuck a pick through his foot in Number Two Shaft; Clint Hamilton broke a leg when caught between two mine cars; David Currie broke his leg in Shaft Number Three; Mace Oiler crushed a leg in Shaft Number Six; a lump of coal fell on cager Tom Hughes's head, knocking him unconscious; Robert Tweed suffered a similar but fatal injury when a piece of slate fell 110 feet from the top of Shaft Number Seven and struck him on the head;

Cary Stokes died of a blow to the head when a large lump of coal plum-meted 170 feet; Frank Goodwin lost a foot at the coal washer and an-other miner, unnamed, was badly crushed in one of the shafts; James Bailey was caught between the timbers and killed while putting a coal car on the cage for hoisting.[47]

Blast injuries, especially, wreaked havoc in a mine and on a human body. A physician described the likely effects of such an accident. "If a miner is injured by a blast in a mine; he catches the blast full in the face, breast, arms and stomach; his flesh is badly torn and lacer-ated, and particles of dirt, pieces of stone and flakes of coal, are driven into the flesh by the violence of the explosion." J. W. Connaughton, who suffered just such an accident in Thurber in 1896, graphically de-scribed the incident that permanently maimed him: "I was mining, digging coal, and was rolling out coal into the road way to be loaded, and there was a blast went off in the room beside mine and the blast caught me and throwed me about ten or fifteen feet, I was whirling around through the air as you was throwing a stick and my foot struck against a prop and was knocked out of the socket, and the blast tore my flesh all up from the edge of my forehead down as low as my thighs."[48]

Because of his accident and the negligent medical care he claimed he received, he testified about the accident's impact on his ability to earn a living: "I am not able to do any labor that requires standing on my feet any length of time, nor walking. I can work very well on my knees. [It] makes me dependent, to a large extent, on mining or some work that I can be on my knees most of the time." He explained that the force of the explosion drove rock, powder, flecks of stone, and coal dust under his skin, resulting in fifty boils that required lancing. A physician remarked that the flecks of coal dust that permanently scarred his skin were "almost impossible to get out when they are flecked in that way . . . on account of the fact that it gets under the skin." Another doctor stated: "You couldn't get that stain out without skin-ning him." Eight weeks after Connaughton's accident he returned to work, and within two weeks the company fired him for unexplained reasons. Such incidents underscored the insecurity inherent in a min-er's work.[49]

Fire was also a perennial threat underground. In February, 1897, while the fifty- to sixty-person night shift in Thurber still worked in Shaft Number Five, a fire erupted at the tipple and spread to the engine, boiler, and fan houses. The fan house offered the only air supply and "man-way" through which the miners could escape certain death. As was expected within the mining community, coworkers risked their own lives to save those trapped below. A "bucket brigade" composed of men and women saved the fan house, while a group of volunteers entered the mine shaft to warn the workers below and to take them up by an old "return way." Miraculously, no one suffered injury.[50]

Herman R. Lantz, who conducted a sociological study of a coal-mining community similar to Thurber, concluded that out of such hazardous conditions and experiences, strong friendships emerged. "The coal mining occupation," he argued, "has much of the same effects as war on a man," creating a powerful bond between those who serve in the pits together. Both Milton Cantor and David Emmons, among other historians, have likewise described this "communal response to the hazards of industry," which intensified an "occupational consciousness" among mine-workers.[51] The mining community's response to a coworker's injury or death in Thurber especially reflected that reality.

The Texas & Pacific Coal Company provided medical care to the injured in their homes or in the small hospital facility that it operated, distributed company coupons for their expenses during the recuperative period, and even donated funds to assist victims' families with such things as funeral expenses; however, no official written policy dictated benefits payments to the injured. The company distributed limited funds out of the hospital account, into which each mine employee paid on a monthly basis, at the complete discretion of a mine superintendent or the general manager. To supplement such aid, miners often collected funds, held benefits for the victim and family, or subscribed a certain amount of coal to be credited to the injured's account. Many also belonged to fraternal organizations or mutual aid societies that not only facilitated the establishment of social bonds between workers but provided injury and death benefits as well.[52]

Finally, superstitions, songs, and stories that miners learned while developing their skill in the pits also promoted a sense of occupational bond. This folklore varied little from Indiana to Texas.[53] Thus, despite the changes that explosive industrial growth brought the nation, continuity within the mining industry ran from one generation to the next and one region and even one ethnic group to another. As a mine assumed the physical features of a city underground, it also exhibited the more abstract characteristics of a community in which shared experiences established a special connection between its temporary residents.

Miner in his room at mine #8, Thurber, Tex., 1906. *Courtesy Southwest Collection, Texas Tech University*

Thurber miners. *Courtesy Southwest Collection, Texas Tech University*

In the pit, Thurber, Tex. *Courtesy Southwest Collection, Texas Tech University*

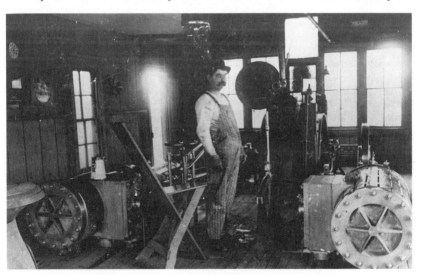

Hoisting engineer, Thurber, Tex. *Courtesy Texas Labor Archives, Special Collections Division, The University of Texas at Arlington Libraries, Arlington, Texas*

Mine #1, Thurber, Tex. *Courtesy Southwest Collection, Texas Tech University*

Unloading at the tipple, Thurber, Tex. *Courtesy Southwest Collection, Texas Tech University*

Group of miners at mine #9, Thurber, Tex., 1906. *Courtesy Texas Labor Archives, Special Collections Division, The University of Texas at Arlington Libraries, Arlington, Texas*

"Black Diamond" train at mine #12, Thurber, Tex. *Courtesy Southwest Collection, Texas Tech University*

III

A Way of Life: Benevolent Despotism
versus Worker Control

*The purpose of the company town is to attract, hold
and control labor. Indeed, it is the question of control which
overshadows all other problems in the company town.*
— HORACE B. DAVIS

In *The World of the Worker,* James
R. Green selected as a primary theme the industrial workers' struggle
to assert some control not only over their work life but also over their
"wider world" at home and at play. His concern, he stated, was "not
to establish a revolutionary tradition where one does not exist, but
rather to describe conflict over power and authority where it did exist."[1]

A company town like Thurber is an especially appropriate and in-
triguing setting for a study of the contest between employer and employee, because the company, which owned virtually everything in the
community, held dictatorial power over its workers' lives. Yet, in addition to the periodic labor unrest that challenged that power, Thurber's
miners, used to a measure of autonomy at work, responded to the re-
strictions of company-town life by creating their own world within the
bounds that the company established. Hence, they functioned not
merely as cogs in a wheel but as active participants in the development
of a way of life that reflected the viability of their ethnic heritage, kinship networks, and individual and mutual aspirations and traditions.

Although the miners' adaptation to life in a company town reflected
the diversity of their ethnic and racial makeup, they still experienced
the unique features of residence in a community in which autocracy
and paternalism existed side by side. As these miners shared an occupational identity that transcended their differences, so the network of
relations that developed in the environment of a company town further solidified the bond of common interest among them.

Company towns like Thurber fell into the category of "dependent

40

communit[ies]," like a feudal manor or a plantation on which one person, family, or business entity owned a large labor-intensive operation.
In addition to the profit motive, in each of these communities the need
and desire to promote "a well-regulated life" for the dependent labor-
ing population also shaped the administration of the enterprise. Owners anticipated the necessities of life and included in the community
the social institutions that they deemed appropriate for the workers.
Implicit, of course, in any such enterprise was the retention of absolute, sometimes harsh, control in the hands of the owner or chief management officer as well as a paternalistic approach to administration
in the interest of maintaining a satisfied and productive work force.[2]
In this type of setting, the relationship between employer and employee
assumed an especially complex nature.

Corporations usually founded these privately owned towns in isolated areas in which a natural resource such as coal, iron, water, metal,
or timber existed in sufficient quantities to attract entrepreneurs intent on exploiting it. To secure labor, most of these companies assumed
responsibility for providing their workers easy access to housing, food,
home furnishings, work materials, educational and religious facilities,
and even entertainment. The founding company usually purchased all
the land within a radius of at least a mile of the primary industrial
operation site, owned all buildings constructed there, and operated
all the businesses established on the company's private property. A fence,
patrolled by armed guards, commonly surrounded the property, en-
abling the corporation to control public access to both residential and
business areas within the compound. Teachers, ministers, and peace
officers recruited to work in the community received a company subsidy of some type that directly tied them to the business enterprise.[3]

The physical scene in these camps rarely impressed visitors with
its beauty. Companies in the late nineteenth century used little fore-
thought in laying out housing or business establishments, so the communities assumed a rather haphazard look. Weathered frame houses
usually painted a uniform red, gray, or yellow dotted the unpaved streets.
Very little greenery broke the monotony of the landscape in the poorer
sections of town or obscured the ever-present reminders of the town's
purpose — belching smokestacks, dust, loud machinery, and day-order-
ing whistles. And the company's presence was everywhere. "As all the
inhabitants are economically and territorially dependent upon the
corporation," an investigative report on company towns concluded,

"every vital activity in the community can be dominated by it. No individual or institution of any consequence escapes." And, the report added, "the head of the plant is the arbiter of every undertaking in the community."[4]

No one who lived in Thurber during Robert Hunter's tenure as general manager doubted the veracity of that statement. "Colonel Hunter had supreme authority in the camp," one resident recalled. "He was practically the company. Whatever he said went; it had to. If it didn't some fellow heard about it."[5]

When the Texas & Pacific Coal Company acquired the Johnson property, a small mining camp already existed there, including a number of privately owned shacks, which the Johnson brothers had permitted the miners to construct on company land. Colonel Hunter demanded that the miners remove the buildings or sell them to his coal company. "A case of Hobson's choice," Gomer Gower termed Hunter's announcement, the offer being "take it or leave it." Gower's father, Thomas, numbered among those who either sold or removed their homes to adjoining land. Hunter recalled in his first annual report to stockholders that the company purchased all of the houses belonging to the old miners "so as to free the property of all rights in outside parties to remain thereon. No one," he finished, "is now allowed to erect a house for any purpose."[6]

While labor problems complicated mining efforts in the first few months after the company acquired the property, Hunter expended more than fifty thousand dollars to construct buildings to house stores and offices, boarding establishments, livery stables, schools, and churches and more than two hundred two-, three-, four-, and five-room houses. The houses looked like employer-built housing in bituminous camps all across the country. The Texas & Pacific Coal Company built the first L- or T-shaped wooden houses in the camp with no thought for symmetry or order, so the front doorway of one house sometimes opened onto the side or back door of another. The result was a rather chaotic appearance in the oldest neighborhoods. The red, brown, or green houses, worn by extreme weather and perennially covered in coal- and red clay dust, sat on rocky soil along unpaved streets with little vegetation of any kind to soften the drab appearance. Inside, the smoke of coal-burning stoves stained walls and ceilings, and the odor of carbide rarely dissipated.[7]

Despite the drabness, residents managed to leave their personal mark on the lots and rent houses they inhabited. The company newspaper encouraged residents who wanted to fix up their yards to use staves from empty barrels to build fences if the standard red picket fence had not already been constructed. Livestock roamed many of the yards. An occasional garden grew in a backyard. The smell of bread freshly baked in outdoor ovens and the pungent odor of fermenting grapes, spicy meats, and special ethnic dishes wafted down from the hills surrounding town and masked the stifling odor of sulfurous fumes, dust, and sweat. Miners drank and socialized in backyard arbors that they built of oak and mesquite limbs and covered in grapevines.[8]

The company rented these houses for $4.00 a month for the first two rooms and $1.00 a month for each additional room, a fee comparable to that charged in company-owned camps elsewhere in the United States. Houses with a finished ceiling, washhouse, or a porch rented according to the number of such amenities. For example, in 1900, a four-room house with porch, washhouse, and finished ceiling rented for $9.00 a month in Thurber; a four-room house with only a washouse for $7.00; a five-room house with porch and washhouse for $8.00; a six-room house with a porch for $6.00; and a six-room house with a washhouse for $8.00. Once the company introduced electricity into the pits in 1894 and strung wires and installed fixtures in the residential areas (at no charge to residents), Thurberites paid $.25 per month for each electrical globe or fixture. When the number of miners exceeded the number of houses, workers paid $1.50 a month for lodging in a tent. The Hotel Knox, which opened in 1894, charged $2.00 to $2.50 a room per day. Company lodging houses specifically built for single employees rented for $18.00 a month.[9]

Although company rent books indicated that housing in the residential area in which a majority of southern and eastern Europeans resided contained the fewest amenities, the homes rented by the Italians often had the largest number of rooms. This reflected the Italians' inclination to earn extra income by offering room and board to single males. In Thurber, almost 70 percent of Italian households maintained boarders, one bed after another filling bedrooms.[10]

The largest number of boarders that the 1900 census counted in any one household in Thurber was nine; the average was five. Most of these boarders had emigrated from Italy. Over two-thirds of the boarders in coal miner households lived in a residence headed by an Italian. The Fantini residence, for example, housed seven boarders in addition to four family members. Alex Fantini paid the company six dollars a month in rent. The four-room "cottage" with washhouse that the Morietta family rented housed seven boarders in addition to two family members. The company charged Morietta seven dollars a month. Five boarders lived in the Gerotti residence with four family members. The house had four rooms and a washhouse.[11]

This situation corresponded closely to that in other industrial communities in which a married man, usually a recent immigrant himself, took in three to four boarders. Under the boarding boss system a boarder paid anywhere from sixteen to twenty-eight dollars a month for clean clothes, daily meals, freshly prepared carbide lamps, and cramped sleeping quarters. In more than a third of these households all but one room was used for sleeping; even the kitchen often substituted as a bedroom after the evening meal. Although crowded, most of these households did not maintain so many boarders that personal relationships could not develop. In fact, such group living arrangements in so many miner households actually contributed to the cementing of occupational bonds forged in the mines.[12]

The mining population tended to live together not only in individual households but also in distinct neighborhoods, divided along ethnic and racial group lines, as the population rapidly grew. Managers normally assigned housing according to availability rather than intentionally segregating residents. Yet, separate ethnic and racial housing arrangements quickly developed, since the cheaper housing closest to the mines naturally attracted mineworkers and family members also apprised their kin and friends when they became aware of vacancies so they could rent a residence nearby.[13]

Although the 1900 census included enough indications of ethnic integration to suggest that ethnic divisions in Thurber's neighborhoods were not absolute, southern and eastern Europeans generally populated the north and south sides of Hill #3 (closest to Mine Number Three) or Italian Hill (as the census taker in 1910 designated it) on the village's west side. This residential area was closest to the mining operations by 1900. Sometimes conflict between northern and southern Italians divided Italian neighborhoods in industrial communities, but no such tension appears to have complicated life on Italian Hill. It is likely, however, that residents grouped themselves, as circumstances made it possible, according to village and regional loyalties. Many Irish lived at the base of nearby Stump Hill (so-called because of the large number of tree stumps there), while the 1900 census and company rent books indicated that American-born and English, Scots, and Welsh miners and brick plant workers lived in some proximity to one another on Park Row (near the baseball park) to the north and east of town. Residents regarded the latter as a somewhat more desirable neighborhood because of its greater distance from the mines.[14]

The black population lived at the far eastern end of the camp. Although segregated housing, schooling, religious services, and even amusement reduced white and black contact, blacks still shopped with whites at company stores, patronized a company saloon where the races imbibed together, and, in isolated cases, according to 1900 census records, lived in apparent proximity to whites. The census even recorded a black boarder, who was not a servant, in a white household. The old Johnson miners greatly resented the black strikebreakers whom Hunter imported in 1888 and 1889 and may have tried to intimidate them, but no mass racial disturbances ever occurred in the community.[15] Like their ethnically diverse counterparts on Italian and Stump hills, black miners too shared the common experience of residing in a community in which a profit-making institution provided virtually all services and controlled access to the mining camp.

A six-foot, four-wire barbed fence, erected in the winter of 1888–89, enclosed the nine-hundred-acre camp compound. A locked gate on each side of the fence, patrolled by armed guards, kept outsiders from entering the enclosed area. A common feature in company towns, the intimidating fence prevented undesirables, union organizers in particular, from mixing with the population inside. Peddlers and local farmers seeking a ready market for their goods also often fell victim to the fence, which protected a company's monopoly on trade with the inhabitants.[16]

More than one resident in Thurber claimed that Colonel Hunter compelled his employees to shop at the company's stores and prohibited local merchants and farmers from competing with them. Hunter, however, denied it. "It is certainly a fact," he stated, "that all the people who lived, by my permission, within the enclosure there at Thurber, traded at our stores," but "we do not compel them to trade there. They trade where they please. Of course," he added, "I expected the majority of our employes would trade there. It is [also] very true that all those stores were established there for profit and gain, and that the company expected to sell [to] the people who lived in there, so long as they would behave themselves and pay the money, whether they were employees or not, if they were not objectionable."[17]

In fact, farmers regularly sold produce and livestock inside the fence. A legal confrontation between Hunter and local residents who could not even get ready access to the post office in Thurber had forced him to unlock the gates. Nonetheless, company patrol of the premises continued, and Hunter used his considerable authority to ban or order removal of anyone he deemed unacceptable.[18]

Gomer Gower claimed that when peddlers entered the camp to sell goods, "company men" followed them and noted the names and house numbers of purchasers. One woman related the story that her mother hid items purchased outside the village under her skirts on reentering the fenced compound to escape detection. Whatever the reality, any intimidation tactics Hunter may have employed failed to keep the residents from purchasing some goods from sources other than those directly controlled by the company. Because of a periodic labor shortage, the company simply could not afford to dismiss workers for so insignificant a reason.[19]

Even if the company did not overtly force employees to buy at company stores, trade there might as well have been compulsory. It was common in the Southwest for companies to require miners to purchase their explosives only from company stock. Besides, the coal company's stores held an enormous competitive edge over any independent establishments. The availability of credit to employees between paydays encouraged shopping at the only stores that accepted company scrip. The mercantile also maintained a large stock of goods ranging from blasting powder to caskets and musical instruments and could and would order virtually anything a customer requested. The presence of multilingual clerks to assist the large foreign population and the construction of a separate store on the far-flung Italian Hill offered a less-intimidating atmosphere than stores in nearby towns. As a result, most of the wages the corporation paid out quickly reentered company coffers through the company stores.[20]

The mercantile company's direct access to information on employees' earnings and on the coal company's anticipated production demands, which would influence those earnings, also gave store managers the ability to extend or limit credit accordingly. This significantly diminished the potential for losses. That the company collected employees' debts through payroll deduction further protected the stores from the kind of problems that often drove independent enterprises out of business quickly.[21]

Whether Thurber's "pluck me's," as labor activists called company stores, gouged customers is unclear. The *Texas Miner* advertised prices that it claimed were one-fourth to one-third lower than those in other local communities and actively courted potential purchasers outside Thurber. Reports to company stockholders even contained references to price reductions because of stiff competition outside the camp. Although charges of high prices in company towns usually headed the list of residents' complaints and provided fodder for labor agitators, an investigation into the bituminous coal industry by the Immigration Commission in 1911 discovered that allegations of excessively inflated prices and inferior quality stock in company stores were not provable. "In the majority of cases," the commission reported, "the reverse is true, the employee being able to secure from the company as good, if not better, articles for the same or a less price than would be charged by an independent store." The United States Coal Commission report in 1925, however, contradicted that finding, estimating that company store prices ran at least 7 percent higher than those at independent stores in one Alabama district it examined.[22]

Whether the result of slightly higher prices or of a monopoly on trade, the company stores in Thurber fulfilled Hunter's expectation of profit in their very first year of operation. The stores produced a 17 percent return, assuring that income from the mercantile establishments would cover the interest on all outstanding company bonds. According to the company newspaper, between 1893 and 1894, the mercantile business increased 150 percent, or from $2,206 on one date in 1893, to $5,369 on the same date the following year. Between 1900 and 1903, the net profits of the Texas Pacific Mercantile & Manufacturing Company amounted to between $92,000 and $115,000.[23]

The fence that symbolized the company's monopoly on trade also represented the dictatorial control of the general manager. When saloon operator Thomas Lawson ran afoul of Hunter, the Colonel wielded all his power to remove him from the camp. Hunter ordered his clerks, engineers, and office employees, "on pain of discharge," not to patronize the saloon. He further instructed his storekeepers to refuse Lawson, his saloon employees, and their families goods from all stores except the drugstore. Hunter also halted water and ice delivery to the saloon, prohibited Lawson's use of the livery stable and telegraph office, and denied him the privilege of cashing scrip received in payment for saloon charges. The ice cream shop even refused service to the wife of one of Lawson's barkeepers. "In fact," Lawson testified, "the entire saloon was boycotted by the camp . . . as far as selling goods was concerned."[24]

Hunter explained under oath that he pursued such action because Lawson "was endeavoring in every way to break up my camp and persuading my miners to leave when I need them badly. . . . That is the reason why I wanted him out of the camp the same as you gentlemen would want a mad dog out of your way where you had children."[25] Contractual obligations complicated Hunter's efforts to destroy Lawson's business, however. In most other cases he simply fired troublesome employees and left unwanted intruders in the hands of a company-subsidized police force.

Hunter discovered he could not always depend on local authorities to assist him when trouble, especially labor disputes, flared. A county sheriff sympathetic to the miners created an exacting obstacle to restoring peace and quiet on Hunter's terms. A local constable refused to cater to the company's wishes during the Colonel's dispute with Lawson in 1890. In 1895, the chief law officer in Thurber, a special commissioned Texas Ranger, objected to the practice of turning over fines to a constable who exhibited considerable antipathy toward the Rangers.[26] Lacking the consistent support of local law officials, Hunter, like so many other nineteenth-century industrialists, sought outside assistance and hired his own police force.

The extent of Hunter's subsidy of law officers is evident from the very first financial records he maintained after acquisition of the Johnson property. Between December, 1888, and July, 1889, the months of the most heated labor unrest in the camp, the Colonel approved disbursements of $150 on the average from a special police account. By 1900, a constable and assistant appeared on the payroll as company employees.[27]

Hunter also corresponded frequently with state officials, particularly the adjutant general of the Texas Rangers, who ordered Company B of the Frontier Battalion to Thurber on numerous occasions. During one such period of upheaval, the adjutant general confidentially ordered Capt. S. A. McMurry to interview both sides in the dispute and to assure labor leaders that there would be no trouble as long as they obeyed the law. The Rangers, however, typically performed their duties on behalf of the coal company and developed long-term ties with it. In fact, after one ten-day visit of the Rangers to Thurber, the Colonel posed with them for photographs. Vouchers submitted to the adjutant general indicated that Company B purchased considerable supplies and horses in town as well; this easy access to needed goods on the frontier could have shaped the Rangers' "loyalty."[28]

Hunter received permission by 1891 to headquarter several special commissioned Rangers in the camp, reasoning in part that the location of company property in more than one county complicated law enforcement for local authorities. He also hired a number of former Rangers to work for the company. The *Texas Miner* described the chief officer of Hunter's commissioned force, William Lightfoot, who had served as a captain in the Fort Worth Police Department for several years: "They say that [he's] a high and a hard kicker, and can swipe the bull's eye every trip, changing feet alternately with the poetry of motion. Moral: When he has cause to tell you to leave camp, and does tell you, you'd better go shy on back talk. See?"[29]

In 1894, the company also organized a rifle team, the R. D. Hunter Rifles, composed of twenty-five "picked" men whom Captain Lightfoot commanded. "The object," the *Texas Miner* recorded on December 8, "is recreation, amusement, to familiarize themselves in the handling of fire-arms, and — business." The team drilled weekly, practicing quick shooting among other things. "To see not one, but dozens of the men pump a target, the size of a man, full of holes, and put a shot just where they wanted to, and without taking aim, and with the quickness almost of a flash of lightning, demonstrated to us what practice would accomplish under proper directions," effused a writer for the December 15 edition.

"The boys" apparently spent large quantities of ammunition during their drills, but the company regarded the team as a sound investment. "Some fine day it might pay ten thousand times over in dollars and cents to the T.&P. Coal company, to say nothing of ridding the community of a class of men who are a menace to law and order." The paper (December 15) was referring specifically to train robbers who had been menacing the area, but it was not easy to overlook the potential for the use of the rifle team as fence-, mine-, or bodyguards in case of widespread unrest in the community.

The company allied itself closely not only with law officers, but with other justice officials in the community also. Before his commissioning

49

as a special law enforcement officer and his election as justice of the peace for Precinct 7 of Erath County (which included Thurber), J. M. Williams worked for the coal company in one of its stores and ran the livery stable. A previous justice of the peace operated the drugstore, and A. H. Miller, a company manager, also served as a justice of the peace for a number of years.[30]

Furthermore, the "calaboose" that the corporation built in Thurber was, according to the testimony of a county constable, "their [Texas & Pacific Coal Company's] private property." Officers other than those working for the company had to retrieve the keys to the jail from someone in town before using it. The *Texas Miner,* commenting on the generally peaceful condition of the camp, claimed that the jail got little use "except to jug outsiders who steal in at night to try and make trouble with our men."[31]

Law officers often transported the more serious offenders to the county seat in Stephenville for incarceration and trial, although a local court did hear cases in Thurber. The *Miner* (June 30, 1894) described the court, however, as "only a desk in an office where Esquire Williams sits once in a while" and where a brief lockup and assessment of a fine apparently constituted the typical punishment. The company even on occasion paid residents' fines and deducted the amount from their wages, probably to keep them working and out of jail.

Thurber had a reputation as a tough town, which a periodic murder or assault case, arrest of a fugitive, or robbery enhanced, but most charges against residents resulted from considerably less-serious violations. Newspaper accounts and reports that the specially commissioned Rangers filed with the adjutant general listed arrests for aggravated assault, fighting, carrying a concealed weapon, disturbing the peace, petty theft, use of abusive language, gambling, and failure to work the county roads. There was even one case of wife beating, one of assault with a hatchet by a woman against her son-in-law, and an indecent exposure.[32]

One can assume that law officers administered justice on behalf of the corporation that largely subsidized them, but in Thurber the long arm of the law occasionally touched even company officials. Whether there were two William K. Gordons in Thurber is not known, but on July 2, 1896, Lightfoot and his deputy reported the arrest of a William K. Gordon on simple assault charges. An athletic, physically imposing man who enjoyed boxing, the town's resident manager sometimes challenged an adversary to a fight, a characteristic that inspired more admiration and awe than fear among the rough-and-tumble miners.[33]

Hunter himself, whom a resident described as "a little bit more on the hard side than . . . W. K. Gordon," was not above a fight. Sgt. W. J. L. Sullivan, a Ranger in Company B whom Captain McMurry sent to Thurber on Hunter's request in the heat of a labor dispute, wrote a memorable account of an altercation involving Thomas Lawson in which Hunter and Sullivan both participated. Testimony in a lawsuit that Texas & Pacific Coal Company instituted against Lawson confirmed that a skirmish occurred. In a chapter in his memoirs entitled "An Exciting Fisticuff," Sullivan wrote: "About two months after [Lawson resisted arrest for shooting a miner in the saloon], Lawson and his bartender, Malcom, and Col. Hunter, all three met in a drug store. Hunter and Lawson began cursing each other, and I heard the row and rushed into the store just in time to see Hunter burst the bottom of a spittoon out over Tom Lawson's head. Hunter then threw a box of cigars at him, striking Lawson in the ear and scattering cigars all over the floor."[34]

In the meantime, the bartender attacked Sullivan, the company's attorney entered the fracas, and "Hunter was pacing around after Lawson with a heavy rock, but never did get in his lick." Everybody involved, including Sullivan, was arrested and assessed a twelve-dollar fine. Hunter refunded Sullivan's money and then spent two hundred dollars fighting his own case. Although not an ordinary occurrence in Thurber, this incident underscored Hunter's personal brand of justice.[35] The company newspaper (June 30) explained: "There is a tacitly recognized force that no one questions, no one denies—orders are issued and implicitly obeyed as if from the council of ten in Venice."

One would expect that Hunter's dictatorial power extended to local politics. Government investigations into the pattern of life in company-owned camps found that companies did not have to act overtly to control politics, "for the Company is generally the only organized force in the neighborhood." If the company's favorable position did not have its intended effect, however, "direct means" might be deemed appropriate. Supervisors doubled as "ward-heelers" and assumed responsibility for ensuring that workers voted for the company's candidate. The secret ballot, according to the report, did not exist, and dismissal followed an independent vote or outspoken position contrary to company wishes.[36]

Hunter's dispute with the Johnson miners and his attempt to remove them from his camp may very well have directly affected the political scene in Thurber and Erath County, whether intended or not. In the November, 1888, presidential election, the Union Labor party carried the Johnson Mines box, with ninety-three votes to fifty-two for the Democrats and four for the Republicans. In the 1900 presidential election, only one voter in Thurber cast a vote for Socialist candidate Eugene Debs. In the same period the number of votes for the Republican party, which Hunter's newspaper actively supported, increased significantly.[37]

Although Thurber's private ownership precluded the existence of any elected city government, county, state, and national politics played well in the community, and the company displayed a keen interest in election campaigns. The *Texas Mining and Trade Journal* ran election notices in English, Italian, and, occasionally Polish and solicited candidate notices for the newspaper. On February 17, 1900, the paper carried a notice to candidates that read: "Thurber and Thurber Precinct has a voting population of 700, to say nothing of the voters in the county who read the JOURNAL columns weekly. This vote is worth soliciting, and the JOURNAL is the best medium by which to solicit these voters. The vote of the foreigners here is numerous, and it is worth your while to reach it."

Candidates for office commonly visited the camp as election day approached. In November, 1896, William K. Gordon wrote Edgar Marston: "The camp is full of candidates to day and everything points to a hot election to morrow." The candidates' political persuasion seemed to have made little difference, as the visitors ranged from Populists to Democrats and Republicans. In July, 1894, the Populists held their precinct primary in Thurber's town hall. In April, 1895, the first silver convention in the state of Texas, according to the Stephenville paper, was held in Thurber, with two thousand in attendance.[38]

Because of its large population compared to other communities in the area, Thurber could and sometimes did hold the balance of power in county elections. This was particularly evident in the Prohibition elections that the county sponsored. In an 1895 local-option election, for example, those who opposed Prohibition won when the 702 wet votes in Thurber joined the 1,503 wet votes in the rest of the county to defeat the 1,480 dry votes cast countywide. Only twelve Thurber residents voted for Prohibition.[39]

In the 1894 county elections, four Democrats, who carried the Thurber box, lost to Populists. The *Texas Miner* (November 17) hardly regarded it as a disaster, however, for on at least one issue, the free and unlimited coinage of silver, the Populists and local Democrats agreed. The company pledged to "make the personal acquaintance of those [candidates] whom we have not already met."

Indeed, despite the fact that in national politics the company newspaper supported the Republican party, in large part because of its position on the tariff, Hunter's weekly assumed an independent political posture. The paper claimed this qualified it for "Mugwump" status. In its first issue, the newspaper announced: "Our politics will be of the independent sort; we shall have our say of what we believe is for the best interest of the country at large, of the state of Texas, of our county and town in particular," and "our policy will be liberal enough to print anything that our readers may write to us in opposition to our ideas."[40]

One such letter (not printed but reported in an 1895 issue) charged that the coal company was dismissing any employee who did not vote for the local Democratic ticket. In fact, more than one resident claimed that Hunter coerced his employees into voting his position. One recalled premarked ballots, more than one ride to the polls on a single election day, and timely instructions from the priest on the best candidate. Others, however, remembered no such pressure. The company newspaper, whatever the reality, emphatically denied the complaint. "A man in this camp is a free man to do just as he pleases, so long as he attends to his business and is a sober, steady man. A man may be a Populist, Republican, Democrat, or a member of any other blessed organization he pleases, and never a question asked."[41]

The previous year (November 17, 1894), however, the paper had reprinted a *Stephenville Empire* article that commented on another effective means of shaping political leanings inside the camp—the power of the local press. "The power of a good, live newspaper is nowhere more visible than at Thurber," the paper wrote. "Heretofore the mines have been almost solidly Democratic. THE MINER has been dishing out strong Republican doctrine there for the past ten months, and last Tuesday the Democrats only carried it by an astonishingly small majority. This can be attributed more [to] the hard political work of THE MINER than to [any] other source."

Election-eve issues of the Thurber paper confirmed its propensity to preach. The paper editorialized in behalf of its choices for office, formed a "Free Coinage" Club, printing members' names in numerous issues, offered joint subscriptions for a protectionist New York publication and the weekly edition of the *Texas Miner,* and encouraged the formation of a local Republican organization. In fact, in the 1892 presidential election the Republican electors lost the Thurber box by only thirteen votes, while in the county vote the Democratic and Populist party electors each won ten times as many votes as their Republican counterparts. In 1896, voters in Thurber cast their votes overwhelmingly for McKinley (while the county went overwhelmingly Democratic), and four years later McKinley electors suffered defeat at the Thurber box by only thirty-five votes (but lost by a two-to-one margin countywide).[42]

One can only speculate on how many votes Thurber miners cast for company-supported candidates as a result of overt or subtle pressure. By 1900, 54 percent of the adult immigrant males in Thurber held alien, hence nonvoting, status, since the state required one-year residence and the filing of naturalization papers before a noncitizen could qualify for suffrage. But in August, 1895, a Fort Worth organization, the Junior Order of United American Mechanics, raised the issue of "certain parties" in Erath County using the foreign vote to pass a particular election issue. The group adopted a resolution condemning those who had transported 307 unnaturalized foreigners to Fort Worth to declare their intention to seek citizenship, thus earning the right to vote.[43]

About the same time, the *Texas Miner* (July 13, 1895) reported that three hundred "foreigners" had secured their naturalization papers "and are now prepared to vote-'er-straight for the free and unlimited coinage of silver at a ratio of 16 to 1." More likely it was the Prohibition issue for which the company needed "anti" voters. "Foreign speakers" took to the stump in Thurber as the election approached, and Hunter even announced that the company had suspended plans to build one hundred new houses and several coke ovens until the issue was settled. "If local option carries," the *Miner* noted, "the company will . . . place all additional improvements over the line into Palo Pinto county," a not-so-veiled threat that had serious implications for Erath County. In 1904, when Erath County did pass the dry option, the company simply constructed a new saloon just across the county line, as Hunter had promised nine years earlier.[44]

In 1892, the question of the eligibility of newly naturalized voters in Erath County produced a lawsuit on behalf of a defeated candidate. A petition charged that unqualified election judges at Thurber had improperly conducted the election and that forty-seven voters at the Thurber box lacked valid naturalization papers. The petitioners filed suit demanding that the county throw out the entire box, but the plaintiffs subsequently dropped the charges.[45]

Thurber's foreign-born miners held enough potential voting power and, because of their limited ability to speak English, were sufficiently vulnerable that some negative "mouthing around" about the situation periodically occurred in other parts of the county. Interest in politics among the foreign-born population clearly existed if the organization of a Polish Democratic Society in Thurber by 1898 was any indicator. At a pre–election day meeting at which two candidates spoke before a "large and enthusiastic" crowd, the society chairman urged Polish residents "to take a deeper interest in the affairs of the government of their adopted country." It is reasonable to assume that, as such political involvement increased, the company would use its own favorable position to influence the foreign-born miners' vote. Several company officials, for example, A. H. Miller and Lit Williams, whom Thurber residents consistently supported at the polls, also held county offices such as constable, justice of the peace, and county commissioner, which likely further influenced the participation of the voters in the democratic process in Thurber.[46]

Using company influence, whether economic, political, or social, to shape employees' lives fit in with the paternalistic approach to regulating residents' experiences that was common in dependent communities like Thurber. When Colonel Hunter advertised in out-of-state mining regions for miners to come to Thurber, he explicitly encouraged workers with families to immigrate. Not only was he interested in courting a stable work force, he was surely aware of the family's powerful role in the workers' lives and its potential as a means of establishing some control over employees. The company could rely on the family to recruit more workers and to teach them the discipline of life in and outside the mines. Management itself even assumed the role of parent in the corporate family and encouraged that image. In the provision of services and in decision making the company presumed to know better than its workers (the "children" in the family) what was best for all. This parental posture sometimes appealed to recent immigrants, for whom the family unit served as the center of their preindustrial culture. It was even part of the mining tradition for family members to labor and function as a unit. The idea of employer and employee working together as one big family with common interests thus sparked a positive response.[47]

On the other hand, adults quickly took offense at the implication that they lacked the capability to make decisions that affected their everyday lives. The effect of the company's paternalistic behavior became clear: "Individual freedom [was] abrogated in the name of benevolence." The corporate welfare programs which that "benevolence" produced reflected the effort to control worker behavior while providing for the residents' well-being. Contented workers, management reasoned, made loyal and nonunionized workers. Offering employees certain benefits also made employers appear socially responsible and gave them the opportunity to link every aspect of life—at home, work, or play—with the company. In practice, ironically, the presence of relatives, the reliance on the family in the community, and the company's fostering of a feeling of kinship among residents also enabled workers to resist in both subtle and dramatic ways the overpowering presence of the company.[48]

The company newspaper, a basic ingredient in the privately sponsored welfare system employers began to implement in the late nineteenth century, played a considerable role in fostering the image that the company desired. The *Texas Miner* not only reported news of local interest and advertised goods for the mercantile but also touted the company's generosity toward its workers/residents. The paper personalized company officials by reporting their visits and passing along interesting anecdotes about them. Birth, marriage, and death announcements, news of visitors, vacations, and promotions, and editorial statements applauding the company's efforts to protect its employees filled its pages. The *Miner* also printed a section entitled "Our Own Little World," in which it promoted the community and its management, and it included an Italian-language news section. Colonel Hunter received congratulatory attention in most of the issues in the paper's first year of publication. "Onward goes the march of progress and improvement in Thurber," the editor wrote in March, 1894, "and every day sees some new feature inaugurated in our town by the everlasting energy and thoughtfulness of 'our Colonel.' It is just such things, beneficial to all, that shows the large hearted character of him who is ever at the helm, and the sincere desire he has to do everything in his power that will prove a benefit to the community."[49]

The subject of company paternalism in general served as a periodic theme in the weekly newspaper's editions. "Earnest thought for the welfare of the citizens," a February 3, 1894, article stated, "has put in practice rules and regulations that are rigid as the adamant, but framed for the best interests of all." Two months later (April 28) the paper wrote: "It is only egregious fools who will run counter to a company that is doing everything possible for the benefit, comfort and convenience of it's employes." On August 25, it pursued a similar theme with the conclusion that "the management of this great company and the generals of this army of industry never have friction with their employes; when riot runs rampant at other like places, Thurber always remains tranquil, and each and every employe pursues the even tenor of his way, knowing that his interests are safe in the hands of these gentlemen." An October 20 article offered yet another explanation for the purported tranquility: "Our town has less disturbance and trouble than any town we have ever known of—simply because bad men and women cannot live here."

In material terms, by the turn of the century Hunter offered his employees a system of welfare capitalism that provided not only essentials but many free or inexpensive services that neither necessity nor law required. These amenities were at least comparable and often superior to those in coal mining company towns described by the Dillingham Commission in 1911, and the United States Coal Commission in 1920. Inadequate water supply often plagued isolated industrial communities, but when the Texas & Pacific Coal Company purchased the Johnson property, Colonel Hunter arranged for the Texas and Pacific Railroad to haul water in iron railway tanks from nearby Strawn. The company charged ten cents a barrel only for delivery of the water. By the early 1890s, the company had developed its own water supply by constructing a small twenty-acre reservoir called Little Lake and then a larger reservoir, east of town, called Big Lake. The company implemented a sand and charcoal filtration process to purify and clarify water pumped to a tank that several water mains connected to the restaurant, saloon, and livery stable by the middle of the decade. By 1905, the community drew its water from two tanks with a combined fifty-thousand-gallon capacity.[50]

Although the company constructed modern sewage and bathing facilities in the housing opened to occupation between 1900 and 1920, few of the older neighborhoods near the mines in Thurber had either when the mines shut down in the 1920s. There were, however, no indications that the inadequacy or unavailability of modern facilities produced the type of public health problems common in mining camps throughout the country. Family members and boarders sometimes bathed in tubs in the kitchen or outside the house, but many miners bathed after work in downtown bathhouses, where tubs filled long rooms. As rudimentary as these facilities may have seemed, few mining towns even as late as 1920 offered them. Thurber's barbershop, located just south of Main Street in the heart of the camp, charged fifteen cents for a bath and towel; bathers had to carry their own water. Only after unionization did the company build bathhouses at the mines.[51]

At the heart of any private welfare system lay medical, religious, educational, and recreational facilities. In 1893, the Colonel supervised construction of a four- or five-room frame building for hospital care. One bed sat in each room. Within five years, eight cots in a nine-room facility served as hospital beds. Most miners preferred to recuperate at home, so the hospital rarely suffered from overcrowding. The company established a hospital fund with fifty cents deducted from each miner's wages at the monthly payday. The fee paid for free surgical and medical care for employees and their families and financial assistance during the recuperation period. In case of an employee's accidental death, the company paid funeral expenses.[52]

In 1890, Hunter employed his nephew by marriage, Dr. Charles Binney, a young physician in practice just one year, to succeed the two physicians who had served briefly before him. Binney treated about twenty patients a day and performed a considerable amount of surgery. Riding on horseback or in a horse and buggy, he covered about a four mile service area a day and was earning $225 a month after eight years of employment in Thurber. Other doctors apparently did not commonly visit patients within the camp unless invited by a company physician on a consultation basis. Hunter did not prohibit employees from seeking care from doctors in nearby communities, but the inconvenience and additional cash expense (since "free" medical care applied only to services that a company doctor rendered) eliminated that option for many. Unlike in most company towns, Hunter also recruited dentists, who periodically traveled to Thurber and accepted patients at the hotel on a cash or scrip payment basis.[53]

Most residents evidently recognized the adequacy of the medical care they received at the hands of company physicians whom Gomer Gower described generally as "of a high type." Yet employees still expressed ambivalence toward the company doctors. This stemmed in part from the workers' belief that the company turned a profit on such services. A court decision in 1898 supported that perception. After a local court awarded damages to a miner who claimed he received negligent medical care after being injured in a mine blast, attorneys for the Texas & Pacific Coal Company argued on appeal that the company provided medical treatment for its employees as a charity and could not be held liable for negligence. The court rejected the corporation's argument, holding that the Texas & Pacific Coal Company was "a monopoly with accrued profits in taking care of the sick." In 1894, for example, the company had collected $3,307.50 more than it spent out of the hospital fund. In 1895, only $127 over the sum deducted from the miners' wages remained, but two years later the company retained over $1,000 in undistributed funds.[54]

Employees also shared the fear that company physicians visiting them in their homes would collect information that could be used against them. Whether anyone lost a job because of a physician's report is unknown, but minutes from a store managers' meeting indicate why workers believed their concern had some basis in fact. To meet customers' needs more adequately, management proposed that, if in making their rounds, doctors saw a peddler at a house, they should inquire as to why the family preferred purchasing from him and report the response to the store's general manager. The physicians apparently agreed to do this.[55]

In addition to a hospital, the Texas & Pacific Coal Company quickly opened school and church facilities for workers and their families after the mines began production. By the turn of the century, a public school, for which no resident paid taxes, a private Catholic school run by the Sisters of Incarnate Word (Hunter Academy), and a separate public school for black children (the Hunter School) educated school-age residents. To promote assimilation of the large foreign population, the corporation also operated an adult night school program for one dollar a month per person.[56]

Despite the availability of schools, the 1900 census identified only about one-third of the town's school-age children (ages seven to seventeen) as students. It also listed one seven-year-old and one nine-year-old, three ten-year-olds, six eleven-year-olds, six twelve-year-olds, eleven thirteen-year-olds, twelve fourteen-year-olds, six fifteen-year-olds, nineteen sixteen-year-olds, and fifteen seventeen-year-olds employed in the coal pits. This obviously accounted for the smaller percentage of male students as compared to female students in school. Apparently, no males over age fifteen attended Thurber's schools in 1900. In fact, the census reported that only one-fourth of school-age males attended school at all; almost 40 percent of school-age females, however, had enrolled that year.[57]

Education served as one means of socialization and assimilation of foreigners and helped develop a permanent, stable, and loyal work force. Funding for schools depended on attendance, however, so the perennial problem of poor attendance prompted more than one company newspaper article in a single year on the importance of education. The articles aimed, obviously, at a particular audience. "You would not send a miner into the mines without any tools whatever, and expect him to mine coal, and the most important tool to help your children on in the world is an education" (February 3, 1894). Moreover, in contributing to the maintenance of the schools by supplementing teacher salaries and exerting influence on school boards, since company officials often served as school trustees, the company could dominate yet another important aspect of the workers' lives.[58]

For the recreational as well as educational benefit of his residents, Hunter opened a public library in 1892, the first in the county. Corporation officials believed that reading promoted mental improvement and reduced the time spent in less-productive recreational pursuits such as drinking. The company newspaper reported on January 20, 1894, that Thurber's library held fifteen hundred volumes. Check-out privileges required a small deposit, but business there thrived.[59]

In most coal camps, companies designated a building for church services or constructed one especially for that purpose. The various denominations then shared the facilities. In 1899, the *Texas Mining and Trade Journal* listed three denominations holding services on alternate Sundays at the Union Church in Thurber: Methodist, Presbyterian, and Baptist. In 1892, a Catholic church initiated services in a separate location, offering religious instruction in English, Italian, and Polish.

By the turn of the century, the Hunter Morning Star Church and African Methodist Episcopal Church served black residents in their east-side residential area.[60]

The company charged no rental fees for church buildings or for pastors' housing. "No rent by order of W.K.G." periodically appeared in rent books for buildings the company set aside for church activities and parsonages. The Catholic priest's "recompense" from the company included not only a furnished house but also board and livery stable charges. Such allotments most likely applied to the other pastors who resided in the community as well.[61]

One can only speculate on the extent to which company officials applied pressure on the community's clergy. From all indications, Texas & Pacific Coal Company did not recruit any of the pastors who served in Thurber and did not meddle in their business. Someone, official or otherwise, apparently did question the habits of the Catholic priest living in Thurber. Gordon, who by that time had succeeded the retired Hunter, expressed little concern: "The Father is undoubtedly very free and easy going, but this does not seem objectionable to his flock as most of them are pretty much of the same feather.[62]

Situations in most coal camps rarely required as "muscular" an effort as the denial of housing and other subsidies to antagonistic clergy or demands for removal of a pastor. The simple presence of company officials at services may have had an intimidating effect, intended or not. Even without any urging from company officials, churches facilitated Americanization and, in emphasizing the virtues of faithfulness, obedience, patience, honesty, discipline, and hard work, could undermine confrontational behavior and promote the very qualities industrialists desired in employees.[63]

Church activities may have performed an even more significant function in strengthening social ties within the working population. Special revivals, first communions, conversions, musical presentations, weddings, baptisms, funerals and burials, picnics, fund-raisers, and charitable assistance to an ill or injured neighbor played an important part in the workers' world. Festive Italian and Polish wedding celebrations lasted for days in Thurber. Exploding blasting powder announced the birth of a child or the observance of other happy occasions.

Even the saddest occasions reflected the workers' identity. Irish, Italian, and Polish residents held elaborate wakes for their dead. Even though the company likely had embalmed the body, outfitted it in a casket purchased at the mercantile, and transported the deceased in a company hearse to a final resting place, the miners' social station and traditions dictated the appearance of the company's ten-acre graveyard. Broken glass, a child's iron frame bed, ornamental iron fences, wooden or pipe crosses, or broken brick marked graves in Thurber, as they did in peasant villages in Europe and in graveyards across America where families could not afford expensive headstones. Names like Deaton, Keith, Weaver, George, Harris, Green, Smith, and Taylor joined Dudko, Beneventi, Giovanni, Potepan, Fornaszewski, Solignani, Paulowsky, Applehans, Dzelski, Kretschmer, Maletski, and Salazar on grave markers, their inscriptions printed in the various languages spoken in Thurber.[64] These expressions of heritage, mutual concern, and independence also extended to other social activities in the community.

In company towns, management expected to influence the way its employees spent their spare time. Organized recreational events expressed that paternalistic impulse to satisfy employees' needs and wants (as perceived by the company), to raise morale and assure contentment —one of the central goals of welfare capitalism—and to strengthen ties between the company and its employees. Corporations operated saloons and sponsored annual holiday celebrations, athletic teams, community bands, and entertainment in company-owned meeting halls or opera houses.[65] Workers left their personal and cultural imprint on many of these pursuits and created their own diversions, however.

Perhaps no organized recreational event had more "Americanizing" qualities than a game of baseball or a July 4 picnic. The Texas & Pacific Coal Company spent a lot of time and effort in promoting both. The company built a special park on the town's east side and recruited athletically inclined employees to work for the company and to play for its baseball team, the Thurber Colts. Operators expected company teams like the Colts to entertain residents but also to advertise the town and the company. These teams additionally encouraged competitiveness, teamwork, and an appreciation of rules—habits that any company hoped its workers would develop not only at play but also at work. Thurber's team apparently fulfilled the company's expectations, because it attracted crowds from all over the region and proved to be a source of considerable community pride.[66]

Thurberites loved to watch baseball but enjoyed playing it too. They formed their own informal teams (along ethnic, mine, or occupational

lines) and entertained themselves. Next to baseball the miners preferred Italian bocci ball, a game similar to croquet without mallets,
over almost any other sport. Outside the saloon and in backyards at
almost any time of the year residents could hear the crack of wooden
balls striking each other.[67]

Each July 4 the Texas & Pacific Coal Company sponsored a camp-
wide, day-long celebration open to Thurber residents and to neighboring communities as well. A common feature in towns in which
management practiced welfare capitalism, these field days promoted
patriotism and Americanization. They also gave the company the opportunity to display its benevolent side and to foster the image of one
big family. The company furnished all the food and beverages and organized sports contests with cash prizes for cattle roping; soaped-pole
climbing; potato, sack, bicycle, hurdle, and foot racing; musical concerts; dances; parades, and patriotic orations. Even with the holiday's
American theme, however, each ethnic group gathered at separate
points on the picnic grounds and, according to the company newspaper (July 7, 1894), "enjoyed themselves after their own fashion."[68]

The miners had no paid days off, but celebrated a whole variety
of holidays in addition to American Independence Day—some company-
approved, others of the workers' own making. On Columbus Day, May
Day, Cinco de Mayo, and various saints' days and other religious holidays, the beer flowed freely. The parades, songfests, dancing, and feast-
ing, with participants often dressed in colorful folk costumes, reinforced
ethnic pride and a feeling of security in the large immigrant population, which had brought the traditions of these celebrations with them
from their homelands. During these holidays, one resident recalled,
"mining would cease and celebrations were boisterous."[69]

Private social associations that sponsored dances, sporting activities,
dinners, and charitable activities abounded in Thurber. The exclusive
Lotus Club and the Hunter Fishing and Boating Club, which company executives organized in 1895, excluded general membership, but
Thurber's residents established a multitude of their own clubs. Every
imaginable lodge counted members in Thurber, most segregated according to sex, race, and ethnic group. In 1900, a city directory listed
fourteen lodges or organizations with chapters in town. The Woodmen
of the World, Knights of Pythias, Independent Order of Foresters, Independent Order of Good Templars, Ancient Order United Druids,

Societa D'Italia, Star of Italy, Household of Ruth, Mutual Aid and Benefit Society, Oddfellows, Rebekah Lodge, Masons, Redmen, and the African League all held meetings in Thurber in the 1890s.

These lodges and mutual aid societies assumed both beneficial and social purposes. The Good Templars, never very influential in Thurber, pledged to abstain from smoking and drinking and periodically sponsored box suppers and musical and literary programs for members. Lodge meetings, suppers, masquerade balls, parades, banquets, and musical programs kept the town hall, which the company leased to groups for a small fee, occupied nearly every evening.[70]

The Italian organizations, like their American counterparts, offered opportunities for get-togethers as well as monetary assistance in case of illness, injury, or death. They also performed another function by fighting nativist sentiment and encouraging their membership to assimilate into American society. A ball that the Italian chapter of the Ancient Order United Druids held in Thurber in 1900 reflected both of these purposes. "A large number of American ladies and gentlemen were seen [there]," the *Texas Mining and Trade Journal* reported (February 17), "many participating in the festivities."[71]

Whatever the ethnic or racial group represented in them, these clubs and lodges formed an integral part of the after-work world that workers created in Thurber. They succeeded particularly in a setting like Thurber because they affirmed a feeling of community in a very individualistic world and offered safety and fellowship to a group that experienced little of it at work. In sum, "their rich group life not only provided a fleeting escape from arduous jobs; it provided a way by which working people could exert some control over the painful process of entering the urban, industrial world."[72]

By 1895, the Texas & Pacific Coal Company opened an opera house in Thurber and booked a variety of programs to entertain its residents. These ranged from the "Down-East Comedy Drama" to mind reading, Goethe's *Faust*, and *Il Trovatore*. As popular as these programs were, local talent contributed just as much to the community's cultural life. Whatever social segregation separated the various ethnic groups, each appreciated the other's flair for music, especially that of the Italians.[73]

The R. D. Hunter Concert Band, the R. H. Ward Italian Band, and a string band presented weekend concerts throughout the year. On Saturday and Sunday nights, group singing filled the boarding-houses and backyards of residential areas, especially on Hill #3. "Isn't there a wonderful lot of music in a small keg," the *Texas Miner* mused (August 18, 1894). "The airs of every nationality float out upon the breezes every night from the hillsides in this camp." Black musicians also performed in formal and informal concert for black and white audiences.[74]

At the company saloon, Thurber's multiethnic and multiracial mining population discovered another sphere in which it could establish and practice a value system largely of its own making. Saloon-going was a group activity. As many as two hundred to three hundred miners at one time socialized at the saloon or in the adjacent beer gardens in Thurber when the mines closed for the day. Free to relax, share a round of drinks or a keg of beer, gossip, joke, tell stories, complain, and, occasionally, fight, the miners passed their spare time in a democratic setting in which all patrons, regardless of age, religious beliefs, race, or ethnic background, received comparable treatment. Traditions of commonality and reciprocity so central to a coal miner's work in the mines also ordered relations in the saloon.[75]

An independently contracted saloon sat on the property that Hunter bought from the Johnson brothers in 1888. After one buy out, a lawsuit, and more than one fistfight, the Colonel finally gained control over the establishment and ordered construction of a larger building, which became known as the Snake. The company subsequently established a second saloon, the Lizard, on Hill #3 because of its proximity to the mines.[76]

Company rules prohibited gambling on the premises and the sale of liquor on Sunday except by a physician's order. The saloon opened at 5:30 A.M. and closed at 10:00 P.M. Monday through Friday and at midnight on Saturday. Drunkenness inevitably enlivened the scene, especially on payday, when the saloons reached capacity and the buying of rounds kept glasses full. The saloons justifiably earned a reputation for rowdiness. An occasional shooting startled patrons, and arrests for illegal gambling and fighting frequently occupied law officers who patrolled the area.

The saloons never suffered from lack of business. Probably the most patronized establishment in the camp, the saloon netted a profit of 100 to 125 percent in its first six months of operation. It sold as much as three train car loads, or approximately 150 barrels, of beer a month as well as hard liquor, wine, and cigars. Miners bought beer for ten cents a quart and four dollars a keg and by 1894 could even eat lunch there. Sharing a keg of beer in outdoor sheds and arbors that mimicked beer gardens in the Old Country or a quart with friends inside the saloon sealed many a friendship in Thurber.[77]

Leisure activities not only offered the miners a respite from hard work but contributed yet another element to the job-related culture they all shaped and experienced. In combination with the common bonds that linked them on the job, the ups and downs of life in a town owned by a corporation, and a camp history of labor agitation, these group social activities and assertions of independence from the company's incessant presence set the foundation for a dramatic challenge to company authority. This action tapped the resource of shared experiences and crossed racial, ethnic, cultural, gender, occupational, and language lines.

Looking into town, Thurber, Tex. *Courtesy Southwest Collection, Texas Tech University*

Italian family with boarders, Thurber, Tex., 1907. *Courtesy Southwest Collection, Texas Tech University*

General store. *Courtesy Dick Smith Library, Tarleton State University, Stephenville, Texas*

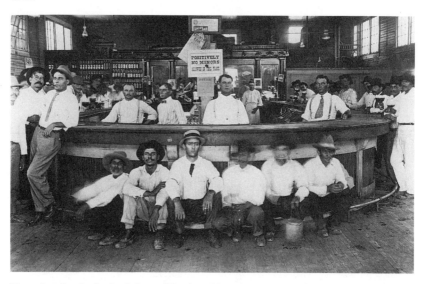

Horseshoe bar in Snake Saloon, Thurber, Tex. *Courtesy Southwest Collection, Texas Tech University*

UMWA Band, Thurber, Tex. *Courtesy Southwest Collection, Texas Tech University*

Thurber baseball team. *Courtesy Dick Smith Library, Tarleton State University, Stephenville, Texas*

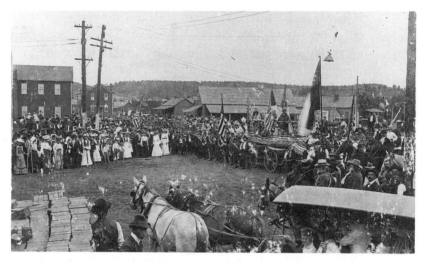

Fourth of July celebration, Thurber, Tex., early 1900s. *Courtesy Texas Labor Archives, Special Collections Division, The University of Texas at Arlington Libraries, Arlington, Texas*

Coal mine #11, Thurber, Tex. *Courtesy Southwest Collection, Texas Tech University*

IV

The Struggle for the Individual
and the Union, 1888–1903

Good bye, Mr. Gordon, we must leave you,
And you bet your life we're glad to go.
Something tells us we are needed —
To the Union Mines we'll go.
Yes the boys with picks are marching,
And we can no longer stay.
Hark! We hear our leaders calling
Good bye, we're away.

— UNION BANNER

For fifteen years after the Texas &
Pacific Coal Company purchased the Johnson assets, a core group of
miners, most of Welsh, Scots, and Irish ancestry, led a protest movement that challenged the very heart of Colonel Hunter's system of operation in Thurber. Their lives most likely paralleled that of Gomer
Gower and his family, as they migrated in and out of eastern, mid-
western, and southwestern mining centers in the United States, following relatives and friends and operators' appeals for skilled workers.
Many of these miners had probably worked underground in Erath and
Palo Pinto counties some time before Hunter even invested in the mining industry there. Their mining experience dated to their childhoods,
and from an early age they understood the usefulness of the strike,
organization, negotiation, solicitation of help from local and distant
allies, and emigration as tools of protest. Using such traditional resistance tactics, they laid the basis for a movement in Thurber that
ultimately bridged ethnic and racial differences and assumed mass pro-
portions in 1903.[1]

Ironically, their actions won success during William K. Gordon's tenure as general manager in Thurber. From the time Gordon went to
work for Hunter in 1889, the civil engineer and self-taught geologist
earned a reputation for fairness among the miners as he rose through

company ranks as mining engineer, superintendent, assistant general manager, and then vice-president and general manager. He lived in the camp with his family and encouraged or at least quietly tolerated the residents' customs, as alien as they must have seemed. He continued and extended Hunter's attempt at welfare capitalism and gave every indication of being an enlightened and benevolent manager.[2]

Even company paternalism, however, could not overcome two important factors: the miners' individualistic impulse to have more control over their work and after-work lives and the mushrooming effect of the rise of the United Mine Workers' union in the Southwest. The result was the development of one of the most dramatic organizational episodes in Texas' early industrial history.

Labor organizations near the site of the Texas & Pacific Coal Company's mining operations had a history at least six years longer than that of the coal company itself. At least three Knights of Labor locals existed in Erath County between 1885 and 1888 (none specifically for coal miners), four in nearby Eastland County between 1883 and 1887, and nine in Palo Pinto County. The local at Gordon, just adjacent to Thurber, represented coal miners from 1882 to 1889.[3]

In 1884, a 186-day strike by 450 miners and laborers to protest a wage reduction closed the mines at Coalville. The walkout, which a Knights of Labor local had called, failed, and the Gould railroad interests proceeded with a 14 percent wage cut. The railroad's mining operation in the area, however, did not survive the financial loss the strike precipitated; in 1886, Gould completely halted coal production there. Even so, the Gordon local still recorded over 200 members in a locale with a population under 1,000. When the Johnson brothers recruited the unemployed Coalville miners the same year the mines folded, they offered the workers a mining rate of $1.50 a ton, $.25 lower than they had received previously. This announcement prompted yet another strike.[4]

For two months the miners remained idle, until the Johnsons granted the local Knights of Labor Assembly the right to appoint a mine committee to negotiate with management in settling disputes. The brothers also agreed to remunerate the miners at the wage paid at Coalville. From that point, good relations between the miners' local and the company continued until William Johnson failed to meet the payroll in 1888, and the company changed hands. For the next four years, these workers agitated and organized in an effort to thwart the new owners' efforts to operate the mines without them.[5]

Hunter never professed any affection for assertive, organized workers and, as he established his domain in Thurber, refused to negotiate on any terms but his own. When the Texas & Pacific Coal Company took possession of the Johnson property, the Colonel immediately posted notices announcing more than a 30 percent cut in the mining rate and almost a 10 percent reduction in the day wage that the Johnson Company had paid. He further made clear his intention to operate the mines on the screened-coal rather than the mine-run basis.[6]

The Colonel also demanded, by Gower's account, that employees "renounce their allegiance to the Knights of Labor and promise not to participate in any sort of union organization efforts." This demand for a yellow dog contract had the same effect as "shaking a red shawl in the face of a bull." When a miners' committee sought a meeting with Hunter, he received them cordially enough but could not conceal his disdain for them. As the miners left, having gained no concessions from the Colonel, Gower recalled that Hunter admonished them: "I will make a dollar look as big as a wagon wheel to you s-o-bs before I get through with you." As a result, none of the old miners applied for Hunter's jobs, forcing him to send his confederates on recruiting tours to mining camps in Indiana, Illinois, Pennsylvania, Kentucky, Missouri, and Kansas.[7]

In a remarkable display of unity, the Johnson miners, in concert with Knights of Labor locals in various mining districts across the country, managed to impede company recruiting efforts for almost three months. Their means of operation were simple but effective. They sent representatives to mining districts and wrote letters to union newspapers. Gower recounted how he helped the local: "There was a sufficient number of us who sought employment in various parts of the country . . . to advise unsuspecting miners of the conditions in Texas. I, myself," he added, "though but an eighteen year old boy at the time, was assigned to the Belleville field in southern Illinois [where a sister and her family resided] for that purpose."[8]

Dan McLauchlan, recording secretary of Knights of Labor Local Assembly 2345, filed several reports on the miners' difficulties with the *Journal of United Labor,* a Knights of Labor publication (May 5, June 23, 1888). After the union committee's unsuccessful meeting with Hunter, McLauchlan claimed that the Texas & Pacific Coal Company was in the market for strikebreakers, who "would be glad to come here and work at any price." McLauchlan asked readers to stay away until a settlement had been reached—"until then," he wrote, "help us by giving Gordon, Texas, a wide berth" (October 25, 1888).

Another McLauchlan letter to the *Journal* (January 3, 1889) explained that working for Hunter meant accepting work at a reduced wage with no input from those who best understood the difficulty of working thin-veined mines. "We have not insisted upon the old price," McLauchlan concluded, "but simply ask that the matter be submitted to arbitration and we [be] given a chance to be heard. This is a poor place to come to for work . . . and all miners are requested to keep away." McLauchlan sent similar letters to another labor newspaper, the *National Labor Tribune* (October 13, October 20, December 15, December 22, 1888), a publication of the National Progressive Union of Miners.

The dispersal of information about conditions at the Johnson mines reaped immediate rewards. Moral and financial support from Knights of Labor locals in the nation's mining districts seriously impeded Hunter's effort to start production. Union members all over the country kept Thurber workers informed of company recruitment activities and sent their own representatives to dissuade miners from working for the Texas & Pacific Coal Company. When company trains arrived in the nation's mining districts, local assembly members infiltrated employment meetings, learned the time of return to Texas, and passed the information to Thurber's local. When the trains reached Fort Worth, a Knights delegation waited to persuade potential employees to leave and with Farmers' Alliance and Knights of Labor national assembly aid, to fund their return. Such activities kept the mines practically shut down until February, 1889, when company officials and Texas Rangers duped labor activists waiting for the train in Fort Worth. They managed to get over 170 miners—many of them black—past the union activists, but a third of these new employees subsequently refused to enter the mines and joined the Knights of Labor after hearing speeches at the Labor Hall.[9]

Frustrated in his initial attempts to import new employees, operate the mines, and maintain absolute control, Hunter resolved to crush the striking miners. Much to his dismay, they congregated at an independently operated saloon in the area and at a meeting hall only a mile from company property on land the Knights of Labor had purchased in 1887. By the end of December, 1888, after gunfire showered the building where the Colonel and his lieutenants were in their offices, the general manager appealed to local and state officials for a contingency of Texas Rangers to be sent "to protect life and property at the mines." The *Dallas Morning News* reported on December 23 that ten of Captain McMurry's company of Texas Rangers had arrived at the mines three days earlier to handle a disturbance caused by the striking miners. Five days later, the paper noted, McMurry wired Adj. Gen. W. H. King in Austin that all was "quiet and orderly" around the mines.[10]

In January, the adjutant general himself visited the camp at Captain McMurry's request. His interview with the Knights of Labor committee convinced him of the sincerity of their pledge to help maintain order against the irresponsible few who had threatened Hunter. Nevertheless, agitation continued. In the interest of protecting Hunter's investment, Texas Ranger Company B maintained a visible presence in Thurber as the strikers continued their efforts to thwart Hunter's attempts to replenish the pits with imported miners. In May, McMurry wrote King that "through the workings of the Knights of Labor & the Strikers, the miners on yesterday demanded ten cents advance per ton on coal, besides several changes in the rules & regulations of the company—none of which Col Hunter says he will agree to—says he will shut down the mines first." McMurry expressed his reluctance to remove his men from the "hard case" in Thurber; "something like a 'slow fever,'" he thought, had started and was spreading there like an epidemic.[11]

In June, 1889, McMurry reported that thirty to forty strikers continued their agitation and were "very much annoyed on a/c of a number of them having been arrested for Rioting, Intimidation, [and] Carrying Pistols." On July 8, McMurry noted that John Clinton, a member of the miners' strike committee, had penetrated the enclosure and beaten two white miners, for which he was promptly detained.[12] Such reports, of course, further convinced state authorities of the accuracy of Hunter's claims against the striking workers.

The Knights of Labor local at Gordon regarded and reported the situation somewhat differently. In June, 1889, George W. Britton wrote the *Journal of United Labor* that the company had tried "all kinds of plans to get us into trouble." The first resulted in drunken men who did not belong to the Order shooting in the streets. "Then," Britton continued, "they [company officials] set up a big howl that the striking miners were rioting, and through that scheme they managed to get a company of State Rangers here. In place of them attempting to keep the peace they have been trying to get some of us into trouble, but so far," he added, "they have made a complete failure" (June 6, 1889). As for the "riot," Britton recorded the report of the Erath County Grand Jury on the matter (*Journal of United Labor,* June 6, 1889): "In regard to the rumored troubles at the coal mines, after a thorough investigation of the same, we are satisfied that there is not, nor ever has been, an organized body of men whose object was to intimidate Colonel Hunter or his employes either by force or threats in the discharge of their duty. The disturbance on December 12 or 13 that caused so much comment was made by a drunken, lawless element, for whose conduct the miners are not responsible."

Union committee members contended that, failing in its attempt to discredit the workers, the company had resorted to arresting the striking workers for vagrancy. "They have already arrested two of our members for a test case, and if they make it stick they say they will have us all behind the bars." Britton concluded with the comment that "if our trouble was settled, it would be but a short time till old 2345 would be booming again. We have had several struggles since we were first organized, but this is the worst we have ever had." Appeals for miners to stay away continued into August, 1889.[13]

Although other writers have contended that the Rangers acted as "referees" in the dispute between Hunter and the miners, it is clear that in the 1889–90 crisis, the underlying reason the adjutant general ordered the Rangers to Thurber was to remove the agitating miners or at least to maintain control over them for the company's benefit. As long as the Rangers remained, the striking miners knew they had little chance to succeed. Shortly before the Rangers left Thurber, McMurry told King, "the strikers still remain in force on the outside, praying for the Rangers to be moved away. They claim that they could soon get clear of 'old Hunter' and the Negroes [the largest number of miners recruited who remained at work], were it not for the Rangers."[14]

The captain's periodic reports, often written on Texas & Pacific Coal Company stationery, displayed an obvious bias against the strikers. McMurry described the Johnson miners' attempts to distribute literature and persuade imported workers to abandon their plans to work for Hunter: "It seemed that they were anxious to do some dirty work, although they possess an unusual amount of 'gall' they did not attempt to get on the train, and I imagine they were very much chagrined when the train did not halt at [the] Depot to give them an opportunity to

76

deliver themselves of their inflammatory speeches and distribute their lying documents." Captain McMurry further charged that his men had been treated with disrespect by both the miners and their family members, although the Rangers by and large had minded their own business.[15]

In his annual report for 1889–90, the adjutant general also expressed sympathy for the company, repeating Hunter's contention that these "so-called strikers" had never been employed by the Texas & Pacific Coal Company but had made the claim to prevent other miners from assuming jobs at low wages in the mines. He also alluded to the economic impact the new business promised the area if development proceeded without impediment. "The opening of abundant beds of coal in this section of a quality to burn and to coke well, the necessary employment of hundreds of hands, the up-building and success of many local enterprises, the influx of population and," he added, "the creation of a home market for many local products; all these desirable things might be expected to begin and grow with the development of coal here, if the company was allowed to proceed peaceably in its enterprises, but to this the so-called strikers objected." King viewed the Rangers' role in moral terms. "Not only in its actual material results is this matter of vast importance, but even more so," he wrote, "in the moral influences exerted by the notice given to all dangerous or lawless combinations of every class and kind that labor shall be free in Texas and that when men will not work themselves they will not be allowed to combine against or violently interfere with those who will and do work."[16]

On several occasions, residents charged the Rangers with abusive acts. Covington A. Hall, general lecturer for the Knights of Labor, claimed in a letter to Atty. Gen. James S. Hogg that a "peaceful law abiding lot of citizens" at Thurber was "being abused, imposed upon and mystreated by a company of State Rangers." Hogg lacked jurisdiction in the matter but advised Hall to take his complaints to the governor. If Hall indeed followed Hogg's suggestion, it had no apparent impact on the Ranger presence there. In June, the strikers filed charges against at least two officers for disturbing the peace when they interfered with the striking miners' attempt to talk to several incoming strikebreakers. At least one of the lawmen was tried and found guilty but fined only one dollar. Despite these incidents, Gomer Gower described the Rangers overall as a "pretty decent bunch of fellows."[17]

Whatever their demeanor, the Rangers' purpose not only in Thurber but in various parts of the state when labor unrest erupted was indisputable. On January 15, 1887, the *National Labor Tribune* singled out Texas' adjutant general for special scorn. In a front-page article headlined "THE ASININE GENERAL OF TEXAS," the paper ridiculed the statements of the adjutant general, in his annual report, on the subject of "oath-bound labor organizations, and the alleged necessity to maintain the militia in fighting shape to resist the encroachments of said organizations." There was no doubt that, while the Rangers remained in Thurber on the adjutant general's orders, Hunter held the upper hand.

In the process, the Colonel expended thirty thousand dollars in company funds and used the power at his disposal to attempt to drive the Johnson miners completely out of the area. A letter from an officer in the Palo Pinto Coal Mining Company to Gov. L. S. Ross demonstrated how far the colonel's influence extended. The company, "acting in unison with Col. Hunter," closed its mines in January, 1889. "Since then," he continued, "we have pretty nearly got rid of all the old miners." The Palo Pinto Coal Mining Company also utilized the Rangers' services with results similar to those in Thurber. "Capt. McMurray [McMurry] sent down three of the Rangers . . . and their presence wrought a marked effect on the men. We have given instructions to have a wire fence put around our village and as all the malcontents have moved about two miles away we don't anticipate any further trouble."[18]

In his fight against the Johnson miners, Hunter also took advantage of the acute problem of dual unionism then complicating organizational efforts in American mining districts. Apparently recognizing the heated jurisdictional battle that the fledgling Knights of Labor District Assembly 135 and the National Progressive [Miners] Union were waging, Hunter convinced representatives of the latter, which in 1890 formed the United Mine Workers, to declare the strike at Thurber over. The organization's willingness to do so reflected its leaders' reasoning that the possible employment of their members in Texas would open the district to successful unionization.[19]

In December, 1888, Hunter contacted the National Progressive Union's *National Labor Tribune,* which by then already had run several recruitment advertisements for the Texas & Pacific Coal Company as well as letters from Dan McLauchlan. Hunter requested that the Progressive Union send a representative to Thurber to investigate conditions at the mines. The union complied, and on Christmas Day, 1888, William Rennie arrived in Thurber. Met by Dan McLauchlan, John Clinton, and Hunter's son-in-law Edgar Marston, Rennie made a lengthy report to the *Tribune*. After meeting with Hunter and the miners' committee and examining the camp, he concluded that the company had not misrepresented the physical conditions around the mines to potential employees. Agreeing with Hunter's position on every point and accusing McLauchlan of spreading "barefaced falsehoods," Rennie concluded with the comment that he knew of "no mining camp where a miner can enjoy more advantages than at the mines of the Texas and Pacific Coal Company." His denunciation of McLauchlan reflected consolidationists' frustration with Knights of Labor locals that, they contended, acted too brashly and without the sanction of district leaders. "It is no wonder the K. of L. has got into bad repute," Rennie finished. Three weeks later the paper boasted about the ongoing movement of miners from DA 135 to the Progressive Union.[20]

Shortly after Rennie's trip, the *National Labor Tribune* (January 5, 1889) declared that under union rules a strike did not exist in Thurber; this opened the way for workers to accept employment there. This, the paper stated, would preserve the "Texas coal field" for unionization and save it from being overwhelmed by cheap Mexican labor. The local strikers, however, rejected the *Tribune*'s decision and wrote letters to the *Journal of United Labor* (January 17) requesting continued support. In response, the Knights of Labor newspaper called for the *Tribune*'s condemnation but took no further action.

In June, 1889, after submission of the local's case to the General Executive Board of the Knights of Labor to effect a settlement, Terence Powderly sent executive board member James J. Holland to confer with Hunter. Hunter told his stockholders that Powderly's adjutant found the company unyielding and already victorious, so the Knights of Labor called the strike "off." Holland claimed the company (which he mistakenly referred to as the Pacific Mining Company) "absolutely refused to treat with me." Accepting the fruitlessness of any further action, he sought employment for the strikers at another mine and recommended that the board terminate its sanction of the strike but continue to warn miners not to seek employment in Thurber. In November, 1889, the Assembly, at its thirteenth regular session, accepted Holland's report and approved his recommendation.[21] Many of the Johnson strikers did drift to other parts of the country, but problems at Thurber remained and activism continued.

In July, 1890, Hunter asked the Rangers to return to Thurber to forestall racial conflict. He claimed that the old strikers were fomenting trouble against the black miners Hunter had employed as strikebreakers the previous year. Fence cutting was the principal manifestation of the problem Captain McMurry reported. With the Rangers' assistance, however, Hunter and the fence held their ground, and within a month normal coal mining operations resumed. Even so, Gower recalled, although Hunter had discharged union members and blacklisted former Johnson employees, the Colonel, in need of skilled miners, agreed in 1892 to reemploy some of them if they refrained from organizing activity. Whatever short-term promises they may have made, the organizational activity did not end, though no unions existed in the community in the 1890s.[22]

In response to the wage reductions that accompanied the 1893 depression in the major coal-producing states and threatened the western and southwestern coal fields, the United Mine Workers' fifth annual convention, in April, 1894, ordered a massive work stoppage. The general labor unrest of that year further heightened industrialists' fears of increased agitation and organization campaigns, employee walkouts, financial losses, and general social and economic chaos. Following in the footsteps of coal producers across the country, in March, 1894, the Texas & Pacific Coal Company reduced the tonnage rate that it paid pit workers from $1.15 to $1.00.[23]

Several months of disorder in the camp followed, capped by a threat on the Colonel's life supposedly made by the owners of a Palo Pinto County saloon just outside the camp fence. The arrest of several "agitators" at a late-night meeting further reflected the unrest in the village. Not surprisingly, in June, Hunter appealed to Adj. Gen. W. H. Mabry for assistance. "Owing to the troubled condition among the miners of the United States at this time, I ask you to appoint about five special rangers to assist in keeping peace at the mines." Hunter refused to admit that any strike had occurred in the pits, although the *Dallas Morning News* (June 6, 1894) reported a work stoppage, but he contended striking miners elsewhere "are sending their walking delegates in here in a clandestine manner."[24]

Hunter may have been correct. The previous month the newspaper in nearby Gordon recounted the story of a miner who claimed that law officers and company officials manhandled him. The *Texas Miner* (May 26, 1894) offered its own account of his "rather 'remarkable'" story. The company, the paper contended, based on its own investigation, knew that the individual in question and his two sidekicks had earned a reputation as agitators but hired them anyway. Law officers arrested them while the three shared drinks in the saloon with several black miners to whom they were delivering their pitch. "The officers simply took him [the complainant] in a hack and outside of camp, and warned him of the unhealthy condition of this camp for an agitator." A week later (June 2) the *Miner* wrote: "Some lazy, good-for-nothing scoundrels steal into camp under cover of night and try to make dissatisfaction with the men," but, the editor claimed, with little success. "Anarchists, agitators, you might as well understand, once and for all, that you cannot fool the Texas & Pacific Coal Company's miners." The June 9 issue of the newspaper similarly denied the existence of any discontent in the camp.

This episode reached a climax at the end of the first week of June, when the imported incendiaries (as the company considered them), one of whom was black, conducted a secret meeting inside the camp. William Lightfoot, hired by the company as an undercover officer to investigate the possibility of a strike, infiltrated the gathering at the Bruce & Stewart Saloon just outside the company compound. In an affidavit submitted to the justice of the peace (who had worked for the company), the captain described the situation. The saloon owners, he believed, held a grudge against Hunter because he had closed a road that allowed residents access from Thurber to the competing drinking establishment. Drawing the miners with an offer of free beer all day, the saloon owners encouraged speech making with the purpose of inciting a strike against the coal company.[25]

The following day the saloon owners and the black "agitator" called a meeting at the old Knights of Labor Hall to which they invited "certain miners in whom [they] had confidence." Lightfoot recollected: "We met in the dark and had no light during the meeting except from a match which I struck to light a cigar." In the course of their speeches, the meeting's organizers urged the miners to strike (like their colleagues in mining districts throughout the country) to protest wage reductions instituted when the demand for coal remained high. In the meantime, law officers, on Lightfoot's information, surrounded the hall and arrested those inside for unlawful assembly. Soon after this incident, the adjutant general's office received at least twenty-five affidavits from a variety of Thurber-area residents, including Hunter, who claimed the miners had no complaints against the company. They blamed the saloon owners for encouraging drunkenness among the workers and providing a meeting place for a few malcontents.[26]

Gomer Gower also recalled the incident. Fearing that his employees were planning to unionize, Hunter hired a spy, Gower related, who identified himself as a member of the Knights of Labor and proposed to organize the workers. The better-informed in the group, Gower pointed out, immediately grew suspicious because they recognized that the Knights had relinquished their jurisdiction to the United Mine Workers. Others, however, expressed some interest, only to have their names reported to the Colonel. During a week's time, possibly at the same time the company solicited the affidavits mentioned earlier, Hunter and his legal staff questioned the miners at the Opera House. The workers apparently satisfied the company that not a single one was interested in organizing a union. "The whole affair was perfectly staged," Gower remembered, "with the Colonel, as always, dressed in his pleated white, spotless shirt plus trousers and coatless, presiding." Despite the intimidating scene, Gower explained, "the untutored miners, being well versed in the art of dealing with spies and evading the hypothetical question of the inquisitors, baffled the Colonel and his aides."[27]

While these events were transpiring, Adjutant General Mabry agreed to send several officers to investigate the trouble in Thurber. But in a confidential letter to Capt. William J. "Bill" McDonald, Mabry intimated Gov. James Hogg's apparent sympathy for the miners. Hogg recognized that the wage reduction, introduced at the very time that strikes elsewhere had forced an increase in the price of coal because of shortages, had prompted the difficulty at Thurber. "Under these conditions," Mabry wrote, "Gov. Hogg is averse to using the strong arm of the state to intimidate workmen whose wages may be below what justly can be paid them as living wages." While awaiting McDonald's report on the situation, Mabry continued that he expected his two representatives to maintain order, which, he counseled "you can best do . . . by going quietly to the leaders, and tell[ing] them that no lawless acts will be tolerated; that peace," he concluded, "and the majesty of the law will be preserved and maintained at all hazards."[28]

When the adjutant general received the officers' initial report, he rejected it because the report failed to recount events on both sides of the issue. This made it impossible for the state's chief executive and the adjutant general to understand the situation completely. "A full and impartial report of the grievances on the part of the men employed by the Coal Company, or other persons connected with the mines, is desired." Four days later, with an acceptable report in hand that claimed the miners had no real grievances except the presence of bothersome agitators, Mabry still refused to send any additional men. "Owing to the Governor's dislike to any appearance of coercion, until it is necessary to maintain peace, law, & order, no rangers will be sent to that point at present."[29]

Interestingly enough, in a personal letter to Mabry, Hunter expressed his satisfaction with the Ranger presence, albeit limited, in and around the camp. The *Texas Miner* (June 16, 1894) likewise applauded the Rangers' assistance. The paper attributed the "driving away [of] the cut-throat element of outside agitators and dynamiters who were terrorizing our miners and mine workers" to the prompt action taken by the governor and the adjutant general. Mabry's confidential orders notwithstanding, Ranger W. J. L. Sullivan reported to Thurber with two of his "boys" on June 12 (four days before Mabry refused to send the Rangers there in full force) "to help keep down a Strike at that plase." He also recorded the arrest of one person on June 20 "for threatening to blow up the coal mines."[30]

Hunter finally sought the posting of special law officers to the camp to ensure law and order. Within a month of the trouble at the saloon, secret investigator Lightfoot, followed several months later by Malcolm "Lit" Williams, initiated the procedures required for appointment as "Special Rangers" stationed in Thurber. Their monthly reports from the middle of 1894 through 1899 described no strike-related difficulties in the camp, despite the United Mine Workers' July 4, 1897, nationwide strike and stepped-up organizational activities throughout the Southwest.[31]

Agitation in Thurber, however, apparently did not cease. In April, 1896, the *Texas State Labor Journal* wrote a series of articles charging armed officers in the coal town with the robbery and intimidation of residents. The paper also blasted the company for cheating the miners out of their just wages by using the screen basis for weighing their coal output, docking them excessively for dirty coal, and charging unreasonable prices at the camp stores. At a mass meeting of purportedly five hundred to six hundred miners at the Opera House, a committee on resolutions drafted a series of statements refuting all of the labor paper's charges. According to a document of resolution that the committee sent to the adjutant general, the miners in attendance unanimously adopted the committee report. The committee head worked as a pit boss in Thurber and had contributed one of the affidavits claiming the miners had no complaints in 1894.[32] The accuracy and significance of this curious document are subject to question, considering the events that took place seven years later. Gower did not comment on it.

When Colonel Hunter retired in 1899 and turned the company over to Edgar Marston and William K. Gordon, the United Mine Workers of America had reached a turning point in its history. Although the union counted only 9,731 members in 1897, in the wake of the disastrous 1894 strike, the miners' organization called a work suspension on July 4, 1899. Over 100,000 miners responded, walking out of the pits in the nation's central mining district. Falling wages, the introduction of labor-saving machinery, unemployment, and the resulting effects on the coal-mining population had generated a greater militancy among miners, unionized or not, for which operators had not prepared.[33]

Plagued with overproduction, cutthroat competition, falling prices, and instability in the industy, mine owners in the Central Field agreed to meet in joint conference with representatives of miners' locals. They expected to find a joint solution to their problems and to establish the machinery that could forestall strikes. With this success and recognizing that the key to survival was a strong, national organization that would function as a counterforce to the operators, the United Mine Workers, under the leadership of John Mitchell, committed itself to an aggressive organizational effort. By 1899, union organizers had moved west of the Mississippi River and in that same year made important inroads in organizing the Southwest Field (including Arkansas, Indian Territory, and Texas).[34]

In Texas by 1900, the coal mines at Lyra, Strawn, Rock Creek, Alba, and Bridgeport, all within a seventy-mile radius of Thurber, could be counted as union camps. Gordon wrote Marston in January of that year that things were "quiet" with his miners after a spate of difficulty with the drivers. He expressed disappointment, however, that "Bennett over at Strawn [several miles northwest of Thurber] is allowing the Union to get a very strong foothold there. . . . Besides," he added, "it gives this organization a starting point in Texas, which could have been so easily prevented had he opposed it in its infancy."[35]

Thurber was one of the holdouts in the area, but the history of labor agitation there, the intensive organizational activity that apparently realized success in nearby mining camps and across the Southwest, and mine operators' recognition that districtwide union agreements could actually help stabilize the industry paved the way for Thurber's succumbing to the inevitable. Furthermore, although company officials may have felt some security in the large number of non-English-speaking immigrants in Thurber, whom employers typically regarded as docile and less inclined to join unions, the United Mine Workers early recognized the reality of sometimes militant multiethnic and multiracial mining populations and quickly adapted to them. In 1891, when the *United Mine Workers' Journal* began publication, it printed its weekly editions in a number of languages. Organizers who spoke foreign languages worked those areas with a high concentration of immigrant workers. Such a policy paid important dividends. "New" immigrant groups in Utah, Pennsylvania, and other mining centers actively supported strike calls and organization efforts. The miners' union also actively organized mixed locals to include not only immigrant but black laborers as well.[36]

With the intensification of union activity in Texas by 1900, organizers were working the Thurber mines surreptitiously, some even wearing disguises to penetrate the fenced compound. Peter Hanraty, president since 1900 of District 21, United Mine Workers of America, which claimed jurisdiction over the Southwest Coal Field, described his efforts to gain access to closed camps. Having succeeded in employing "guarrilo [guerrilla] warfare" against Oklahoma operators to force them to negotiate, he applied similar techniques in Texas:

> In May of last year [1903] I made my first trip to Texas for the purpose [of] looking over that field and to find out the conditions of the miners and to lay plans to organize them, Thurber . . . being the best fortified place against organized labor in the United States. I had to keep my identity unknowen and my movements very *secret,* for Fourteen Years the company had been very successful in keeping Organized Labor from getting a foothold there. . . . [A]fter making a thorough investigation and realizing the importance of organizing Thurber I layed my plans and set about to execute them. In June . . . I sent an Organizer there

who spoke several different Languages, to work in the mines with instructions how to act, and after twelve days he left and told me it was impossible to Organize them. I then sent a Mexican there: what became of him I do not know, as he never reported, nor have I been able to locate him since. In Aug. I sent Tom Fenolio from Hartford to Thurber with Pacific [specific] instructions how to proceed; he went to work in the mines, and associated with the leading Italians and great credit should be given him for the able and fearless manner he worked among them. Arrangements were made for Labor-day celebration close to Thurber Junction but was changed to Lyra, invitations were sent to Thurber inviting the miners to participate.[37]

The company ordered activists discovered inside the town to vacate the premises, but smoldering discontent and "secret preparations" produced well-organized collective action by Labor Day, 1903. The union's stepped-up activity prompted the company to post an announcement, dated August 23 and written in four languages, that, effective October 1, the Texas & Pacific Coal Mining Company would increase the mining rate from $1.00 to $1.05 a ton and pay bonuses for production of anything over the miners' average monthly production of thirty tons. Additionally, the company proposed to delay the early-morning train departure from 6:30 to 7:00 and granted the miners a nine-hour day.[38]

Few miners failed to recognize what was afoot. A September 3 notice confirmed this perception. "For the information of all employees, notice is given that Thurber will remain a nonunion camp." Anyone who disagreed could "get a settlement at any time."[39]

The miners took these notices as a direct challenge. Fanning the fire were reports of the disappearance of a Mexican organizer (to whom Hanraty referred in his report) and rumors of the discovery of a murdered Mexican, his identification withheld by the company, in the area. Sensing the tension, Gordon took action. On August 30, 1903, the general manager wrote Gov. Samuel Willis Tucker Lanham for a contingent of three or four Rangers who, he felt, as the company's "guests" would "have a most quieting effect on the agitators." Claiming that 98 percent of the workers wanted no union, he charged union activists with fomenting discontent where none existed. Advised explicitly by Adj. Gen. John A. Hulen that their duty was "to keep the peace, and in no event [to] take sides with any faction that may possibly arise," the first group of Rangers arrived on September 5, after the mine workers' union had announced Hanraty's plans for the three-day picnic to begin on Labor Day. To defuse the union's effort, Gordon opened the Thurber Club, the private social retreat normally closed to the miners, for a grand barbecue in celebration of Labor Day.[40]

Not to be outdone, the United Mine Workers seized the opportunity of having the miners all together (some eleven hundred persons, not all miners, assembled there) and instructed a miner's son to ride among them spreading the word that a union organizer waited at Lyra to induct them into the organization. A massive Labor Day celebration at Lyra attracted a crowd of hundreds, although most of the Italians marked the celebration at Thurber, where Gordon had successfully outbid the union for an Italian band to entertain the crowd. At Lyra, after a short speech by Hanraty, a 2½-hour discourse by international United Mine Worker organizer William Wardjon, and a liquor-free barbecue, about sixty miners from Thurber, very likely including members of the old Johnson miner group, joined the organization. Hanraty, Wardjon, and C. W. Woodman, secretary of the Texas State Federation of Labor, who had arrived in Lyra at midnight after an open-buggy ride in the pouring rain, received the new members and sent them back to the company town to "work quietly and wait." To the surprise of even the organizers, "the work of the sixty bore immediate fruit."[41]

On the following day, Thurber's as-yet largely unorganized miners presented Gordon with a set of demands. They called for a mining rate of $1.35 a ton, an increase in day wages, an eight-hour day, bi-weekly paydays, and recognition of the United Mine Workers of America. Although not among their written demands, the miners also made clear their sentiments that the fence and armed guards be removed.[42]

Gordon refused to meet the demands, and the miners boycotted the pits on Wednesday and marched to Lyra to meet union representatives. Wardjon, who had already returned to Fort Worth, made his way back to Lyra on the noon train, and on his arrival there heard a rousing cheer of "Wardjon, Wardjon" from those seeking union membership. "There," Wardjon related, "the men [fourteen hundred strong] congregated in a grove awaiting him—waiting for some one to tell them how to conduct a strike, how to become union men" (*United Mine Workers' Journal,* September 24, 1903).

Seven hundred miners joined the union on the spot, and organizers called another meeting for Thursday at the Palo Pinto Bridge, three miles from Lyra and Thurber. Unionized miners from Lyra led the procession and on their arrival at the bridge found nearly two thousand men and women representing not only miners and their families but brick workers, clerks, carpenters, teamsters, and laborers, all interested in unionization. As a posse of Rangers approached, the crowd, some standing, some seated on the ground, and others clinging to tree limbs, surrounded the speakers, fearing a confrontation. None occurred; the peace officers simply requested that the miners not set off any blasting powder, as was the custom during celebrations, and departed (*United Mine Workers' Journal,* September 24, 1903).

When asked who wanted to join the union, all those who were seated stood, and the organizers, with benefit of interpreters, proceeded to swear in the union's newest converts and to initiate steps to organize all the other company employees. Even local farmers expressed their intent to join a union. Wardjon counseled the miners not to return to work, draw any pay, or remove their tools from the mines until Hanraty advised them further, because under company rules workers had to vacate their homes one week after drawing their final pay. The miners then created a relief committee with all "races" represented, opened a commissary to aid those in need, and promised shelter to anyone forced out of his or her home.[43]

On Hanraty's return the district president told the strikers that if they did not want to work for the company under existing conditions, they should pick up their tools and leave the property. Hanraty explained: "If the company will not treat you as human beings, then leave them in peace. Lacking a say in what your wages are, you are not free men." So emerged the union's plan of action — an exodus, a massive "going away," a tactic that strikers had employed without much success in Indian Territory during the 1894 strike and that reflected an extension of the industrial worker's tradition of quitting as an expression of dissatisfaction.[44]

To succeed, the exodus had to be a peaceful one. "If anyone imposes upon you, let us know and we will see that you are protected under the law. But, let me tell you," Hanraty continued, "if you do any one wrong, I will be the first to see that you are sent where you belong." The workers complied without exception. No violence or drunkenness aggravated the tense scene. To those ready to depart Thurber, the United Mine Workers offered shelter, assistance, new employment, and transportation and even promised to supervise the stock of those leaving if quarantine laws at their destinations would affect them. Gordon offered the miners train service to the mines, accompanied by Rangers, to collect their tools. All miners who requested their pay received it in cash. Tools that the company offered to purchase and personal property too cumbersome to transport sold cheaply.[45]

All together, at least five hundred miners left Thurber, most of them single Italians who sought employment elsewhere in the United States or who returned to Italy. The dramatic departure crippled the company, since only eight or nine men refused to strike, and the limited recruitment efforts initiated by the company had failed miserably. In one case, eighteen miners from Pennsylvania imported by the company marched to Lyra as soon as local residents described the situation in Thurber to them. Once there, union organizers convinced them to leave and paid their return passage. C. W. Woodman recalled that out of several trainloads of strikebreakers transported to Thurber, only three miners actually reached the camp. Others refused to work the mines on learning of the strike. The trio who continued the trip to the town finally joined the union and earned the nickname "the $30,000 men," since they were all that remained of the strikebreakers it had cost the company thirty thousand dollars to recruit.[46]

Almost two weeks into the strike, Edgar Marston arrived in Thurber in his private railroad car. Once there he met with the unshaven, unbathed Hanraty, Wardjon, and Woodman, who had been working and sleeping in a nearby wooded area during the crisis. Marston asked that the mine workers' union not call out the miners at Rock Creek, where a subsidiary of the Texas & Pacific Coal Company employed 150 men. In return he agreed to recognize the union at Rock Creek. The company having taken the first step, union officials promised not to transport any more workers from the area, inferring that Marston would recognize the union in Thurber if the employees halted their departures. Marston then agreed to participate in an upcoming Fort Worth meeting between Southwest Coal Field operators and union representatives.[47]

From September 23 to September 26, Marston met with national, regional, and local union leaders. They finally signed an agreement granting the miners an immediate 15 percent raise (to $1.15 a ton), biweekly paydays, and an eight-hour day for day laborers. The company also agreed to collect union dues, assessments, fines, and initiation fees, an agreement that subsequent payroll records confirm. The miners additionally received the right to have a checkweighman oversee the weighing of each miner's output and, although the screened mining system continued, the company narrowed the bars that determined the amount of coal retained for weighing. The company further agreed to pay for certain deadwork. In return, the union promised to return the workers to the mines and to solicit four hundred to five hundred miners, if needed, to replace employees who had departed permanently.[48]

The negotiations not only successfully addressed the miners' concerns about their work, the strike also influenced company policy in regard to those features of a company town that, even after Hunter's retirement, had continued to frustrate residents. The fence surrounding Thurber, the symbol of an autocracy that even in its paternalism affronted human dignity, came down. After the strike, the company allowed employees to live outside the town, tolerated independent merchants and peddlers, who freely advertised and sold their goods in the camp, and accepted residents' requests to seek the care of physicians other than those employed by the company if they so chose. Additionally, Marston's annual report for 1903 proposed that the mercantile company be operated more independently of the coal company, since the company stores served as a perennial topic at union meetings.[49]

Fifteen years of activism produced a victory in Thurber that both the individual and the union shared. The company won as well, for few serious labor difficulties threatened the mines' operation in the next twenty years. The events that occurred there, however, assumed a greater significance than the immediate impact on Thurberites. Similar scenes were played out in other bituminous and anthracite coal–mining regions across the United States. As a result, by the early 1900s, the United Mine Workers' Union was a powerful force in the Southwest and elsewhere. In Texas before the Thurber strike there were only three hundred organized miners. With the miners' success in Thurber and surrounding mining communities, "a powerful and militant organization" enforced the closed shop in Texas' mining district for over twenty years. By April, 1909, the total United Mine Workers' Union membership in Texas locals had reached twenty-two hundred.[50]

Thurber's miner activists constituted only one group of labor agitators in Texas who protested their working conditions in this same time period; longshoremen, railroad workers, cowboys, cotton handlers, and streetcar workers all expressed their discontent. The mine workers' locals, however, were an especially important group. Among the largest in the country, they played an influential role in the Texas Federation of

Labor, which successfully fought the open shop movement in Texas until the 1920s. The state organization not only endorsed labor's traditional tactic, the strike, but also mobilized its resources to lobby successfully for legislation to protect Texas' industrial workers. Laws that the state legislature passed in the early 1900s, under pressure from organized labor, included prohibition of the use of coercion against employees who did not patronize company stores, institution of safety standards in mines, establishment of sixteen as the minimum age for mineworkers, a declaration of scrip payment as illegal, and passage of an anti-blacklisting law. Gomer Gower declared that during this time "labor . . . was in the saddle in Texas." In the same period, Thurber could also lay claim to the distinction of being, in Gower's words, "one of the most pleasant mining communities in the country."[51]

V

Boom to Bust in Unionized Thurber

*Thurber was said to be the only little city wherein every
worker was a due[s]-paying member of his respective
union. So it continued for nearl[y] 20 years when oil came
into general use and coal shrunk to practically nothing.
   The ending of Thurber, and other coal camps in Texas,
was a tragedy. Homes broken up, no place to turn for re-
employment — and, a kinder hearted, more loyal citizens
were never grouped together.*
                              —C. W. WOODMAN

For almost twenty years after the 1903 strike, Thurber continued to operate as a single-industry community owned by a powerful corporation. The nature and conduct of the largely immigrant mining population changed little. Under the administration of Edgar Marston and William K. Gordon, the system of welfare capitalism initiated by Colonel Hunter expanded. For the most part, a benignant attitude characterized employer-employee relations both on and off the job. By the standards of the day, Thurber fit the picture of a model company town. In the 1920s, however, circumstances compelled the company to shut down the mines. Ironically, the model mining community closed the decade on the verge of becoming a ghost town.

In the ten-year period that followed the United Mine Workers' organization of pit workers in and around Thurber, coal production grew by leaps and bounds. In 1904, Gordon reported an output of 322,922 tons from the company's mines at Thurber; in 1912, the mines produced more than twice that amount. During the same period, the company opened five new shafts and abandoned production in only two of the older pits. The coal business in Texas was booming — record-breaking, in fact — as the annual geological surveys indicated, despite predictions by some in 1903 that the excessive wage demands of organized coal workers would ruin the industry.[1] Thurber's mining population likewise multiplied.

The 1910 census recorded 3,805 residents in Thurber; since 1900, the town's population had grown by 49 percent. Support enterprises similarly expanded to meet employees' needs. A mercantile that included dry goods, market, hardware, drug, and grocery departments replaced the lone general store that had provided goods and services to the miners originally. The company built an ice plant, electric light plant, auxiliary general store, saloon, livery stable, dairy, hotel, and cashier, paymaster, auditing, and general company offices. The corporation also maintained twenty miles of railroad track between the mines and town, a social club for company executives, an opera house, a sanitation department, a hospital, wood and lumberyards, a machine shop, pumping station, cotton gin, photography studio, newspaper office, fire department, library, shoe repair shop, and a brick plant. In addition, the Texas & Pacific Coal Company provided all residential housing and buildings for three public schools, six churches, a Methodist resettlement house, and meeting halls for the multitude of community organizations to which employees and their families belonged.[2]

Coal miners and their families still dominated the camp population. Of the approximately 1,600 males listing occupations, two-thirds described themselves as miners. This number represented almost a 30 percent increase in the total number of males who identified themselves as coal diggers in 1900. Another 140 males in 1910 worked in mine-related jobs, including timberman, pusher, road cleaner, flat trimmer, spragger, trapper, brakeman, machine helper, motorman, check puller, teamster, engineer, inspector, fireman, and weighman; this reflected the increasing occupational specialization occurring in the mines and the sophistication of the enterprise in Thurber. The brick plant employed less than 10 percent of the male working population. The other enterprises in Thurber still existed largely to serve the mining operation and its employees and their families.[3]

The makeup of the mining population in Thurber in 1910 reflected, as it had in 1900, the growing influence of southern and eastern European immigrants and, at least in Texas, of Mexican laborers on the mining industry in the Southwest. By 1910, 84 percent of Thurber's miners claimed a foreign birth, compared to 66 percent in 1900. Half of all these miners had emigrated from Italy. Mexico and Poland contributed the next-largest percentages (see table 7).[4]

Thurber gave little appearance of being a melting pot as the 1910s opened. The Methodist church's home missionary program even op-

TABLE 7

Ethnicity and Assimilation Components in the Coal-Mining Population, Thurber, Texas, 1910

Nationality	Number	% All Coal Miners	% English-Speaking	% Alien	% Naturalized	% Pending	% Less Than 10 Years	% Le[ss] Than Year
		Ethnicity of Coal Miners			Citizenship		Residency in U.S	
Italian	546	51.0	1	95.0	4.8	0.2	81	51
Polish	108	10.0	20	89.0	7.0	4.0	80	57
Mexican	124	12.0	10	100.0	0.0	0.0	43	15
Australian	40	4.0	22	95.0	5.0	0.0	77	38
Hungarian	27	3.0	7	96.0	0.0	4.0	81	59
French	10	0.9	50	80.0	10.0	10.0	40	0
English	8	0.7	100	29.0	71.0	0.0	0	0
Scots	7	0.6	100	29.0	57.0	14.0	14	14
German	4	0.3	100	25.0	25.0	50.0	0	0
Belgian	3	0.3	100	100.0	0.0	0.0	66	67
Welsh	3	0.3	100	0.0	67.0	33.0	0	0
Bohemian	2	0.2	100	100.0	0.0	0.0	100	100
Swedish	2	0.2	100	0.0	100.0	0.0	0	0
Spanish	2	0.2	0	100.0	0.0	0.0	100	100
Irish	1	0.1	100	0.0	100.0	0.0	0	0
Swiss	1	0.1	100	0.0	0.0	100.0	0	0
Lithuanian	1	0.1	0	0.0	0.0	100.0	0	0
Norwegian	1	0.1	100	0.0	0.0	100.0	100	0
South American	1	0.1	0	NA	NA	NA	100	0
Total Foreign-born Miners	891	84.2	8	92	6	2	72	45

NOTES: NA = Not Available
SOURCES: Twelfth Census, 1910, MS; computer analysis of data base for Thurber, Texas, 1910.

erated a settlement house there after 1908, targeted at the foreign population. Only a fourth of all miners in the community spoke English. Ten years earlier, just under 50 percent of the miners were fluent in the English language. Less than a third of immigrant miners in Thurber had been residents of the United States for more than ten years when the census was taken in 1910, and fewer than 10 percent of them had indicated their intent to settle permanently in this country. Many of their family members remained abroad. On paydays an extra five or six money order clerks worked to accommodate the long lines of miners sending money to relatives in Europe. The lack of a physical and emotional attachment to the United States coupled with a tendency to live in segregated neighborhoods and to move frequently meant that assimilation happened slowly, if at all.[5]

Factors like these limited opportunities for members of Thurber's foreign-born population ever to occupy "middle-class" positions. Only four persons of immigrant background—three from Mexico and one from Canada—worked as brick plant workers. Although one of four doctors, two of six ministers, one salesman, one bookkeeper, and one saloon employee claimed Italian birth, the census described no other person of southern or eastern European or Mexican birth filling any white-collar position. Persons of immigrant background who held such jobs outside the mines generally represented the "old" immigration. Underground, the company rewarded the most-experienced coal diggers, usually of British background, with supervisory positions[6] (see table 8). Characteristics of Thurber's typical miner had changed little in ten years. He continued to labor in his room in the coal shaft, and his social life centered on family, friends, and activities on Italian or Stump hills.

Not unexpectedly, race, like ethnicity, persisted in the post-1900 period as a segregating and occupation-limiting factor. The total black population in Thurber underwent a negligible increase, from just over 250 in 1900 to 275 in 1910. Eighty-four black males identified themselves as coal miners; another 25 listed mine-related positions for their occupations. The remainder worked in menial jobs, although one black professional, a teacher, lived in Thurber (table 8). Segregated housing and social activities still separated the races, but blacks joined the same two local miners' unions to which whites belonged.[7] Occupation continued to link ethnic and racial groups both inside and outside the mines, despite the apparent deepening of ethnic and racial consciousness in the community. An awareness of class differences within the population, especially after 1918, also prevailed.

The growth of support enterprises in Thurber opened the door for the appearance of a larger middle class. According to the 1910 census, these individuals, largely of U.S. or British birth, generally lived in proximity to one another in company lodging rooms or in the residential area closest to town. Brick bungalows and more-attractive lots distinguished the middle-class neighborhood from the drab frame houses elsewhere.[8]

TABLE 8
Occupations by Ethnicity and Race,
Thurber, Texas, 1910

Occupation	Foreign Born in Occupation		Blacks in Occupation	
	Number	% of Total	Number	% of Total
Coal miner (see table 1 for nationalities)	891	83	84	8
Saloon employee Italian (1) Polish (1)	2	40	0	0
Cook	0	0	1	50
Preacher Italian (2) Swedish (1)	3	50	0	0
Salesman Italian (1)	1	4	0	0
Carpenter Polish (1) Swedish (1)	2	11	0	0
Day laborer Mexican (1)	1	6	0	0
Servant Welsh (1) Swedish (1)	2	40	2	40
Waiter	0	0	4	80
Brick plant worker Mexican (3) Canadian (1)	4	3	1	0.8
Fireman in mines Swiss (1)	1	20	0	0
Weighman Scots (1)	1	20	0	0
Meat cutter German (1)	1	6	0	0
Manager German (1) Scots (1) Irish (1) Norwegian (1)	4	24	0	0
Doctor Italian (1)	1	25	0	0

TABLE 8 — *continued*

Occupation	Foreign Born in Occupation		Blacks in Occupation	
	Number	% of Total	Number	% of Total
Railroad worker	8	33	0	0
German (4)				
Swiss (1)				
English (2)				
Irish (1)				
Teacher	4	31	1	8
French (1)				
Irish (2)				
Russian (1)				
Machinist	1	9	0	0
Scots (1)				
Teamster	1	6	2	13
Hungarian (1)				
Miscellaneous mine worker*	12	13	0	0
German (1)				
Austrian (1)				
Mexican (2)				
Polish (2)				
French (5)				
Norwegian (1)				
Bookkeeper	2	20	0	0
Italian (1)				
English (1)				
Clerk	1	7	0	0
French (1)				
Woodcutter	3	75	0	0
Mexican (3)				
Porter	1	12	7	88
Italian (1)				
Stable worker	1	7	0	0
Polish (1)				
Miscellaneous plant worker†	1	5	0	0
Polish (1)				
Mine engineer	2	11	0	0
English (2)				

NOTES: *Timberman, pusher, road cleaner, flat trimmer, spragger, trapper, brakeman, machine helper, motorman, check puller
†Ice plant, water plant, dairy, electrical plant
SOURCES: Thirteenth Census, 1910, MS; computer analysis of data base for Thurber, Texas, 1910.

The "big bugs," as one Thurberite called company executives, arrived in town in larger numbers during 1918. That year the company turned its attention to oil prospecting and drilling and, reflecting that new interest, changed its name to Texas Pacific Coal and Oil Company. These officials resided with their families on "silk stocking row," or New York Hill, where life with such luxuries as telephones and automobiles assumed a quite different meaning than on Italian and Stump hills to the northwest. Brick sidewalks, landscaped yards, and large brick homes contrasted sharply with the chaotic, drab, dusty appearance of the miners' neighborhoods. Membership in the Thurber Club, a particular mark of elite status, relieved the doldrums of life in a not-so-sophisticated coal town by offering special sporting privileges, including hunting, fishing, and billiards, a reading room, and a location for elaborate and elegant parties.[9]

Few residents failed to notice the social distinctions. The wife of a Methodist minister who lived in Thurber for four years in the 1910s wrote: "The . . . co. officials had good houses; otherwise the houses were mostly of the same pattern, painted dark green if painted at all, making a very drab appearance." Another resident related: "The working people, they weren't anything according to the upper classes. . . . It was a big family, but there were classes."[10]

Unlike the elite on New York Hill and the middle-class Thurberite on Park Row, a group living experience continued among the miners, even though half of them were not married and at least another 20 percent were widowed or married but living without a spouse (see tables 9 and 10). The boarding system had actually expanded by 1910. Just

TABLE 9
Marital Status of Coal Miners,
Thurber, Texas, 1910

Marital Status	% of Total Reported
Single	50
Married	46
Living with spouse	31
Not living with spouse	15
Widowed	4
Divorced	less 1

SOURCES: Thirteenth Census, 1910, MS; computer analysis of data base, Thurber, Texas, 1910.

98

TABLE 10

Household and Family Structure of Coal Miners,
Thurber, Texas, 1910

Type of Household	% of Coal Miner Households
Nuclear — 2 parent	30
Nuclear — 1 parent	2
Extended — 2 parent	11
Extended — 1 parent	2
Augmented — 2 parent	24
Augmented — 1 parent	1
Mixed adult group, including married couples with no children	30

NOTES: A nuclear family is defined as parent(s) and child(ren); an extended household as parent(s), child(ren), and other relatives; an augmented household as parent(s), child(ren), and nonrelatives (Walkowitz, *Worker City, Company Town,* p. 113).
SOURCES: Thirteenth Census, 1910, MS; computer analysis of data base, Thurber, Texas, 1910.

over 50 percent of Thurber's coal miners boarded in a household. More than two-thirds of these boarders had emigrated from Italy, and the largest number of miner households with boarders could still be found on Italian Hill, where an average of five boarders resided in homes that offered room and board. This situation conformed to the pattern in Italian households nationwide but also indicated the effects of ongoing immigration into Thurber and the growing pains that a rapidly developing community with inadequate housing experienced.[11]

Cramped living quarters and a lack of privacy were conditions of life in most mining towns, but the introduction of more modern utilities in Thurber gradually improved the quality of life. With natural gas, less coal dust filled the air inside and outside. When the brick plant converted from coal to gas for firing brick, the *Stephenville Empire* (March 3, 1916) announced: "No longer does a great pall of smoke which could be seen for miles, hang over Thurber." Newer neighborhoods also had piped running water.[12]

Modern amenities arrived last, if at all, in the poorer neighborhoods before the mines shut down in the 1920s, but, unlike in many coal towns in other parts of the country, no extraordinary public health problems plagued the community. In 1912, Marston employed Dr. Thomas Darlington, a well-known sanitation expert from New York, to examine conditions in Thurber. In his report Darlington emphasized the need to rid the area of flies and mosquitoes and, according to the *Stephenville Empire* (November 29), advised marked improvement in residents' living habits. The paper noted that the company intended to replace the older houses in the mining neighborhoods to control sanitation better. Within a month (December 20) the paper announced that the Texas & Pacific Coal Company had initiated a cleanup in the mining town, with prizes offered to the best workers.

No unusual patterns of contagious disease threatened health in the community, although occasional epidemics spread through the population, drawing the attention of local newspapers. An outbreak of meningitis in Thurber in 1912 may have prompted Marston's sanitation study. In 1916, physicians placed thirty-nine houses under quarantine because of smallpox infection. The influenza epidemic that swept the nation in 1918–19 invaded Thurber as well. But diseases that flourished where tainted water supplies, inadequate sanitation facilities, overcrowded housing, and inadequate medical care confounded efforts to maintain public health did not disturb Thurber's residents on any significant scale. By the 1910s, the standard of public health in Thurber exceeded that of many mining towns in other parts of the country.[13]

Thurber's Good Templar Society argued that the consumption of alcohol constituted the town's most serious infectious ailment, but the advocates of abstinence never succeeded in winning many converts among residents in the hard-drinking town. The saloon earned the company a considerable profit and, as a gathering place, performed a vital ethnic and occupational social function. Before federal law dictated the closing of saloons, Thurberites, with the company's blessing, either defeated county dry elections or imbibed at the saloon that the corporation transported across the county line when Erath County did vote dry.[14]

Residents even brewed their own concoctions, like the Italian brandy graspa (or grappo), from grapes the mercantile imported in large quantities. Well after Prohibition, old habits died very slowly. Raids in and around Thurber inevitably uncovered bootleg enterprises. In October, 1917, authorities netted three barrels of beer in a house operating as a saloon. In 1921, a two-day raid on twenty-one locations in Thurber netted ten arrests and the destruction of 2,200 gallons of fruit mash, 1,170 gallons of wine, and 790 gallons of beer. Law officials estimated the value at ten thousand dollars. In 1922, a contingent of Texas Rangers arrested two Italians, one of whom possessed "two barrels of beer which was 200 pints and fourteen quart bottles" and the other "nine gallons of wine, twenty-one pints and 8 quarts of beer."[15]

Reports of gambling dens and illegal cockfights also attracted considerable attention in the area as late as 1923 (*Stephenville Tribune,* March 30, 1923). Neither bootlegging nor illegal gaming necessarily typified everyday life for most of Thurber's population, but publicity surrounding such activities contributed to the wild image Thurber carried with it into the second decade of the twentieth century. No one associated Thurber with a tame way of life.

The hard-working and hard-living miners in Thurber also used their union meetings as a gathering place, and they became as important to their social lives as the saloon, social club, or lodge. Despite their religious, ethnic, and racial differences, coal miners met on a fairly equal footing at the union hall. The United Mine workers' Union had organized both an American and an Italian local in Thurber, but many non-Italians, including Americans—white and black—joined the latter because its frugal management resulted in lower dues and more benefits. At this weekly after-work "gob pile," workers shared grievances, established the machinery to assist ill and injured coworkers, and escaped the operator's supervision. Occupational assimilation and initiation for new mine employees also occurred here, since Thurber's closed-shop system required that all miners join the union immediately on employment.[16]

Despite a history of labor conflict in and around Thurber, no major upheavals of the type that preceded the miners' organization in 1903 seriously complicated employer-employee relations at Thurber's mines before 1921. Periodic problems, however, especially between an Italian group and the company, perplexed Gordon and United Mine Workers' officials alike. Thus, even after unionization, the miners asserted a measure of autonomy from both company and union control by taking their share of mass holidays and refusing to work if they held a grievance. The complexity of union-company agreements also encouraged a distrust of union officials and operators among the rank and file.[17] The result was an occasional lapse of discipline among unionized workers, despite the prohibition of walkouts and strikes during contract periods.

In 1908, Gordon wrote Marston that February's output easily would have reached forty-three thousand tons, "had the miners not taken a holiday on the first." On another occasion, he related, Italian miners claimed that a hoisting cage in poor condition threatened their safety and that the company weighman had insulted their check weighman. They declined the trip underground. Even a union district official who journeyed to Thurber on Gordon's request failed to resolve the problem, which by then, the general manager claimed, had spread to Italians in other shafts. Because of the need to meet the railway's need for coal, Gordon finally accepted the company weighman's resignation.[18]

Gordon blamed the difficulties on radical influence among the Italians and their frustration with the local union. "The Italians are becoming very restless, and under the influence of a small number of Socialists and Anarchists, are desirous of kicking out of the traces, with the U.M.W. of A. and affiliating with some other union body, which I believe to be the Industrial Workmen [Workers] of the World." He also believed that the Italians were using the whole series of events to test the miners' union. "The leaders of the Italians told me that their people had become tired of the union, as the latter had no respect or regard for them, other than to receive their monthly dues."[19]

Gordon's evaluation of the rebellious element may have had some basis in fact. At the very time Gordon expressed his concern about radical union activities, the Industrial Workers of the World had organized three locals in Texas coal fields. Socialist sympathizers paraded, lectured, met, taught, and voted in Thurber. Red sashes and carnations, one Italian resident recalled, decorated numerous participants in the annual May Day parade in the community. The company rent book for 1907 included a notation for a rent-free (by "order of W.K.G.") Ballance House Socialist Club in the Italian neighborhood as well as a "Socialist School," which also paid no rent. In national and state elections, a small group of voters in Thurber consistently cast their votes for Socialist candidates after 1903. More important, Socialists probably exerted considerable influence at Thurber's union hall, since they often controlled union politics in mining communities where a large disfranchised foreign population resided.[20]

It is furthermore likely that subtle if not overt ethnic tension existed in Thurber, as it did throughout the labor movement (the United Mine Workers' progressive stance on that issue notwithstanding), and that devotion to the letter of a union contract did not hold much appeal when aggravations at the pit threatened expectations of steady, safe work and decent pay. Whatever the reasons for the Italians' protests, the image of the submissive, disinterested foreigner did not fit in Thurber. Throughout the post-1903 period, Italian miners in Thurber occasionally exasperated both the company and the parent union.

In 1906, Gordon privately proposed to Marston that the corporation, in conjunction with the United Mine Workers, hire more English-speaking miners. Otherwise, he warned, the company faced the possibility of incessant tie-ups in production or even demands to recognize another union even less-acceptable to Marston and associates. The general manager further speculated on the advisability of sinking the next coal shaft at a sufficient distance from Thurber to warrant establishing a new village. "By so doing, we can split or divide the working force into two units, which would give us some advantage in the time of labor troubles."[21]

By 1908, the Italian insurgency prompted Thurber's general manager to threaten to "use dissatisfaction with [the] Italians to force an agreement" with the United Mine Workers. Gordon may have hoped to use the problem of dual unionism in the coal fields to manipulate the United Mine Workers, but he also derived some pleasure in observing the union's difficulty. "While I realize that the local officers of the U.M.W. of A. seem to be up a tree when it comes to handling rebellious members, there is some little satisfaction in ridiculing them, and," he wrote, "in constantly keeping the condition as prominently before them as possible."[22]

Following a resurrection of the company's difficulties with the Italian miners in 1909, Marston contacted former United Mine Workers' Union president John Mitchell, by then affiliated with the National Civic Federation, and asked his assistance. This was part of a pattern that had developed after the 1903 strike. Marston and Mitchell corresponded on numerous occasions and developed a friendly social relationship. Mitchell sent Marston's son Hunter a copy of his book on organized labor when he learned that the young man had expressed some interest in the subject. Mitchell socialized with the industrialist, received an invitation to Hunter Marston's marriage, and even sought the wealthy capitalist's financial advice. Marston, in turn, often freely expressed his opinion on difficulties he encountered with his employees in the coal community and asked Mitchell's advice both during and after the latter's tenure as president of the mine workers.[23] From all indications, this relationship worked to both the company's and the workers' advantage.

In 1910 and 1912, for example, as the date for contract negotiations with Texas' miners approached, Marston used Mitchell as a sounding board for his frustrations concerning their wage demands. Marston never lived in Thurber and rarely visited there, but he contended: "I believe the miners at Thurber are happier, and as a whole more contented and enjoy life equally, if not better, than at any mining camp in the country." He could not understand why they still demanded a 10 percent wage increase. In 1913, Marston complained to Mitchell about the miners' raising the issue of paying a monthly fee for the services of company physicians.[24]

In response to such letters, Mitchell, who encountered considerable hostility within the United Mine Workers for his affiliation with the National Civic Federation and his links to business leaders, often argued the workers' position in measured and conciliatory terms. In regard to the company doctor issue, Mitchell frankly stated: "No man should be required to accept the services of a physician if he or his family be ill, in whom he has no confidence, and certainly he should not be required to pay for the services of a physician if he refuses to accept service from such physician." Marston may not have agreed but apparently listened, and when the company allowed its employees to consult other physicians, their business flourished.[25]

Mitchell even officially arbitrated three labor disputes in Thurber. In 1910, Gordon claimed he had information that one of the miners' locals had approved a resolution calling for a mine shutdown on workdays following any five-minute delay in the arrival time of the train that carried the miners home from the shafts. On November 1, after a train delay the afternoon before, the miners took a holiday. After Gordon submitted one appeal after another to union officials demanding assessment of a penalty on the union, and witnesses to the alleged illegal walkout filed depositions on the matter, Mitchell agreed to arbitrate.[26]

After hearing each side, he denied the company's complaint, accepting the union representatives' contention that the miners traditionally observed All Saints' Day on November 1 by not working. "However," Mitchell added, "I am convinced that the members of the local unions . . . should in the future notify the company in advance when it is their intention in a body to remain at home in the observance of a holiday" and that both parties agree on which days mine employees would celebrate with a general day off.[27] Mitchell shrewdly solved the dispute so that both sides won and both sides lost—and each made its point.

Mitchell also refereed disputes over the screen-weighing system and the pay scale for engineers at the pits. In the former, he refused to assess a penalty on either side; in the latter, he denied the requested pay increase but advised that one be implemented in upcoming contract negotiations. The following year representatives of both the miners and the operators again requested Mitchell's aid in arbitrating a dispute, but without explanation, he declined.[28]

Ongoing concerns about the scrip system and work-related injuries, in addition to the issues just noted, also periodically eroded amicable miner/operator relations in Thurber. The Miners' Cooperative Store in Thurber Junction (Mingus) filed a complaint in Palo Pinto County in 1911 relating to the "custom" in Thurber of the company's "issuing checks or coupons in exchange for labor." The Texas Pacific Mercantile & Manufacturing Company's refusal to redeem the "checks" for purchases at the cooperative store had prompted the action, a repetition of one filed several years previously in behalf of a group in nearby Strawn. Apparently, nothing come of the complaint, for the "check" system in Thurber operated well into the 1920s.[29]

Even with mine safety improvements dictated by state law or union contract, mine workers still lived and labored in fear of explosion, roof collapse, hoisting and underground car accidents, and fire in the pits. In a June, 1916, letter to Edgar Marston, Gordon mentioned six injury damage suits that employees had filed against the coal company, one involving the traumatic loss of a miner's leg. At least seven suits pertaining to work injuries or deaths caused by a fall of coal or hoisting and underground car accidents reached the civil appeals courts between 1906 and 1919.[30]

Accident victims ranged from a badly bruised seventeen-year-old miner who fell into a coal chute at Mine Number One to an apparent heart attack victim found dead at Shaft Number Ten. A nineteen-year-old died after an empty car crushed his left leg, a fifty-two-year-old suffered a foot "mashed to a pulp" by a car wheel, a brakeman was killed on a coal train, an electric motor tore a man's arm from his body, and the explosion of a twenty-five-pound can of blasting powder injured seven and killed two. Unlike the pre-1903 period, however, union benefits as well as worker's compensation, employer liability funds, court-ordered damage assessments, and organization benefit payments often recompensed victims or their families when such traumatic incidents occurred. Miners or their families no longer depended solely on limited aid from lodges or coworkers who "passed the hat" or on the unwritten policy of assistance that had helped the needy in Thurber previously.[31]

Despite ongoing disagreements over such issues as safety, weighing procedures, car shortages, and wages, few strikes between 1904 and 1919 significantly reduced output or the miners' income. Contracts usually ran two years, concluded in even years, at which time a brief shutdown might result if negotiations stalled. The USGS reported negligible strike activity in Texas mines between 1904 and 1917, but in line with the national scene, slightly more in the even years of contract renewal, particularly 1906, 1910 (when a strike lasting three months did decrease production by 100,000 tons), and 1916. During 1916, the *Stephenville Empire* (September 22) ominously and prophetically predicted: "If the company can not get a fair deal from its men it is said it will shut down its mines, and go into other lines of business."[32]

This comment followed three important occurrences. In its 1914 report on the nation's mineral resources, the United States Geological Survey blamed the decrease in coal production in the Southwest on "the great increase in Texas and Oklahoma in the production of petroleum, which because of its fall in price . . . has displaced a considerable quantity of coal and lignite as fuel, both on the railroads and in the industries." The same year as the survey's publication, the *Stephenville Empire* (January 22) reported an oil strike in January, 1915, by the Texas & Pacific Coal Company just three miles west of Thurber's neighbor community of Strawn. The well produced one hundred barrels of oil a day and raised hopes throughout the area. "Excitement is intense," the paper noted.[33]

In May of that year Marston wrote Gordon a confidential letter that in retrospect spelled the beginning of the end for the mining industry in Thurber: "The Texas & Pacific Railway are going to introduce oil and the best we shall do is to get an order for what coal they use at $2.25, so you see the necessity of cutting down every expense possible. I don't want any money spent for any further improvements and," he concluded, "we must turn our attention to two things, viz: (1) decreasing cost of output and (2) increasing our oil supply." He also remarked on his pleasure at the upturn in brick plant profits, another corporate enterprise, like the mercantile company, that Marston expected might rescue the corporation. The Texas & Pacific Coal Company's "phenomenal oil development in the Ranger and Strawn oil fields" by fall, 1917, and the corporation's name change to Texas Pacific Coal and Oil Company in 1918 sealed the fate of a community dependent on coal production.[34]

Before oil captured the company's attention, Texas' bituminous coal miners averaged a work year of 229 days, 2½ months short of a full 308-day year of activity. The typical bituminous miner in Texas produced in that same period 383 tons a year and 1.39 tons daily (see table 11). Union contracts offered a safer workplace, a shorter workday, a greater sense of worker control over mine operations and wages earned, as well as slightly more job security. But the profession remained a precarious one both above and below ground.[35]

Thurberites, including coal miners, earned sufficient sums to deposit savings with the Texas & Pacific Coal Company, and some regularly sent money to relatives elsewhere.[36] This suggested that two weeks of steady work, frugal income management, few unanticipated expenses, no property taxes, comparative shopping, and extra money–making enterprises in the home might allow a family or an individual to set aside a sum biweekly or monthly. Nevertheless, the effects of a lengthy separation from the mines could have serious financial consequences. Days lost because of strikes, delays, accidents, holidays, car shortages, equipment breakdowns, inclement weather, and a multitude of other factors could still exact a toll on a miner's income. In the early 1920s, an unexpected event, which finally depopulated almost the entire town, forced the coal miners into other occupations or to coal pits in other parts of the country.

As the war years ended and the industrial bonanza that wartime production requirements had stimulated waned, workers turned from expressions of patriotic harmony to aggressive concern for their pocketbooks. Operators, on the other hand, sought a reduction in wages to reflect the end of the immediate postwar boom in 1920 and proposed separate district agreements so contracts would better reflect special conditions in outlying districts like Texas. Expecting some relief from the rapidly rising cost of living and a reward for their sacrifice, bituminous coal miners all over the country, who had worked throughout the war with no pay increases, demanded unprecedented contract improve-

TABLE II

Texas Bituminous Coal Mine Production,
Thurber, Texas, 1904–23

Year	Average Number of Days Worked	Average Tons/Year/ Miner	Average Tons/Day/ Miner	Total Production (tons)	Tonnage Rate ($)	Estimated Average Yearly Income/Miner ($)
1904	223	344	1.86	774,815	1.150	395.60
1905	253	399	1.68	809,151	1.150	458.85
1906	233	430	1.90	839,985	1.225	526.75
1907	255	300	1.18	940,337	1.225	367.50
1908	266	326	1.23	1,047,407	1.225	399.35
1909	NA	NA	NA	1,112,228	NA	NA
1910	242	330	1.36	1,010,944	1.275	420.75
1911	230	269	1.17	1,083,952	1.275	342.97
1912	248	341	1.37	1,197,907	NA	NA
1913	261	353	1.35	1,247,988	NA	NA
1914	246	402	1.63	1,218,160	1.325	532.65
1915	241	NA	NA	1,197,792	NA	NA
1916	217	350	1.61	1,025,093	NA	NA
1917	274	450	1.64	1,259,276	NA	NA
1918	273	457	1.67	1,074,183	2.000	914.00
1919	228	331	1.45	734,087	2.000	662.00
1920	243	324	1.33	545,227	2.400, 2.650	777.60
1921	121	336	2.77	210,638	2.000	672.00
1922	190	250	1.31	265,179	2.000	500.00
1923	131	NA	NA	175,332	NA	NA

NOTES: NA = Not Available

According to the U.S. Census, Texas workers involved in manufacturing earned an average of $449 a year in 1904, $540 a year in 1909, and $1,080 a year in 1919.

SOURCES: *Mineral Resources of the United States, 1904–1923;* footnote 38; *Thirteenth Census of the United States: Manufactures,* 1909, vol. 9, p. 1213; *Census of Manufactures,* 1914, vol. 1, p. 1483; *Fourteenth Census of the United States: Manufactures,* 1919, vol. 9, p. 1469.

ments. District 21 was no exception. In 1919, a bitter strike in the bituminous fields crippled the nation's coal production and closed Thurber's pits for a month.[37]

Following the recommendations of the bituminous coal commission charged by Pres. Woodrow Wilson with developing equitable wage rates for bituminous coal miners throughout the nation, Texas operators in the spring of 1920 awarded their miners a 20 percent increase over the

1919 agreement. Six months later Texas miners launched another strike that netted them a $.25 raise in the tonnage rate (to $2.65).[38] The following year, however, their negotiating fortunes faded.

When the operators proposed a 25 percent reduction in wages in 1921, the miners countered with a smaller cut in the tonnage and day rates. The company refused their offer, contending that the thin-veined Texas coal fields could not compete at union pay scales with the thicker and richer Eastern coal fields or with cheap fuel oil. In response, Thurber's miners declined to work under the company's offer and launched their last major strike.[39] From that point, recalcitrance on both sides doomed any quick strike settlement.

Emboldened by the open-shop mood across the nation and frustrated by the failure to win a suitable agreement with the miners' representatives, Texas Pacific Coal and Oil Company posted a handbill in September, 1921, stating: "On account of the low market price and the slack demand for coal the Company will be unable to operate Mine No 1 at the present time. The following 1918 scale will be paid: Mining rate $2.00 per ton. . . . Employees wishing work should report to . . . [the pit] Boss, Mine No. 10." In addition to a 25 percent wage reduction, the company further demanded that all those occupying company houses who had not paid rent and utility charges settle their accounts within the week or the company would disconnect water, electric, and gas service. Quoted in the industry trade journal *Coal Age,* Gordon reiterated his intention to hold firm. Even at the wages offered, he contended, the company would merely break even. The fight to defeat the closed shop that had ordered employee/employer relations in Thurber for eighteen years had commenced.[40]

A tenacious and tough negotiator at contract conferences with miner representatives, Gordon nevertheless received accolades from union officials for his faithful adherence to agreements before 1921. A geologist, resourceful corporate executive, respected and well-liked town manager, and philosophical and practical foe of labor organizations, Gordon believed that the future of Texas & Pacific Coal Company lay in unorganized oil and not in unionized coal fields. His opposition to labor unions even found expression at the company's oil drilling sites. Months before the famous McCleskey Well on the Ranger Field in Eastland County began pumping oil in 1917 for Texas & Pacific Coal Company, Gordon wrote Marston: "The effort to organize our Oil Field Employes which has been promoted by members of the Thurber-Strawn miners' locals and the Federation of Labor, has been . . . completely defeated by us. . . . The effort to organize," he explained, "was nipped in the bud, when the president and other officials were discharged and ordered out of the field." Gordon prophetically and quite accurately called the deed "one of the most thorough setbacks organized labor has received since it gained its first foothold in these parts."[41]

By 1921, the miners' wage demands, Gordon's oil discoveries (after years of insisting that Marston invest company funds in oil and prospecting where scientific studies rejected the significant presence of oil and gas), the railroads' increasing reliance on cheaper fuel oil, and the economic recession all coalesced. With Marston's blessing, Gordon refused to concede to unionized miners even if coal mining ceased. Not one to mince words on the subject, Gordon wrote: "It is an evident fact that under such conditions, the Coal operators of Texas are being strangled like a mangy dog, and that the bituminous coal industry must either perish or the Open Shop prevail." Marston expressed similar sentiments: "You and I have done our best to build up a prosperous community and if the miners refuse to cooperate to save Thurber, we shall have to take our medicine and witness the destruction of our attractive settlement."[42]

Their decision really hinged, however, on another factor. Coal no longer reigned over the industrial economy of the Southwest. Therefore, those who tapped the mineral discovered that they were as dispensable as the commodity they produced—in sharp contrast to their situation only three years earlier. Local union president Lawrence Santi reasoned: "The company got oil hungry. They could just turn on a spigot and get oil. They forgot their coal." John Spratt, Sr., one of Texas' foremost economic historians and a onetime resident of Mingus, Thurber's neighboring community, succinctly explains: "As a Texas industry, coal mining owed its existence exclusively to the railroads; and, as an industry, it died when the railroad switched to oil-burning locomotives."[43] Texas' thin bituminous coal veins, which demanded so much of miner and operator alike, lacked appeal when previously coal-dependent markets looked to petroleum for fuel.

Gordon and Marston anticipated the shift and, with the financial resources accessible to a corporation like the Texas & Pacific Coal Company, gambled successfully, easing the company from one primary enterprise to another without significant loss. The miners and their representatives may have recognized the danger signals, but even backed by a national organization dedicated to the protection of their occupational interests and emboldened by a presidential commission inquiry that recognized the miners' wartime contribution, Thurber's coal diggers lacked the power and resources to persevere. They could not force the mines' reopening, and closed mines translated into no income. Dedication to principle and profession succumbed to the demands of basic need. By 1922, Thurber stood on its last legs as a mining community.

In April, 1922, another coal strike closed the nation's bituminous mines, but Texas' limited coal operations, according to *Coal Age,* continued unscathed. "Recent developments in the national coal strike have not affected Texas mines. Most of the larger mines in Texas are operated on an open-shop basis. In the vicinity of Thurber," the journal noted, "the Texas Pacific Coal & Oil Co. is the largest operator. One mine of this company has been in operation since a few weeks after the strike was called, an agreement having been reached. Another is being operated on the open shop basis. The two mines in operation are working about 200 men, against a normal working force of about 800 men." By 1925, a total of only 748 mine employees oversaw production of 182,680 tons of bituminous coal in Texas. Hispanic surnames filled the mine payroll books in Thurber, and the company no longer deducted union dues from its employees' wages.[44]

Annual reports that Marston filed with his stockholders between 1919 and 1937 emphasized the diminished importance of the mines to the corporation, especially after further labor difficulties developed. Oil news dominated the reports from the time that the McCleskey well set off the oil boom at Ranger. After 1926, when yet another strike disrupted production throughout the Southwest, the company mined no coal.[45]

Many miners left the community as early as 1919, dispersing into California, Illinois, Kentucky, Pennsylvania, and Missouri; others returned to Italy. Between 1921 and 1922, their numbers dropped dramatically as the tent city at the old Strike Town where the Johnson miners had waged their underground war against Colonel Hunter evolved into an underfunded, uncomfortable, and inadequate home for unionized miners who refused to accept nonunion work. Those who stayed in the area or who left temporarily only to return years later farmed or found other employment. In the 1930s, the company finally dismantled the last pieces of the once-thriving community.[46]

For thirty-eight years a diverse population had shared the fears, concerns, traditions, pride, sorrows, anger, and independent attitudes of an occupation that dominated community life at the underground "place," in the saloon, the meeting hall, and the home. Mining in Thurber was always more than a way of work; it also enveloped the workers' way of life. Circumstances, not choice, finally ended the miners' intimate relationship with the coal town. One resident expressed what many in the throes of changing conditions in Thurber in the 1920s must have felt: "I didn't leave Thurber. Thurber left me."[47]

This resident's impression of being deserted by the town was borne out by the town itself. Abandoned mines, mine dumps, the TP symbol on the gate of an overgrown graveyard gate, and a few buildings on what was once Main Street recalled the operation of the Texas & Pacific Coal Company. A more viable reminder persisted in names of area residents—Kostiha, Santi, Costa, McKinnon, Havins, Conn, Solignani, and Franks—and in the memories of those like Italian miner and union activist Lawrence Santi, who reminisced: "I came to this country from Florence, Italy. I was 16. Worked in coal mines near Trinidad in Colorado. Then I came here (to Thurber). At one time we had 1,200 miners in those mines. You could go down and look down the tunnel and their lights would be going in and out in unison. That's how beautiful they worked. It was tough when they closed it all down."[48]

Conclusion

It is a good sign when men will defend good conditions
just as emphatically as they condemn bad conditions.
—JOHN MITCHELL

The miners' living and working experience in Thurber during the almost forty years of coal mining there corresponded closely with the picture of life and work in American bituminous coal–mining communities drawn by the government-commissioned Dillingham Report in 1911, and the Coal Commission Report in 1925. A large non-English-speaking population of predominantly southern and eastern European extraction labored in Thurber's mines and resided in drab company housing in ethnic enclaves filled with Old World atmosphere. Company control extended well beyond the workplace into the workers' everyday lives, since the corporation that owned the mines also owned the town in which the workers lived. Workers used scrip at company stores to buy cradles for newborns and caskets for the dead and relaxed after work at the company saloon or meeting hall. Mining techniques varied little from other locations where thin coal veins predominated, and "the miner's freedom" dictated behavior both below and above the ground at the same time that management insisted on autocratic control. Ruinous competition and falling prices periodically threatened the company's financial stability, and attitudes dating back a generation or more shaped the workers' response to company efforts to cope with the uncertainties of the coal mining business. In these regards, Thurber was not very different from hundreds of coal mining towns across America.

According to both government reports noted earlier and statistics maintained by the United States Geological Survey, coal-mining communities in late nineteenth- and early twentieth-century America also experienced considerable labor agitation as unionization efforts escalated.[1] Thurber followed a similar but not identical pattern. In Colorado, Utah, West Virginia, Illinois, Pennsylvania, and other coal-producing states, violent encounters between operators and workers attracted regional and national attention. With little fanfare, however, after years of worker activism, Thurber unionized in 1903 without a single confirmed report of a violent act on either side. Despite occasional disputes during the period 1903 to 1921, model relations generally existed between management and workers.

The explanation lay in several conditions that influenced not only what happened in Thurber's coal mines and at the contract negotiation table but also everyday living experience in the community. These factors contributed, as well, to the development of an environment that distinguished Thurber from the typical coal-producing company town in the early twentieth century. Among these factors, management's attitude toward its laborers held particular importance. Edgar Marston's enlightened though paternalistic management style and the personal and pragmatic approach that W. K. Gordon assumed in supervising the town's operation defused the kind of intense, frustrated opposition that spawned explosive encounters between operators and workers elsewhere. After years of hard-nosed opposition to labor activism during Hunter's tenure, the company recognized and conceded defeat to union forces in 1903, without protracted battle and human suffering. Good business sense rather than altruism or weakness dictated that response. Districtwide agreements encouraged stability in an industry plagued by cutthroat competition, and the United Mine Workers had already made important inroads in Texas and elsewhere across the Southwest.

Even Gordon, who vehemently opposed unionization, accepted the inevitable. His fair treatment of the departing strikers in 1903, and his refusal to use the company's private police force and state law officers in such a way as to incur the workers' wrath impressed even union officials. Until the 1920s, both Marston and Gordon had a reputation among labor leaders for honoring work agreements. On June 4, 1910, at the conclusion of a contract dispute, the Fort Worth–based *Union Banner* reported: "At no time was there the slightest disposition manifested on the part of the operators to take advantage of the [work] suspension to spread dissension among the men. We doubt," the article continued, "if in the whole mining regions of the country there is a set of operators and miners who are on as friendly terms as in Texas." Although such rhetoric served an important public relations function, few communities could boast such cordial relations at contract renewal or any other time.

Operator Marston's interesting relationship with United Mine Workers' president John Mitchell further distinguished him and his business enterprise from those described in government studies. A December, 1903, telegram from Marston to Mitchell expressed the operator's desire to "discuss with you [Mitchell] Texas situation."[2] Marston sought advice from Mitchell, occasionally vented his frustration at him, used Mitchell as a sounding board, encouraged a social relationship between the two, and asked for direct assistance in settling labor disputes. Mitchell, in turn, supplied information, listened to and gingerly counseled Marston, and sought financial advice. It is evident, whatever the intent of the two men in establishing this relationship, that the miners in Thurber generally benefited from this link to one of their own, regardless of disagreements that subsequently estranged Mitchell from the United Mine Workers' Union.

Like a growing number of operators in the twentieth century, Marston also clearly appreciated the role that American Federation of Labor unions played as a buffer against more radical organizations like the Industrial Workers of the World, an organization that had won some members in Thurber by 1907. The result was a fairly close working relationship between union representatives and company officials, to the point that work stoppages led by rebellious Italian miners prompted a coordinated effort by company and union officials to discipline the group that both sides viewed as malcontents.

Although Marston operated Thurber as an absentee owner, unlike many operators, he occasionally visited his town and demonstrated a genuine interest in the community and its welfare. The considerable correspondence between the New York operator and his general manager on every subject from building new arbors near the saloon to coal production levels, personnel problems, contract negotiations, and worker complaints indicated that Thurber represented more to Marston than just a faraway business investment.

Marston, furthermore, continued and expanded the system of welfare capitalism initiated by his father-in-law. Workers' access to electric power, natural gas, medical and dental care, a library, an opera house, recreational facilities, consumer products of all kinds, and company-sponsored holiday events placed Thurber in the category of a model company town, according to standards set in the Dillingham and Coal Commission reports. Whatever their grievances or objections to paternalistic treatment, residents readily admitted that they enjoyed amenities and opportunities often unavailable even in nearby communities. This type of management stood in sharp contrast to communities like Ludlow, Colorado, where the operators' lack of interest and inattention to local operations contributed to one of the most shocking occurrences of violence in America in the early twentieth century.[3]

Although involved in community and business affairs at Thurber, however, Marston never developed the personal relationship with Thurberites that a resident general manager could. Employees naturally identified the company with the highest company official with whom they had contact. Gordon served the company well in that regard. He lived with his family in Thurber, maintained a high profile in town, and developed as much of a personal relationship with the workers as circumstances allowed. His approach to operating the community generally gained the miners' respect — even if they disagreed with him. He could use his fists as well as any rough-and-tumble miner. In an emergency he joined rescue teams, risking his own well-being. He invited individual airing of complaints and adapted to and accepted the unusual habits and practices that ethnic and racial diversity produced. Although he occasionally complained privately about the foreign element, he did not encourage nativism. He also fulfilled contractual obligations. Gomer Gower recalled that "Mr. Gordon went more than half way in many instances in demanding that the mine foremen observe the terms of the agreement in their dealings with the miners."[4]

Gordon also exhibited a pragmatic side that benefited both the company and its employees. In 1906, for example, he wrote Marston about a state mine bill to which labor and business leaders had agreed. "It developed there," he wrote, "that a bill of some kind would surely pass the Legislature, as the governor and several legislators have pledged themselves to it, so we concluded that the best thing under the circumstances was to agree with the labor leaders to a measure which would do us the least harm." Like Marston, Gordon also epitomized the paternalistic manager. That image apparently served him well even during times of crisis. It was reported that some miners wept and expressed their affection for the general manager as they departed the community during the 1903 strike.[5]

Although the injection of outside law authorities into labor disturbances often aggravated an already volatile situation, Thurber did not suffer the tragic consequences that sometimes resulted from confrontations between strikers and law officers. Local and state officials did not grant the company wholesale use of law officers, although Texas governors generally complied with operators' requests for assistance. More than one local sheriff or constable resisted company calls for help, and at the state level an adjutant general in the Hogg administration ordered a company of Rangers stationed in Thurber during a labor dispute to listen to both sides and practice moderation. Although a point of real irritation to the strikers, the Rangers, even in the Hunter days, generally performed their duties on the company's behalf without much use of force. After the success of the 1903 strike and the subsequent decline in labor unrest until the 1920s, state law officers rarely involved themselves in Thurber's affairs.

In that same time period, labor leaders actively participated in state politics, winning passage of a comprehensive mine bill and other labor-related legislation. From all indications, the Texas & Pacific Coal Company complied with the laws. In states like Colorado and Utah, coal companies refused to comply with such legislation, and state officials did not force them. This contributed as much as any other factor to the development of a volatile and tense situation that spawned industrial warfare. Thurber did not fit in that mold.

The miners and the union that organized them also shaped the scene in such a way as to reduce the risk of violence and to create an atmosphere somewhat different from the typical mining town. Despite the years of labor agitation in a frontier setting, where the use of a rifle was second nature, no pattern of violence among coal miners existed to set the stage for an explosive showdown at Thurber. At the height of the disturbance in 1903, labor leaders like Pete Hanraty and William Wardjon recognized the wisdom of utilizing peaceful resistance, which would cripple the company without giving the union's critics ammunition. Union organizers counseled restraint, and without exception employees practiced it. The union's strategy of removing the strikers from Thurber to jobs elsewhere provided a safety valve, too, for pent-up emotions and frustrations. The United Mine Workers' recruitment of organizers who spoke a variety of foreign languages also facilitated the effort to maintain control over a mixed population and concomitantly offered assurance to non-English-speaking immigrant miners.

Thus, the theme of unity and conciliation that John Mitchell emphasized during his tenure as a United Mine Workers' official reaped its particular reward during organization days in Thurber. Throughout the country, workers' demands for union recognition produced the greatest resistance from operators and the bitterest and most violent confrontations between employee and employer. Thurber's passage through this battlefield with few scars, a testament to the company, the union, and the workers, paved the way for conciliatory relations later.

Even certain physical features about Thurber differentiated it from other coal communities. A rapidly growing population — nearly four thousand by 1910 — fostered an urban atmosphere and reduced the sense of isolation that characterized the typically small-town and rural settings in which most American coal miners lived. In fact, to the locals who lived on the edge of the Texas frontier, Thurber was civilization — the largest city between Fort Worth and Abilene. Additionally, after the 1903 strike, the company actively solicited business from nearby townspeople and farmers. This encouraged a feeling of openness and even civic pride among Thurberites, who recognized that their town was an economic, political, and social center for Erath, Eastland, and Palo Pinto counties, a status that few coal-mining communities enjoyed.

The physical environment, which on the one hand determined the very qualities that made Thurber a typical bituminous coal–mining region, at the same time also distinguished it from the norm. The weather, though sometimes severe, generally made it possible for Thurber miners to work an average of at least one month longer than the bituminous coal miner elsewhere. The thin coal vein that complicated the work below ground somewhat mitigated this advantageous situation, but more workdays lessened complaints about slack time. Because of the geological formations around Thurber, little water and few dangerous gases invaded the mines, reducing at least the potential for mine disasters. A good water supply eliminated some of the public health problems with which many coal towns had to contend. The availability of natural gas by the 1910s for home use and to operate the brick plant reduced the cloud of coal dust that had hung in the air, coating everything, and produced a healthier and cleaner atmosphere. In relative terms, then, by the first decade of the twentieth century, Thurber offered its residents a better place to work and live than many of the coal communities described in government studies twenty years later.

Even the thin coal vein that determined Thurber's existence in the first place had its peculiar effect. Hand mining was difficult under such conditions, machine mining, often impractical. Thurber's mines operated under modern standards, but the late introduction of machine mining there because of the small workplace allowed more traditional mining practices and attitudes to prevail longer than in most of America's bituminous coal–mining regions. This may partially explain one of the most noteworthy features of work and life in Thurber—civic pride in and loyalty to the community. The miners' traditional connection to their rooms or places underground developed into an attachment to the town above. Over the years, even many of those who had left Thurber remarked on the sense of community that prevailed there.

As a result, for the past one hundred years a community that existed only half that long has attracted an unusual amount of attention, with emphasis generally placed on the notorious features of life there. Yet a miner who had worked "pencil" veins in Pennsylvania, Illinois, West Virginia, or Colorado must have adapted quickly to work and life in Thurber. A strain of continuity ran through most company-owned coal-mining towns. But within a short time of their arrival, particularly as Hunter's days as general manager reached an end and a more "liberal management" held sway, the miners would detect certain differences that would make a long-term impression on them.[6] They would discover that, like the miners themselves, the community exhibited a certain paradoxical nature; it belonged to a group solidly bound by shared experiences but at the same time retained its own unique and individualistic qualities.

Notes

INTRODUCTION

1. Daniel J. Walkowitz, *Worker City, Company Town: Iron and Cotton-Worker Protest in Troy and Cohoes, New York, 1855–84*, p. 12.

2. David Montgomery, "Gutman's Nineteenth Century America," *Labor History* 19 (Summer, 1978): 418.

3. See Eric P. Thompson, *The Making of the English Working Class;* Erick Hobsbawm, *Primitive Rebels and Social Bandits;* and Herbert Gutman, "Work, Culture, and Society in Industrializing America, 1815–1919: An Overview," in *Work, Culture, and Society in Industrializing America: Essays in American Working-Class and Social History,* pp. 3–78. The evolution of American labor history from the Commons et al. approach to that of the new labor history practitioners has been the subject of a multitude of articles and historiographical introductions in recent labor monographs. Among these are Montgomery, "Gutman's Nineteenth Century America"; Robert Zeiger, "Workers and Scholars: Recent Trends in American Labor Historiography," *Labor History* 13 (Spring, 1972): 245–66; David Brody, "The Old Labor History and the New: In Search of an American Working Class," *Labor History* 20 (Winter, 1979): 111–26; David Montgomery, "To Study the People: The American Working Class," *Labor History* 21 (Fall, 1980): 485–512; Robert Ozanne, "Trends in American Labor History," *Labor History* 21 (Fall, 1980): 513–21; Michael H. Frisch and Daniel J. Walkowitz, eds., "Introduction," in *Working Class America: Essays on Labor, Community, and American Society,* pp. ix–xvii; "Introduction," in Walkowitz, *Worker City, Company Town,* pp. 1–15; James R. Green "Preface," in *The World of the Worker: Labor in Twentieth-Century America,* pp. xi–xiv; Jim Green, "Culture, Politics and Workers' Reponse to Industrialization in the US," *Radical America* 16 (1982): 101–28; and Ronald W. Schatz, "Review Essay/Labor Historians, Labor Economics, and the Question of Synthesis," *Journal of American History* 71 (June, 1984): 93–100.

4. Gomer Gower to Mary Jane Gentry, Jan. 18, 1945, in Mary Jane Gentry, "Thurber: The Life and Death of a Texas Town," p. 236.

5. Gomer Gower to Ben L. Owens, Nov. 4, 1940, Mine Workers, Gower Letters, Labor Movement in Texas Collection, 1845–1943 (Barker Texas History Center, University of Texas at Austin), hereafter referred to as Gower Letters. Gomer Gower is listed in the 1910 census for Thurber as married with six children, all male, one of whom was a coal miner (Thirteenth Census of the United States, 1910, Population Schedule, Thurber, Erath County, Texas [microfilm of manuscript copy], hereafter referred to as Thirteenth Census, 1910, MS).

6. Gomer Gower, "Indian Territory Coal Miners," pp. 426–28, 434, Indian/Pioneer History Collection (Archives and Manuscripts Division, Oklahoma Historical Society, Oklahoma City), hereafter referred to as "Indian Territory Coal Miners"; Gomer Gower to Ben L. Owens, Apr. 12, Nov. 4, Nov. 12, 1940, Gower Letters; Ledger, 1887, William Whipple Johnson Papers (Southwest Collection, Texas Tech University, Lubbock, Texas), hereafter referred to as Johnson Papers. The ledger lists six Gowers—father, son, and four Gower in-laws.

7. Numerous authors have described this strike. Among the best accounts are Ruth A. Allen, *Chapters in the History of Organized Labor in Texas,* pp. 96–98; Gentry, "Thurber," pp. 77–95; and James C. Maroney, "The Unionization of Thurber, 1903," *Red River Valley Historical Review* 4 (Spring, 1979): 27–32.

8. Walkowitz, *Worker City, Company Town,* p. 11.

I. LAYING THE FOUNDATION

1. Department of the Interior, United States Geological Survey, *Mineral Resources of the United States,* 1888, p. 367; E. G. Senter, "A Pioneer Texas Industry," *Texas Farm and Ranch* 17 (Jan. 22, 1898), p. 1. This article was quoted in *Texas Mining and Trade Journal,* Oct. 1, 1898 (Secured Collections, Dick Smith Library, Tarleton State University, Stephenville, Texas), hereafter referred to as the *Texas Miner* (its original name) or *Texas Mining and Trade Journal.*

2. Department of the Interior, United States Geological Survey, *Mineral Resources of the United States, 1882,* p. 74, 1891, p. 326; Gentry, "Thurber," p. 4; Annual Report of the Texas & Pacific Coal Company, 1889, p. 1, Miscellaneous (Director's) File, Texas and Pacific Coal Company Records (Southwest Collection, Texas Tech University, Lubbock), hereafter referred to as Annual Report, 1889, and Texas and Pacific Coal Company Records. The Texas Central Railroad ran southeast to west across the southern part of Erath County. The Fort Worth and Rio Grande Railroad ran southwest to northeast across the central part of the county. The Texas and Pacific Railroad crossed the northwestern sector of Erath County (General Land Office, State of Texas, "Map of Erath County"). In 1879, no railroads passed through Erath County (General Land Office, State of Texas, Map, "Erath County, Texas").

3. Annual Report, 1889, p. 1; S. B. McAllister, "Building the Texas and Pacific Railroad West of Fort Worth," *West Texas Historical Association Year Book* 4 (June, 1928): 51; Gentry, "Thurber," pp. 4, 7 ; Gower to Owens, Apr. 12, 1940, Gower Letters.

4. Jonathan Garlock, comp., *Guide to the Local Assemblies of the Knights of Labor,* pp. 505, 636; *Third Annual Report of the Commissioner of Labor,* 1887, "Strikes and Lockouts," pp. 580–83, 806–807.

5. United States Department of the Interior, *Mineral Resources of the United States, 1882,* pp. 74, 733–35, *1883 and 1884,* p. 89, *1885,* p. 11.

6. United States Department of the Interior, United States Geological Survey, *Mineral Resources of the United States, 1885,* pp. 11, 67–68, *1887,* pp. 171, 358, *1889 and 1890,* pp. 147, 170, 271; Annual Report, 1889, p. 15.

7. Robert William Spoede, "William Whipple Johnson: An Enterprising Man," pp. 7, 11, 21, 26, 44, 48; Bill of Sale from J. T. Jowell and N. E. Jowell to W. W. John-

son and H. E. Johnson, Oct. 7, 1886, Legal Documents 1886–87, Deeds Dated 1886–87, Johnson Papers.

8. Data submitted by W. K. Gordon, Sec. V.P. & G.M., for the Texas & Pacific Coal Company's Twenty-Fifth Anniversary Souvenir, Thurber, Texas, July 4, 1913, pp. 1–3, 4, hereafter referred to as data submitted by W. K. Gordon, data submitted for twenty-fifth anniversary by T. R. Hall, Thurber, Texas, July 30, 1913, p. 1, hereafter referred to as data submitted by T. R. Hall, both in Miscellaneous File, Texas and Pacific Coal Company Records; Spoede, "William Whipple Johnson," pp. 52–54; the Johnson Coal Mining Company, Statement, p. 3, Financial Papers, 1888, Financial Documents, L. L. Keller to W. W. Johnson, Dec. 4, 1886, Johnson Papers. Contract is also mentioned in John C. Brown to Johnson Brothers Coal Mining Company, Mar. 24, 1888, Correspondence, 1870–1904, Letters Received, 1870–1904, Johnson Papers.

9. Spoede, "William Whipple Johnson," p. 60; Gomer Gower to Ben Owens, Nov. 4, 1940, Jan. 28, 1941, Gower Letters.

10. John C. Brown to Johnson Brothers Coal Mining Co., Mar. 24, 1888, Correspondence, 1870–1904, Letters Received, 1870–1904, Johnson Papers; Spoede, "William Whipple Johnson," pp. 57, 60–61, 79, 110–11; Gower to Gentry, Aug. 14, 1944, in Gentry, "Thurber," p. 228. Johnson accused his associate Harry Taylor of surreptitiously conspiring with R. D. Hunter to take the mines away from him. Strained relations between Johnson, who established several more mining enterprises in the area after the sale of his first mining company to Hunter in 1888, and the Texas & Pacific Coal Company developed almost from the date of sale. The latter company's monopoly on the coal trade with the Texas and Pacific Railroad and the difficulty other mining companies had in competing with such a strong, dominating corporation explain the poor relationship.

11. *Dallas Morning News,* Nov. 8, 1902; Jimmy M. Skaggs, "To Build a Barony: Colonel Robert D. Hunter," *Arizona and the West* 15 (Autumn, 1973): 245–50, 252–56; Joseph G. McCoy, *Historic Sketches of the Cattle Trade of the West and Southwest,* pp. 30–31, 34, 36.

12. R. D. Hunter to H. M. Taylor, Nov. 25, 1887, Correspondence, 1870–1904, Letters Received, 1870–1904, Assay Report from Eliott C. Jewitt to W. W. Johnson, Nov. 6, 1886, Financial Papers, 1886, Financial Documents, Harry [Taylor] to Mes. Johnson Bros., Aug. 1, 1887, Agreement between W. W. Johnson and R. D. Hunter, June 26, 1888, Document of Sale, Johnson C.M. Co. and T.&P.C. Co., Oct. 6, 1888, Legal Documents, all in Johnson Papers; Journal A, Texas and Pacific Coal Company, Oct., 1888–June, 1893, p. 2, Oct. 6, 1888, p. 4, Nov. 5, 1888, Financial Material, Texas and Pacific Coal Company Records; Spoede, "William Whipple Johnson," pp. 57–58.

13. Gower to Gentry, Aug. 14, 1944, in Gentry, "Thurber," p. 229. The investors in the Texas & Pacific Coal Company selected that name because of the proximity of the railroad to the purchased site. The Texas & Pacific Coal Company and the Texas and Pacific Railroad were separate companies with no corporate link (*Dallas Morning News,* Sept. 20, 1903).

14. Annual Report, 1889, p. 2; Gower to Owens, Nov. 12, Nov. 4, 1940, Gower Letters; Gower to Gentry, Aug. 14, 1944, in Gentry, "Thurber," p. 228.

15. Gower to Owens, Nov. 12, 1940, Jan. 28, 1941, Gower Letters; Gower to Gentry, Aug. 14, 1944, in Gentry, "Thurber," pp. 228–29.

16. Spoede, "William Whipple Johnson," pp. 55–60.

17. R. W. Weitzell to R. D. Hunter, Oct. 1, 1888, Correspondence, 1870–1904, Letters Sent, 1888–97, Johnson Papers; *Texas & Pacific Coal Company* v. *Thomas Lawson,* case no. 346 (Nov., 1895), p. 301, Supreme Court of Texas Records, 1838–1945 (State Archives, Texas State Library, Austin), hereafter referred to as *Texas & Pacific* v. *Lawson;* Annual Report, 1889, p. 3.

18. Gower to Owens, Jan. 28, 1941, Gower Letters.

19. Gordon stated that the company incorporated on September 27, 1888. Hunter wrote that the company was formed on October 6, 1888. The company's annual report in 1937 concurred with Hunter. Data submitted by W. K. Gordon, p. 3; Annual Report, 1889, pp. 1, 3, 6; Texas Pacific Coal and Oil Company, Annual Report, 1937, n.p., Texas and Pacific Coal Company Records; James T. Padgitt, "Captain Joseph C. Lea, the Father of Roswell," *West Texas Historical Association Year Book* 35 (Oct., 1959): 61; *Texas & Pacific* v. *Lawson,* p. 268; Document of Sale, Johnson C. M. Co., and T.&P.C. Co., Oct. 6, 1888, Legal Documents, Johnson Papers.

20. Gower to Owens, Nov. 4, 1940, Gower Letters; Time Book, Mixed Time, Nov., 1888–Mar., 1889, Financial Material, Texas & Pacific Coal Company, Texas and Pacific Coal Company Records, hereafter referred to as Time Book.

21. *Texas & Pacific* v. *Lawson,* pp. 301, 317–20, 397–401, 408, 512–13.

22. Ibid., pp. 319, 320; Annual Report, 1889, pp. 4–5, 15.

23. Data submitted by W. K. Gordon, p. 3; U.S. Department of the Interior, Census Office, *Compendium of the Eleventh Census, Population: 1890,* p. 391; Twelfth Census, 1900, MS; computer analysis of data base, Thurber, Texas, 1900, author's collection, hereafter referred to as computer analysis of data base, Thurber, Texas, 1900. Dr. Vernon L. Williams, Abilene Christian University, provided me with invaluable assistance in applying computer-based quantification methodology to this project. The History Department, University of Houston, facilitated my access to the university's computer system. All analyses of Twelfth Census data in this study are based on the information provided in the census on all 2,559 residents in Thurber. I did not draw conclusions based on random sampling but on an analysis of the total population.

24. *Compendium of the Eleventh Census,* p. 508; U.S. Department of the Interior, Census Office, *Twelfth Census of the United States Taken in the Year 1900, Population,* pp. 784, 787.

25. Ledger, 1887, Legal Documents and Ledgers, Johnson Papers; Texas & Pacific Coal Company, Mine Payrolls, 1890–1926, Financial Material, Texas and Pacific Coal Company Records (microfilm in my possession), hereafter referred to as Mine Payrolls; Twelfth Census, 1900, MS; computer analysis of data base, Thurber, Texas, 1900; Gower to Owens, Nov. 4, 1940, Gower Letters; see Time Books, 1890–98, for appearance of increasing number of Italian names. The designation of "Polish" was given to those respondents who listed Poland Austria, Poland Germany, Poland Russia, and Russia Poland as country of birth; the designation of "Austrian" was given to those who listed Austria-Hungary as place of birth, and the designation of "Hungarian" to those who listed Hungary-Austria as place of birth.

26. *Reports of the Immigration Commission: Immigrants in Industries,* 61st Cong., 2d Sess., Senate Doc. no. 633 (serial 5667), part 1: "Bituminous Coal Mining," vol.

1, pp. 21–23, hereafter referred to as *Immigrants in Industries,* "Bituminous Coal Mining."

27. Ibid.; Glenna Mathews, "An Immigrant Community in Indian Territory," *Labor History* 23 (Summer, 1982): 376, 378; see also Frederick Lynne Ryan, *The Rehabilitation of Oklahoma Coal Mining Communities,* pp. 27–28; Douglas Hale, "European Immigrants in Oklahoma," *The Chronicles of Oklahoma* 53 (Summer, 1975): 196; Kenny L. Brown, "Peaceful Progress: The Italians of Krebs," *The Chronicles of Oklahoma* 53 (Fall, 1975): 333, 339; Philip A. Kalisch, "Ordeal of the Oklahoma Coal Miners," *The Chronicles of Oklahoma* 48 (Autumn, 1970): 332.

28. Twelfth Census, 1900, MS; computer analysis of data base, Thurber, Texas, 1900; Betty Boyd Caroli, *Italian Repatriation from the United States, 1900–1914,* pp. v, 85, 93–94.

29. Twelfth Census, 1900, MS; computer analysis of data base, Thurber, Texas, 1900.

30. Twelfth Census, 1900, MS; computer analysis of data base, Thurber, Texas, 1900.

31. Green, *The World of the Worker,* p. 15; Twelfth Census, 1900, MS; computer analysis of data base, Thurber, Texas, 1900.

II. THE SUBTERRANEAN COMMUNITY

1. George Korson, *Coal Dust on the Fiddle: Songs and Stories of the Bituminous Industry,* p. 121.

2. *Report of the United States Coal Commission,* 68th Cong., 2d Sess., Senate Doc. no. 195 (serial 8402–8403), part 3, "Bituminous Coal—Detailed Labor and Engineering Studies," pp. 1055, 1325, hereafter referred to as *Report of the United States Coal Commission,* "Bituminous Coal"; Carter Goodrich, *The Miner's Freedom: A Study of the Working Life in a Changing Industry,* pp. 19, 30, 56–59.

3. Data submitted by W. K. Gordon, pp. 8, 9; Annual Report, 1889, p. 8; W. K. Gordon to Mary Jane Gentry, June 23, 1944, quoted in Gentry, "Thurber," pp. 28–29; Gomer Gower to Mary Jane Gentry, July 14, 1944, quoted in Gentry, "Thurber," p. 29; *The Texas Miner,* Nov. 3, 1894, advertisement for "100 good long wall miners."

4. Data submitted by W. K. Gordon, p. 4 ("pencil streaks"); *Report of the United States Coal Commission,* "Bituminous Coal," pp. 1055 ("low"), 1056; Gower to Gentry, July 14, 1944, Aug. 14, 1944, in Gentry, "Thurber," pp. 29, 228; Gower to Owens, Nov. 4, 1940, Jan. 28, 1941, Gower Letters; Johnnie Franks interview, Apr. 1, 1967, Thurber, Texas Collection (Southwest Collection, Texas Tech University, Lubbock, Texas), hereafter referred to as Thurber Collection.

5. Goodrich, *The Miner's Freedom,* p. 20 ("place"); *Report of the United States Coal Commission,* "Bituminous Coal," pp. 1054–55; Gordon to Gentry, June 23, 1944, quoted in Gentry, "Thurber," pp. 28–29; Gower to Gentry, July 14, 1944, in Gentry, "Thurber," p. 29; "The Thurber Story" by George Carter (from the files of Mrs. Pinky Wylie), p. 5, Miscellaneous File, Thurber Collection, hereafter referred to as "The Thurber Story" by George Carter; *Texas Mining and Trade Journal,* Oct. 1, 1898; John McCorkle interview, Aug. 10, 1967, Thurber Collection; Sammie F. Booth, Roscoe Hayden Sherrill, Biographical Data Information Sheet and Questionnaire (based on interview), Thurber Collection, hereafter referred to as Biographical Data Information Sheet; Korson, *Coat Dust on the Fiddle,* p. 132.

6. Homer Greene, *Coal and the Coal Mines,* pp. 116-18, 119; Weldon B. Hardman, *Fire in a Hole!* Joe McKinnon, Sherrill, Biographical Data Information Sheets; Walter Kostiha interview, Mar. 5, 1980, Geno Solignani interview, Mar. 5, 1980, Franks interview, Thurber Collection; *Report of the United States Coal Commission,* "Bituminous Coal," p. 1054; Korson, *Coal Dust on the Fiddle,* pp. 116-20, 227.

7. *Report of the United States Coal Commission,* "Bituminous Coal," p. 1054; Korson, *Coal Dust on the Fiddle,* pp. 132-33; Sherrill, McKinnon, Biographical Data Information Sheets; Solignani, Franks interviews, Thurber Collection: Green, *Coal and the Coal Mines,* pp. 118-20, 227.

8. Gower to Owens, Jan. 28, 1941, Gower Letters; data submitted by W. K. Gordon, pp. 30-41; *Report of the United States Coal Commission,* "Bituminous Coal," p. 1054.

9. *Report of the United States Coal Commission,* "Bituminous Coal," pp. 1054, 1055; Sherrill, Biographical Data Information Sheet.

10. Korson, *Coal Dust on the Fiddle,* pp. 122, 131, 132.

11. Ibid., pp. 133, 134; Greene, *Coal and the Coal Mines,* pp. 227-28; Bruce T. Havins, Daisy Conn, John McCorkle, Johnnie Franks, June Graham Terry, Fortunata Mary Nardini Marchioni Meislohn, Ruth Elaine Calloway Costa, Sherrill, Biographical Data Information Sheets; Kostiha interview, Thurber Collection.

12. *Report of the United States Coal Commission,* "Bituminous Coal," pp. 1243, 1325; Goodrich, *The Miner's Freedom,* pp. 31, 37, 55; Korson, *Coal Dust on the Fiddle,* p. 130; *The Texas Miner,* Jan. 27, 1894; Greene, *Coal and the Coal Mines,* pp. 114, 121-22; Tamara K. Hareven, "Family and Work Patterns of Immigrant Laborers in a Planned Industrial Town, 1900-1930," pp. 56-58, discusses the workers' activity in locating employment for relatives; McKinnon, Biographical Data Information Sheet; Kostiha, Franks, Solignani interviews, Thurber Collection; *Immigrants in Industries,* part 4, vol. 2 (serial 5667), "The Bituminous Coal Mining Industry in the Southwest," p. 70, hereafter referred to as *Immigrants in Industries,* "The Bituminous Coal Mining Industry in the Southwest"; *J. W. Connaughton v. Texas & Pacific Coal Company,* case no. 3161 (1899), Court of Civil Appeals, Second Supreme Judicial District of Texas (Fort Worth), trial transcript (Clerk's Office, Texas Court of Civil Appeals, 2d District, Fort Worth, Texas), p. 31, hereafter referred to as *Connaughton v. Texas & Pacific.* The Texas & Pacific Coal Company appealed the lower court's decision in the case to the Court of Civil Appeals in Aug., 1898, resulting in the case's being listed as *Texas & Pacific Coal Company v. J. W. Connaughton.* The transcript used by the appeals court recorded testimony in the original case, in which the corporation was the defendant—hence the listing of Connaughton as plaintiff. Connaughton was also spelled "Connaughten" in documents filed in the Court of Civil Appeals.

13. Homer Lawrence Morris, *The Plight of the Bituminous Coal Miner,* p. 68; Walton H. Hamilton and Helen R. Wright, *The Case of Bituminous Coal,* p. 112; Goodrich, *The Miner's Freedom,* p. 75; Korson, *Coal Dust on the Fiddle,* p. 136.

14. Mine Payrolls, Oct. 1890. The percentage of inside workers who actually mined coal at Thurber compared closely to the 70 percent that the United States Coal Commission estimated digging coal in 1923, and the 60 percent of mine employees whom companies paid at tonnage rates (*Report of the United States Coal Commission,* "Bituminous Coal," pp. 1054-55).

15. Goodrich, *The Miner's Freedom,* pp. 20, 39, 97; Korson, *Coal Dust on the Fiddle,* p. 177; Greene, *Coal and the Coal Mines,* p. 114; *Report of the United States Coal Commission,* "Bituminous Coal," p. 1903; William K. Gordon to Edgar L. Marston, Jan. 10, 1900, William K. Gordon, Jr. Papers (William K. Gordon, Jr., Fort Worth, Texas), hereafter referred to as William K. Gordon, Jr. Papers.

16. *Report of the United States Coal Commission,* "Bituminous Coal," pp. 1052–53; Michael Ray McCormick, "A Comparative Study of Coal Mining Communities in Southern Illinois and Southeastern Ohio in the Late Nineteenth Century," p. 78.

17. *Report of the United States Coal Commission,* "Bituminous Coal," p. 1944; Goodrich, *The Miner's Freedom,* p. 33.

18. The *Texas Miner,* Sept. 15, Dec. 15, 1894; William K. Gordon to Robert D. Hunter, Nov. 17, June 9, 1896, William K. Gordon, Jr. Papers.

19. William K. Gordon to Edgar L. Marston, July 6, 1900, William K. Gordon, Jr. Papers; Gentry, "Thurber," p. 35; Goodrich, *The Miner's Freedom,* p. 35.

20. Gentry, "Thurber," pp. 33, 34; John Franklin Jordan, Sammie Booth, Biographical Data Information Sheets; Daisy Conn interview, Aug. 7, 1967, Thurber Collection.

21. Korson, *Coal Dust on the Fiddle,* p. 21, 122, Gentry, "Thurber," pp. 35, 36; *Immigrants in Industries,* "Bituminous Coal Mining in the Southwest," p. 70; Goodrich, *The Miner's Freedom,* pp. 33, 57–58.

22. William K. Gordon to Edgar L. Marston, Dec. 21, 1899, Edgar L. Marston to William K. Gordon, Dec. 21, 1899, William K. Gordon, Jr. Papers.

23. Gower to Gentry, Aug. 14, 1944, in Gentry, "Thurber," pp. 229, 230; data submitted by W. K. Gordon, p. 32; Jordan, Biographical Data Information Sheet.

24. "Thurber on Strike," *United Mine Workers' Journal,* Sept. 24, 1903, United Mine Workers, 1889–1940, Labor Movement in Texas Collection, hereafter referred to as *United Mine Workers' Journal.*

25. Gower to Gentry, Aug. 14, 1944, in Gentry, "Thurber," p. 230; data submitted by W. K. Gordon, p. 32.

26. Jordan, Biographical Data Information Sheet; "Thurber on Strike," *United Mine Workers' Journal,* Sept. 24, 1903.

27. Arthur Suffern, *Conciliation and Arbitration in the Coal Industry of America,* pp. 25, 26.

28. Korson, *Coal Dust on the Fiddle,* p. 175; the *Texas Miner,* Feb. 10, 1894; *Dallas Morning News,* Sept. 27, 1903.

29. Suffern, *Conciliation and Arbitration,* p. 28; *Report of the United States Coal Commission,* "Bituminous Coal," p. 1111.

30. *Report of the United States Coal Commission,* "Bituminous Coal," pp. 1132–1333; data submitted by W. K. Gordon, p. 29; *Seventeenth Annual Report of the United States Geological Survey, 1895–1896,* part 3, pp. 296–97, 302–305, 307–308, 522; *Nineteenth Annual Report of the United States Geological Survey, 1897–98,* part 6, pp. 323, 521–22; *Twentieth Annual Report of the United States Geological Survey, 1898–99,* part 6, pp. 324–26, 489; *Twenty-first Annual Report of the United States Geological Survey, 1899–1900,* part 6, pp. 348, 357, 501; Department of the Interior, United States Geological Survey, *Mineral Resources of the United States, 1901,* pp.

287–88, 290, 297, 433–34, *1902*, pp. 299, 318, 429–30. The USGS report for 1902 was the last examined, since it covered the year immediately preceding the massive Thurber strike.

31. William K. Gordon to Robert D. Hunter, Aug. 19, 1897, William K. Gordon, Jr. Papers; *Report of the United States Coal Commission,* "Bituminous Coal," p. 1905; Korson, *Coal Dust on the Fiddle,* p. 14.

32. William K. Gordon to Robert D. Hunter, Jan. 26, 1897, Feb. 3, 1897, June 18, 1898, William K. Gordon, Jr. Papers; the *Texas Miner,* Feb. 20, 1897, describes the disastrous fire at Mine Number Five.

33. *Report of the United States Coal Commission,* "Bituminous Coal," pp. 1945–46.

34. William K. Gordon to Robert D. Hunter, June 9, 1898, William K. Gordon to Edgar L. Marston, July 6, 1900, William K. Gordon, Jr. Papers.

35. McKinnon, Biographical Data Information Sheet; Mine Payrolls, Oct., 1890.

36. Goodrich, *The Miner's Freedom,* p. 14; Eric D. Weitz, "Class Formation and Labor Protest in the Mining Communities of Southern Illinois and the Ruhr, 1890–1925," *Labor History* 27 (Winter, 1985–86): 89–90; Gutman, *Work, Culture, and Society in Industrializing America,* pp. 22–25.

37. *Report of the United States Coal Commission,* "Bituminous Coal," pp. 1054, 1055; Mine Payrolls, Oct. 1890.

38. Mine Payrolls, Oct., 1890.

39. *Nineteenth Annual Report of the United States Geological Survey,* pp. 334–35, 521; *Connaughton* v. *Texas & Pacific,* p. 30; *Dallas Morning News,* Sept. 27, 1903; Gower to Gentry, Aug. 14, 1944, Gentry, "Thurber," pp. 233–34; Mine Payrolls, Oct., 1900.

40. *Report of the United States Coal Commission,* "Bituminous Coal," p. 1056; *Nineteenth Annual Report of the United States Geological Survey,* pp. 330, 332–35.

41. Mine Payrolls, Oct., 1890, and Oct., 1900.

42. Ibid.; the *Texas Miner,* July 7, 1894.

43. Mine Payrolls, Oct., 1890, and Oct., 1900.

44. Minutes, Directors and Stockholders Meeting, Texas Pacific Mercantile & Manufacturing Company, Sept. 28, 1894, Texas and Pacific Coal Company Records; *Texas & Pacific* v. *Lawson,* pp. 334–35; *Connaughton* v. *Texas & Pacific,* pp. 47–48; Gower to Owens, Nov. 12, 1940, Gower Letters; Gentry, "Thurber," p. 124.

45. *Report of the United States Coal Commission,* "Bituminous Coal," pp. 1655, 1713–15; Glenna Mathews, "An Immigrant Community in Indian Territory," p. 378; *Immigrants in Industries,* "The Bituminous Coal Mining Industry in the Southwest," p. 69.

46. Jane Graham Terry said, "We lived by whistles." Terry, Halley Comet Jordon Patton, B. Havins, Meislohn, Biographical Data Information Sheets; Solignani interview, Thurber Collection.

47. The *Texas Miner,* Jan. 20, Jan. 27, Feb. 3, Mar. 24, July 24, 1894, Apr. 13, 1895; the *Stephenville Empire,* Sept. 3, 1892, Apr. 14, 1893, Oct. 9, 1896.

48. *Connaughton* v. *Texas & Pacific,* pp. 31, 122.

49. Ibid., pp. 35, 36, 44, 46, 55, 57, 67.

50. The *Texas Miner,* Feb. 20, 1897; Donald L. Miller and Richard E. Sharpless,

The Kingdom of Coal: Work, Enterprise, and Ethnic Communities in the Mine Fields,
p. 133.

51. Herman R. Lantz, *People of Coal Town,* pp. 143, 144; David M. Emmons, "Immigrant Workers and Industrial Hazards: The Irish Miners of Butte, 1880–1919," *Journal of American Ethnic History* 5 (Fall, 1985): 41; Milton Cantor, "Introduction," in Cantor, ed., *American Working Class Culture: Explorations in American Labor and Social History,* p. 16. In their history of the anthracite coal industry in Pennsylvania, Donald L. Miller and Richard E. Sharpless describe the impact of dangerous mine conditions on the workers underground: "Despite their independence, miners were noted for their group solidarity. Highly individualistic though they might be, the working conditions of the mines forced them into close dependency on each other. They had to cooperate under dangerous circumstances" (*The Kingdom of Coal,* p. 132).

52. *Connaughton* v. *Texas & Pacific,* pp. 72, 81, 83–88, 91–92, 100–101, 114–15; the *Texas Miner,* Jan. 20, Sept. 1, Sept. 22, 1894; the *Texas Miner,* Feb. 20, 1894, listed the lodges in the community, and the *Texas Miner,* Feb. 24, 1894, announced the first meeting of a mutual aid and benefit society.

53. Korson, *Coal Dust on the Fiddle,* pp. 20–21.

III. A WAY OF LIFE

1. Green, *The World of the Worker,* pp. xii, xiii, 8.

2. Ruth E. Sutter, *The Next Place You Come To: A Historical Introduction to Communities in North America,* pp. 141, 144, 145; David J. Saposs, "Self-Government and Freedom of Action in Isolated Industrial Communities," pp. 7, 9, 11, 18 (microfilm set of 15 reels, reel 11, University of Houston Library, Houston) in material submitted by John R. Commons of the United States Commission of Industrial Relations to the State Historical Society of Wisconsin from U.S. Senate, *Industrial Relations; Final Report and Testimony Submitted to Congress by the Commission on Industrial Relations Created by the Act of August 23, 1912* (Document no. 415, 64th Cong., 1st Sess., 1916), hereafter referred to as Wisconsin microfilm set.

3. Saposs, "Self-Government and Freedom of Action in Isolated Industrial Communities," pp. 4–5; Leifur Magnusson, United States Department of Labor, Bureau of Labor Statistics, *Housing by Employers in the United States,* pp. 15, 17, 19, 21; *Report of the United States Coal Commission,* "Bituminous Coal," pp. 1426, 1427.

4. Saposs, "Self-Government and Freedom of Action in Isolated Industrial Communities," pp. 4–5; Magnusson, *Housing by Employers in the United States,* pp. 12–13; *Report of the United States Coal Commission,* "Bituminous Coal," p. 1441; *Immigrants in Industries,* "Bituminous Coal Mining in the Southwest," p. 64.

5. *Texas & Pacific* v. *Lawson,* p. 359.

6. Gower to Owens, Nov. 4, 1940, Gower Letters; Annual Report, 1889, p. 5.

7. Annual Report, 1889, p. 6; Gower to Owens, Nov. 12, 1940, Gower Letters; B. Havins, Biographical Data Information Sheet; Gentry, "Thurber," pp. 133–34; Sanborn Fire Insurance Map for Thurber, 1905, Sanborn Fire Insurance Map Collection (Barker Texas History Center, University of Texas at Austin—hereafter referred to as Sanborn Fire Insurance Map Collection), identified frame and brick buildings and unpaved roads in 1894; the *Texas Miner,* July 14, July 28, 1894. Weather conditions

are described in, for example, the *Texas Miner,* Aug. 18, Sept. 8, Nov. 3, 1894, Feb. 9, Feb. 16, June 1, 1895.

8. The *Texas Miner,* Mar. 10, 1894; Gentry, "Thurber," pp. 191–95; Solignani, Franks interviews, Thurber Collection.

9. Rent Book, Texas & Pacific Coal Company, 1900–1901, Financial Material, Texas and Pacific Coal Company Records, hereafter referred to as Rent Book; *Immigrants in Industries,* "Bituminous Coal Mining in the Southwest," p. 65; Magnusson, *Housing by Employers in the United States,* p. 13; Gower to Owens, Nov. 12, 1940, Gower Letters; *Texas & Pacific* v. *Lawson,* p. 470; Kostiha interview, Thurber Collection; the *Texas Miner,* June 9, Sept. 29, 1894. The July 21, 1894, edition wrote: "Owing to the shortness of cottages, a large number of good and substantial tents have been placed at their disposal."

10. Twelfth Census, 1900, MS; computer analysis of data base, Thurber, Texas, 1900; Rent Book, 1900–1901.

11. Twelfth Census, 1900, MS; computer analysis of data base, Thurber, Texas, 1900; Rent Book, 1900–1901.

12. Twelfth Census, 1900, MS; computer analysis of data base, Thurber, Texas, 1900; Francis P. Valiant, "Living Arrangements and Conditions of Industrial Workers," pp. 627–29, 631, 633, 636, Wisconsin microfilm set, reel 11; Franks interview, Thurber Collection; Meislohn, Biographical Data Information Sheet; *Immigrants in Industries,* "Bituminous Coal Mining in the Southwest," pp. 53–54, 58; Gentry, "Thurber," p. 191; Eliot Lord, John J. D. Trenor, and Samuel J. Barrows, *The Italian in America,* p. 113; Mathews, "An Immigrant Community in Indian Territory," pp. 386–87.

13. Earl Brown, William Gordon, Jr., Booth, Costa, Plummer, Jordon, Biographical Data Information Sheets; Hareven, "Family and Work Patterns of Immigrant Laborers," p. 59; *Immigrants in Industries,* "Bituminous Coal Mining in the Southwest," p. 71.

14. Twelfth Census, 1900, MS; computer analysis of data base, Thurber, Texas, 1900; Gentry, "Thurber," pp. 135, 141–42, 187–88; Rent Book, 1900–1901; Thirteenth Census, 1910, MS; Booth, Plummer, Biographical Data Information Sheets; Conn. McCorkle, Franks interviews, Thurber Collection; the *Texas Miner,* July 7, 1894; Gentry, "Thurber," pp. 137–41; Gower to Owens, Nov. 4, 1940, Gower Letters. United States Department of the Interior Geological Survey, Map, Strawn East, Texas Provisional Edition, 1984, shows both Italian and Stump hills. Fire Insurance Map for Thurber, 1905, shows Park Avenue north and east of Main Street. Map, "Thurber Texas, 1920," in my possession, shows Polander Hill on the south side of Italian Hill and Stump Hill south of both. The railroad spur cut Italian Hill in half.

15. *Fort Worth Gazette,* Dec. 27, 1889 (State Archives, Texas State Library, Austin), hereafter referred to as *Fort Worth Gazette;* Twelfth Census, 1900, MS; Costa, Gordon, Jr., and Plummer, Biographical Data Information Sheets; *Texas & Pacific* v. *Lawson,* pp. 184, 383, 536; S. A. McMurry to W. H. King, Apr. 6, 1889, R. D. Hunter to W. H. King, July 5, 1890, General Correspondence, Adjutant General Records, State Archives, Texas State Library, Austin, hereafter referred to as Adjutant General Records; the *Texas Miner,* Mar. 10, July 7, Sept. 8, 1894; the *Stephenville Empire,* July 9, 1892. The *Texas Miner,* Jan. 27, 1894, mentioned two public schools, one "colored and

[one] white." *Texas Mining and Trade Journal,* Sept. 16, 1899, included a "General Directory" for the community that listed a "colored church," the Hunter Morning Star Church, and seven "colored" lodges.

16. Gower to Gentry, Jan. 18, 1945, in Gentry, "Thurber," p. 235; McCorkle and Solignani interviews, Thurber Collection; "The Thurber Story" by George Carter; Jordan, Biographical Data Information Sheet; Gower to Owens, Nov. 4, 1940, Gower Letters; *Texas & Pacific* v. *Lawson,* p. 268; Saposs, "Self-Government and Freedom of Action in Isolated Industrial Communities," pp. 13–14.

17. *Texas & Pacific* v. *Lawson,* p. 271; Gower to Gentry, Aug. 14, 1944, Jan. 18, 1945, in Gentry, "Thurber," pp. 232, 235–36; "The Thurber Story" by George Carter; Gower to Owens, Nov. 12, 1940, Gower Letters.

18. *Texas & Pacific* v. *Lawson,* pp. 261, 271, 531, 562; the *Texas Miner,* Jan. 27, 1894; the *Stephenville Empire,* July 16, 1892.

19. Gower to Owens, Nov. 12, 1940, Gower Letters; Gentry, "Thurber," pp. 113–14; *Texas & Pacific* v. *Lawson,* p. 271.

20. The *Texas Miner,* Sept. 15, Sept. 22, Feb. 17, 1894 (advertised boxing gloves); *Texas Mining and Trade Journal,* Feb. 20, 1897, Sept. 16, 1899; *Immigrants in Industries,* "Bituminous Coal Mining in the Southwest," p. 65; *Report of the United States Coal Commission,* "Bituminous Coal," p. 1462; Gentry, "Thurber," pp. 112–13.

21. *Report of the United States Coal Commission,* "Bituminous Coal," p. 1462.

22. Gower to Owens, Nov. 12, 1940, Gower Letters; *Immigrants in Industries,* "Bituminous Coal Mining in the Southwest," p. 65; the *Texas Miner,* Jan. 20, Jan. 27, May 5, 1894; Gentry, "Thurber," pp. 108, 110; *Report of the United States Coal Commission,* "Bituminous Coal," p. 1460.

23. Gentry, "Thurber," p. 121; the *Texas Miner,* Jan. 5, 1894; Gower to Owens, Nov. 12, 1940, Gower Letters.

24. *Texas & Pacific* v. *Lawson,* pp. 261, 284, 286, 287, 328, 335, 530.

25. Ibid., p. 286.

26. S. A. McMurry to W. H. King, Apr. 6, 1889, Oct. 7, 1890, William Lightfoot to W. H. Mabry, July 23, 1895, General Correspondence, Adjutant General Records; *Texas & Pacific* v. *Lawson,* pp. 188–89, 615–17.

27. Mine Payrolls, Oct., 1900; Journal A, Texas and Pacific Coal Company, Oct. 1888–June 1893, Financial Material, Texas and Pacific Coal Company Records.

28. Telegram and letter, R. D. Hunter to W. H. King, July 5, 1890, R. D. Hunter to W. H. Mabry, June 5, 1894, telegram, Erath County Judge J. L. Humphries to Gov. L. L. Ross, Dec. 13, 1888, Deputy Sheriff T. W. Freeman to W. H. King, Mar. 13, 1889, S. A. McMurry to Gen. W. H. King, Apr. 9, 1889, F. S. Cronk to Capt. L. P. Sicker, Sept. 30, 1889, Dec. 18, 1889, Feb. 24, Sept. 5, 1890, S. A. McMurry to Capt. L. P. Sicker, May 23, 1890, General Correspondence, W. H. Mabry to W. J. McDonald, June 11, 1894, Letter Press Books, Apr. 26–July 4, 1894, all in Adjutant General Records. Freeman wrote King, "Mr. Sam Platt of Capt. McMurray's Co will be Sheriff Shands Deputy to the Mines when the Rangers leave. Col Hunter and Mr Shands are good friends" (the *Texas Miner,* June 23, 1894).

29. The *Texas Miner,* Aug. 18, Sept. 1, Dec. 15, 1894. All of the following citations are from Adjutant General Records: Thomas Scurry to T. W. House, Feb. 27, 1899, Thomas Scurry to William Lightfoot, Mar. 15, 1899, W. J. M. McDonald to W. H.

Mabry, June 20, 1891, Lightfoot to Adjutant General, Feb. 21, 1899, General Correspondence; Thomas Scurry to J. M. Britton, Mar. 15, 1899, Letter Press Books, Feb. 17, 1899–Apr. 28, 1899; J. M. Britton, Application for appointment as special ranger Mar. 10, 1899, Ed. S. Britton, Descriptive List, June 23, 1891 (occupation listed as weighmaster), William Lightfoot, Descriptive List, Mar. 10, 1889, Aug. 9, 1894, William Lightfoot, Application for appointment as special ranger, July 26, 1894, Lit Williams, Application for appointment as special ranger, Nov. 21, 1894, General Service Records. "These special rangers, Lightfoot and Williams, have been in the habit in the camp of executing criminal process independent of any other officer or officers. In other words they have assumed and have been acting as special officers and exercising all their powers and privileges" (John W. Wray to W. H. Mabry, June 16, 1894, Gen. Cor.).

30. Affidavit, June 16, 1894, General Correspondence, Ed S. Britton, Application, Mar. 10, 1899, lists A. H. Miller as Justice of the Peace Precinct Seven, General Service Records, Adjutant General Records; *Texas & Pacific* v. *Lawson,* p. 133.

31. *Texas & Pacific* v. *Lawson,* pp. 521, 523; the *Texas Miner,* June 30, Aug. 25, Sept. 29, 1894.

32. All of the following citations are in General Correspondence, Adjutant General Records: Ed S. Britton to W. H. Mabry, Aug. 7, 1891; William Lightfoot to Captain McDonald, Sept. 4, Oct. 1, 1894; William Lightfoot to W. H. Mabry, Dec. 6, 1894; William Lightfoot and Lit Williams to W. H. Mabry, Mar. 31, Nov. 6, 1895, Apr. 1, 1896, Aug. 2, 1897. The *Texas Miner,* Aug. 25, Sept. 1, Sept. 8, Sept. 29, Nov. 3, 1894.

33. Lit Williams and William Lightfoot to W. H. Mabry, July 2, 1896, General Correspondence, Adjutant General Records; Gordon, Jr., Biographical Data Information Sheet; Gower to Owens, Jan. 28, 1941, Gower Letters; Franks interview, Thurber Collection.

34. Franks interview, Thurber Collection; W. J. L. Sullivan, *Twelve Years in the Saddle for Law and Order on the Frontiers of Texas,* pp. 33–34, 35, 36; *Texas & Pacific* v. *Lawson,* pp. 137–38.

35. Sullivan, *Twelve Years in the Saddle,* p. 36.

36. Saposs, "Self-Government and Freedom of Action in Isolated Industrial Communities," pp. 45, 46–47.

37. General Elections, 1886–1904, Texas Election Returns, Erath County, 1886–1924 (Local Records Depository, Texas State Library, Secured Collections, Dick Smith Library, Tarleton State University, Stephenville, Texas), hereafter referred to as Erath County Election Returns.

38. W. K. Gordon to Edgar L. Marston, Nov. 2, 1896, W. K. Gordon, Jr. Papers; *Texas Mining and Trade Journal,* Feb. 17, 1900; the *Texas Miner,* Feb. 10, May 19, June 16, July 14, Aug. 18, Sept. 22, Oct. 13, Nov. 3, 1894; the *Stephenville Empire,* Apr. 26, 1895.

39. Prohibition Election, July 27, 1895, Erath County Election Returns; the *Stephenville Empire,* Nov. 13, 1896, Aug. 2, 1895.

40. The *Texas Miner,* Jan. 20; see also Feb. 3, Feb. 17, Mar. 10, May 26, June 2, June 16, June 23, Nov. 17, 1894, Feb. 2, 1895.

41. The *Texas Miner,* Feb. 2, 1895; Jordan, Biographical Data Information Sheet; Franks interview, Thurber Collection; Gower to Gentry, Aug. 14, 1944, in Gentry, "Thurber," p. 232.

42. The *Texas Miner,* Feb. 2, Feb. 9, June 1, 1895; Thurber Returns, General Elections, 1892, 1896, 1900, Erath County Election Returns.

43. Roscoe Martin, *The People's Party in Texas: A Study in Third-Party Politics,* p. 102; the *Stephenville Empire,* Aug. 16, 1895; Twelfth Census, 1900, MS; computer analysis of data base, 1900, Thurber, Texas.

44. Gentry, "Thurber," p. 128; Prohibition Election, June 15 (?), 1904, Erath County Election Returns.

45. The *Stephenville Empire,* Dec. 16, Dec. 30, 1892, Apr. 21, May 26, 1893.

46. The *Stephenville Empire,* Dec. 30, 1892; *Texas Mining and Trade Journal,* Oct. 1, 1898. See Thurber Returns, General Election, Nov. 8, 1898, Erath County Election Returns, which note that Miller was running for justice of the peace and Williams for constable in Precinct 7.

47. Advertisement placed by the Texas & Pacific Coal Company in the *National Labor Tribune,* Dec. 8, 1888, for two hundred miners, "married men preferred"; the *Texas Miner,* June 2, 1894; Tamara K. Hareven, "Family Time and Industrial Time: Family and Work in a Planned Corporation Town, 1900–1924," *Journal of Urban History* 1 (May, 1975): 369–71, 373.

48. John Kleinig, *Paternalism,* pp. 3, 4; Melton Alonzo McLaurin, *Paternalism and Protest: Southern Cotton Mill Workers and Organized Labor, 1875–1905,* pp. 38, 47; Jacqueline Dowd Hall, Robert Korstad, James Leloudis, "Cotton Mill People: Work, Community, and Protest in the Textile South, 1880–1940," *American Historical Review* 91 (April, 1986): 255, 264; Stuart Brandes, *American Welfare Capitalism, 1880–1940,* pp. 18, 62–65; Hareven, "Family Time and Industrial Time," pp. 374–75, 384.

49. See, for example, the *Texas Miner,* Mar. 10, Jan. 27, Sept. 1, Oct. 20, Nov. 24, 1894; *Texas Mining and Trade Journal,* Feb. 20, 1897.

50. Conn, Franks interviews, Thurber Collection; "The Thurber Story" by George Carter; Jim Southern, Jordan, Biographical Data Information Sheets; *Texas & Pacific v. Lawson,* pp. 269–70; Sanborn Fire Insurance Map for Thurber, 1905, Sanborn Fire Insurance Map Collection; the *Texas Miner,* Jan. 20, Jan. 27, Mar. 10, 1894; *Report of the United States Coal Commission,* "Bituminous Coal," pp. 1430, 1432; *Immigrants in Industries,* "The Bituminous Coal Mining Industry in the Southwest," p. 72; Gentry, "Thurber," pp. 153–54; Brandes, *American Welfare Capitalism,* pp. 5–7; Saposs, "Self-Government and Freedom of Action in Isolated Industrial Communities," p. 7.

51. McCorkle, Kostiha, Franks interviews, Thurber Collection; "The Thurber Story" by George Carter; *Report of the United States Coal Commission,* "Bituminous Coal," p. 1435; Gentry, "Thurber," p. 133.

52. *Connaughton v. Texas & Pacific,* pp. 74, 88–89, 95–96, 100–101, 114–115, 134, 137.

53. Ibid., pp. 74, 100–101, 134, 137.

54. Gower to Owens, Nov. 12, 1940, Gower Letters; *The Texas Civil Appeals Reports: Cases Argued and Adjudged in the Courts of Civil Appeals of the State of Texas during the Months of December, 1898, and January, February and March, 1899,* pp. 642–45, 646; *Connaughton v. Texas & Pacific,* p. 70; the *Texas Miner,* June 23, July 27, 1895; *Texas Mining and Trade Journal,* Feb. 17, 1900; *Report of the United States Coal Commission,* "Bituminous Coal," p. 1478.

55. Gentry, "Thurber," p. 159.

56. The *Texas Miner,* Mar. 10, Sept. 8, Dec. 8, 1894; *Texas Mining and Trade Jour-*

nal, Sept. 23, 1899; P. Havins, Gordon, Jr., Biographical Data Information Sheets; Franks interview, Thurber Collection; Brandes, *Welfare Capitalism,* p. 39. Erath County school records for 1888–89 list a school at the Johnson Mines Community, General School Fund, Erath County Texas, Book for 1888–89, Book 5, Erath County Records (Local Records Depository, Texas State Library, Secured Collections, Dick Smith Library, Tarleton State University, Stephenville, Texas), pp. 47, 96–97, hereafter referred to as Erath County Records.

57. Twelfth Census, 1900, MS; computer analysis of data base, Thurber, Texas, 1900.

58. The *Texas Miner,* Nov. 17, 1894; Hareven, "Family Time and Industrial Time," p. 370; Saposs, "Self-Government and Freedom of Action in Isolated Industrial Communities," p. 5; Gentry, "Thurber," p. 161; Jordan, Gordon, Jr., Biographical Data Information Sheets. An article on June 2, 1894, in the *Texas Miner* stated: "The school trustees are men employed in connection with the mines." County school records confirmed this. Robert McKinnon, for example, was a pit boss, A. H. Miller a company manager, and William Lightfoot the company-appointed community police captain; all were school trustees.

59. The *Texas Miner,* Mar. 30, 1895; Gentry, "Thurber," p. 160; Brandes, *Welfare Capitalism,* pp. 60–61.

60. *Report of the United States Coal Commission,* "Bituminous Coal," pp. 1478–79; *Texas Mining and Trade Journal,* Feb. 20, 1897, Sept. 9, 1899, Feb. 17, 1900; Gentry, "Thurber," p. 162; Cav. Valentine J. Belfiglio, *The Italian Experience in Texas,* p. 79.

61. Rent Book, 1900–1901; W. K. Gordon to E. L. Marston, Jan. 10, 1900, William K. Gordon, Jr. Papers.

62. Gordon to Marston, Jan. 10, 1900, William K. Gordon, Jr. Papers.

63. Brandes, *Welfare Capitalism,* pp. 68–71, 72.

64. Hall, Korstad, and Leloudis, "Cotton Mill People," p. 264; Roy Rosenzweig, *Eight Hours for What We Will: Workers and Leisure in an Industrial City, 1870–1920,* p. 225; Brandes, *Welfare Capitalism,* pp. 64, 77, 79; Shirley Brittain Cawyer and Weldon I. Hudson, comps., *Erath County, Texas Cemetery Inscriptions,* vol. 3, pp. 211–20; Franks interview, Thurber Collection; "The Thurber Story" by George Carter; Jordan, Booth, Brown, Brock, Meislohn, Biographical Data Information Sheets; see also Gentry, "Thurber," pp. 185–200; Michael Q. Hooks, "Thurber: A Unique Texas Community," *Panhandle-Plains Historical Review* 56 (1983): 1–17; T. Lindsay Baker, *The First Polish Americans: Silesian Settlements in Texas,* pp. 128, 130; Belfiglio, *The Italian Experience in Texas,* p. 86; the *Texas Miner,* Jan. 20, Feb. 3, Feb. 24, June 16, Sept. 29, Oct. 6, 1894.

65. *Report of the United States Coal Commission,* "Bituminous Coal," p. 1479; Robert Goldman and John Wilson, "The Rationalization of Leisure," *Politics and Society* 7 (1977): 157, 159, 177.

66. Brandes, *American Welfare Capitalism,* p. 78; Goldman and Wilson, "The Rationalization of Leisure," p. 159; Gentry, "Thurber," p. 174.

67. Gentry, "Thurber," pp. 174, 194–95; Solignani, Conn interviews, Thurber Collection.

68. The *Texas Miner,* June 30, 1894, July 13, 1895; Brandes, *American Welfare Capitalism,* pp. 80–81.

69. Meislohn, Jordan, Biographical Data Information Sheets; Franks interview, Thurber Collection; Belfiglio, *The Italian Experience in Texas,* pp. 84, 87.

70. The *Texas Miner,* Feb. 3, Feb. 17, Feb. 24, Mar. 17, May 26, June 16, July 21, Nov. 3, 1894, June 20, 1895. The *Texas Miner,* July 27, 1895, announced the Templars' formation. See By-Laws of the R. D. Hunter Fishing and Boating Club, Printed Material, Willie M. Floyd Papers, 1920-68 (Southwest Collection, Texas Tech University, Lubbock), hereafter referred to as Floyd Papers; *Texas Mining and Trade Journal,* Oct. 28, 1897, Feb. 17, 1900; Minnie Sims, Plummer, McKinnon, Southern, Biographical Data Information Sheets; "The Thurber Story" by George M. Carter; McCorkle interview, Thurber Collection.

71. Philip F. Notarianni, "Italian Fraternal Organizations in Utah, 1897-1934," *Utah Historical Quarterly* 43 (Spring, 1975): 173, 187; Belfiglio, *The Italian Experience in Texas,* p. 18; Virginia Yans-McLaughlin, *Family and Community: Italian Immigrants in Buffalo, 1880-1930,* pp. 130-31, similarly describes the function of Italian mutual aid societies.

72. Green, *The World of the Worker,* p. 8.

73. The *Texas Miner,* Mar. 23, July 30, 1895.

74. The *Texas Miner* July 28, 1894; *Texas Mining and Trade Journal,* Feb. 20, 1897, Sept. 9, Nov. 11, 1899, July 28, 1894; Gower to Owens, Nov. 12, 1940, Gower Letters; Conn, Franks interviews, Thurber Collection; Jordan, Biographical Data Information Sheet; Baker, *The First Polish Americans,* p. 134; Belfiglio, *The Italian Experience in Texas,* p. 84.

75. Rosenzweig, *Eight Hours for What We Will,* pp. 51, 53-54, 58, 64-65, 224; *Texas & Pacific* v. *Lawson,* p. 521.

76. Gentry, "Thurber," pp. 126-29.

77. *Texas & Pacific* v. *Lawson,* pp. 183-84, 246, 383, 453, 456, 521, 603; the *Texas Miner,* Feb. 10, Apr. 28, 1894; Gower to Owens, Nov. 12, 1940, Gower Letters; Conn interview, Thurber Collection; Gentry, "Thurber," p. 129. Gordon suggested to Marston that the company construct arbors and sheds near the two saloons (Edgar L. Marston to W. K. Gordon, Dec. 15, 1899, William K. Gordon, Jr. Papers).

IV. THE STRUGGLE FOR THE INDIVIDUAL AND THE UNION, 1888-1903

1. Gower, "Indian Territory Coal Miners," pp. 426-28, 434; *Immigrants in Industries,* "Bituminous Coal Mining," pp. 21-23; "The Bituminous Coal Mining Industry in the Southwest," pp. 10, 14-16. The "old" Johnson miners included men with names like Armstrong, Anderson, Brooks, Brown, Clinton, Curry, Cunningham, Duncan, Davis, Evans, Ford, Gentry, Grant, Hale, Hughes, Kelley, Lester, McLaughlin, McGee, McMillen, Moor, Mitchell, O'Neal, O'Connor, Pierce, Parker, Riley, Roark, Stewart, Scully, Thomas, Tudor, Williams, Weaver, and Young (Johnson Brothers Coal Mining Company, Ledger, 1887, Johnson Papers).

2. "William Knox Gordon," *Fort Worth and the Texas Northwest,* p. 155; Gower to Owens, Jan. 28, 1941, Gower Letters; Gordon, Jr., Biographical Data Information Sheet.

3. Garlock, *Guide to the Local Assemblies of the Knights of Labor,* pp. xxiv, 495–96, 505, 636.
4. Gower to Owens, Apr. 12, 1940, Gower Letters; *Third Annual Report of the Commissioner of Labor, 1887,* pp. 582–83, 806–807, 989; Gower to Gentry, Aug. 14, 1944, in Gentry, "Thurber," p. 228.
5. Gower to Gentry, Aug. 14, 1944, in Gentry, "Thurber," pp. 228–29; Gower to Owens, Nov. 4, Nov. 12, 1940, Gower Letters; Spoede, "William Whipple Johnson," pp. 57–59.
6. Gower to Gentry, Aug. 14, 1944, in Gentry, "Thurber," pp. 229–30.
7. Gower to Gentry, Aug. 14, 1944, in Gentry, "Thurber," pp. 229, 230; Gower to Owens, Nov. 4, Nov. 12, 1940, Gower Letters; see *National Labor Tribune,* Dec. 22, 1888, for a letter from Dan McLauchlan; Annual Report, 1889, p. 3; *Texas & Pacific v. Lawson,* pp. 301, 318, 397–400; Journal A, Financial Material, Texas and Pacific Coal Company Records.
8. Gower to Owens, Nov. 4, 1940, Gower Letters; Gower to Gentry, Aug. 14, 1944, in Gentry, "Thurber," p. 230.
9. Gower to Owens, Nov. 4, 1890, Gower Letters; S. A. McMurry to W. H. King, Feb. 11, Feb. 17, Feb. 21, Apr. 6, 1889, General Correspondence, Adjutant General Records; Annual Report, 1889, pp. 3–4; Gower to Gentry, Aug. 14, 1944, in Gentry, "Thurber," pp. 230–31. The *Journal of United Labor,* Jan. 10, 1889, included a letter of thanks for donations to the local.
10. Annual Report, 1889, pp. 3, 4; *Dallas Morning News,* Dec. 23, Dec. 28, 1888; the *Stephenville Empire,* Dec. 22, 1888; *Fort Worth Daily Gazette,* Dec. 23, 1888; J. L. Humphries to Gov. L. S. Ross, Dec. 13, 1888, S. A. McMurry to W. H. King, Dec. 20, 1888, General Correspondence, Adjutant General Records.
11. S. A. McMurry to W. H. King, May 8, May 23, 1889, Dec. 28, 1888 (telegram), General Correspondence, Adjutant General Records; *Fort Worth Daily Gazette,* Jan. 2, Jan. 6, 1889; Monthly Returns, Company B, Frontier Battalion, Dec. 31, 1888, Adjutant General Records.
12. McMurry to King, Apr. 6, June 6, July 8, 1889, General Correspondence, Adjutant General Records.
13. The *Journal of United Labor,* June 6, July 18, Aug. 1, 1889.
14. Gentry, "Thurber," p. 53; McMurry to King, July 2, 1889, General Correspondence, Adjutant General Records.
15. S. A. McMurry to W. H. King, Feb. 2, Feb. 17, 1889, General Correspondence, Adjutant General Records.
16. *Report of the Adjutant General of the State of Texas for 1889–1890,* pp. 26, 27, 28.
17. C. A. Hall to Attorney General Hogg, June 2, 1889, Mine Workers United, 1889–1940, Labor Movement in Texas Collection; Gower to Owens, Nov. 4, 1940, Gower Letters; J. S. Hogg to C. A. Hall, June 6, 1889, Mine Workers United, 1889–1940, Labor Movement in Texas Collection; the *Journal of United Labor,* June 6, 1889.
18. J. G. Watkins to Governor Ross, Mar. 26, 1889, Harton Walker to W. H. King, Mar. 29, 1889, General Correspondence, Adjutant General Records; Annual Report, 1889, p. 5.

19. *National Labor Tribune,* Jan. 12, 1889; "With so many miners needing . . . employment is it not shameful that our efforts to secure a new union district should meet with obstruction among miners?"

20. *National Labor Tribune,* Oct. 20, Dec. 8, Dec. 15, Dec. 22, 1888, Jan. 5, Jan. 26, 1889.

21. Annual Report, 1889, p. 5; Knights of Labor, *Proceedings of the General Assembly of the Knights of Labor of America Thirteenth Regular Session, November 12–20, 1889,* p. 9; *National Labor Tribune,* Jan. 19, 1889.

22. Telegram, R. D. Hunter to W. H. King, July 5, 1890, note, S. A. McMurry, July 7, 1890, S. A. McMurry to W. H. King, July 12, 1890, all in General Correspondence, Adjutant General Records; Gower to Gentry, Aug. 14, 1944, in Gentry, "Thurber," p. 232; Gower to Owens, Apr. 12, Nov. 4, 1940, Gower Letters.

23. Frank Julian Warne, *The Coal Mine Workers: A Study in Labor Organization,* pp. 212–14; Gower to Gentry, Aug. 14, 1944, in Gentry, "Thurber," p. 233.

24. *Dallas Morning News,* June 4, June 5, 1894; R. D. Hunter to W. H. Mabry, June 5, 1894, General Correspondence, Adjutant General Records.

25. *Dallas Morning News,* June 6, 1894; affidavit by William Lightfoot, June 18, 1894, General Correspondence, Adjutant General Records.

26. Affidavit by William Lightfoot, June 18, 1894, General Correspondence, Adjutant General Records; see also Harry W. Furman to W. H. Mabry, June 6, 1894, F. B. Boles, June 15, 1894, John R. Graves, June 15, 1894, Jas. Wassell, June 15, 1894, J. J. Caradine, June 16, 1894, W. F. Carman, June 16, 1894, W. K. Gordon, June 16, 1894, H. B. Hale, June 16, 1894, D. C. Heatherington, June 16, 1894, Evan Jones, June 16, 1894, Thomas W. Jordan, June 16, 1894, Joe Kendzora, June 16, 1894, Robt. McKinnon, June 16, 1894, J. F. Mann, June 16, 1894, W. H. Mann, June 16, 1894, Ben Matthews, June 16, 1894, Jas. Matthews, June 16, 1894, J. B. Pendleton, June 16, 1894, M. Ready, June 16, 1894, James R. Williams, June 16, 1894, Col. R. D. Hunter, June 18, 1894, Wesley Lewis, June 18, 1894, Andrew Ramage, June 18, 1894, S. P. Smith, June 18, 1894.

27. Gower to Gentry, Aug. 14, 1944, in Gentry, "Thurber," pp. 232, 233; Gower to Owens, Nov. 12, 1940, Gower Letters.

28. W. H. Mabry to W. J. McDonald, June 11, 1894, Letter Press Books, Apr. 26–July 4, 1894, Adjutant General Records.

29. Mabry to McDonald, June 12, June 16, 1894, in ibid.

30. Report, W. J. L. Sullivan, June 31, 1894, R. D. Hunter to W. H. Mabry, June 10, 1894, W. J. McDonald to W. H. Mabry, July 1, 1894, General Correspondence, Adjutant General Records.

31. J. W. Maddox to W. H. Mabry, July 2, 1894, N. A. Stedman to W. H. Mabry, July 2, 1894, E. A. Euless to W. H. Mabry, July 3, 1894, William Lightfoot to W. H. Mabry, July 7, Oct. 31, Dec. 6, 1894, Sept. 3, 1895, Robert H. Ward to the Adjutant General, Aug. 6, 1894, William Lightfoot and Lit Williams to W. H. Mabry, Feb. 6, Feb. 28, Mar. 31, May 5, June 1, July 12, Aug. 3, Oct. 10, Nov. 6, 1895, Apr. 1, May 1, June 1, July 2, Aug. 9, Oct. 2, Nov. 30, 1896, Feb. 3, May 6, June 8, July 4, Aug. 2, Oct. 1, Dec. 2, 1897, William Lightfoot to W. H. Owens, Aug. 6, 1894, all in General Correspondence, Adjutant General Records; William Lightfoot, Application, July 26,

1894, Lit Williams, Application for appointment as a Special Ranger, Nov. 21, 1894, both in General Service Records, Adjutant General Records.

32. Resolutions dated May 1, 1896, Thurber, Texas, Affidavit by Robert McKinnon, June 16, 1894, General Correspondence, Adjutant General Records. George N. Beach, editor of the *Texas State Labor Journal* wrote Mabry, "Will you kindly inform me if there is a military organization in Thurber recognized or armed by the state? If so, when was it organized and by whom is it officered?" I located no reply in the Adjutant General's General Correspondence: George N. Beach to W. H. Mabry, Apr. 24, 1896.

33. Suffern, *Conciliation and Arbitration,* pp. 44-45.

34. Ibid., pp. 45, 50-51, 53-54.

35. W. K. Gordon to E. L. Marston, Jan. 10, 1900, William K. Gordon, Jr. Papers; C. W. Woodman, Secretary of the Texas State Federation of Labor, wrote J. E. Enness in Bridgeport, Texas, in 1902, asking the union there to assess its members $.25 to help support a lobbyist in Austin. Enness apparently refused, prompting Woodman to respond, with some understanding: "As you say, the drain on your treasury to support the miners has been heavy." This letter indicates both the existence of a state-affiliated miners' union approximately sixty miles from Thurber in 1902, and labor upheaval that necessitated some financial response by the local union. In his letter Woodman also acknowledged receipt of $1.80 for the per capita membership assessment. The federation's annual tax was $.06 per member (C. W. Woodman Papers, Collection 163 [the Labor Archives, Special Collections, University of Texas at Arlington, Arlington, Texas], hereafter referred to as Woodman Papers).

36. Suffern, *Conciliation and Arbitration,* pp. 39, 45; Chris Evans, *History of United Mine Workers of America from the Year 1860 to 1890,* vol. 1, pp. 639, 641; Gutman, *Work, Culture, and Society in Industrializing America,* pp. 31, 124, 157-58; Allan Kent Powell, *The Next Time We Strike: Labor in Utah's Coal Fields, 1900-1903,* p. 53; Victor Greene, *The Slavic Community on Strike: Immigrant Labor in Pennsylvania Anthracite;* David Robert Wynn, "Trade Unions and the 'New' Immigration: A Study of the United Mine Workers of America, 1890-1920," pp. 109, 158-59, 161, 165, 171, 232, 248.

37. Report to the Delegates of the Sixth Annual Convention of District 21 (n.d.), Statements/Speeches P. Hanraty, Biographical Data, Pete Hanraty, untitled speech/report on the organization of miners in Indian Territory, all in Peter Hanraty Papers (Oklahoma Historical Society, Oklahoma City), hereafter referred to as Hanraty Papers.

38. Gower to Owens, Apr. 12, 1940, Gower Letters; *Dallas Morning News,* Sept. 11, 1903; the *United Mine Workers' Journal,* Sept. 24, 1903. See Maroney, "The Unionization of Thurber, 1903," Allen, *Chapters in the History of Organized Labor in Texas,* pp. 96-98, Gentry, "Thurber," pp. 77-95, for the best secondary accounts of the strike.

39. *Dallas Morning News,* Sept. 11, 1903.

40. W. K. Gordon to S. W. T. Lanham, Aug. 30, 1903, John A. Hulen to J. H. Rogers, Sept. 3, Sept. 5, 1903, all in General Correspondence, Adjutant General Records; the *United Mine Workers' Journal,* Sept. 24, 1903; *Dallas Morning News,* Sept. 18, 1903; Gower to Owens, Apr. 12, 1940, Gower Letters.

41. *Dallas Morning News,* Sept. 11, 1903; Gower to Owens, Apr. 12, 1940, Gower Letters; *United Mine Workers' Journal,* Sept. 17, 1903.

42. *United Mine Workers' Journal,* Sept. 17, 1903; *Dallas Morning News,* Sept. 11, 1903.

43. *Dallas Morning News,* Sept. 11, 1903; the *United Mine Workers' Journal,* Sept. 24, 1903.

44. *Dallas Morning News,* Sept. 13, Sept. 20, 1903; untitled speech or statement by Pete Hanraty on organization of miners in Indian Territory, Hanraty Papers; Hall, Korstad, Leloudis, "Cotton Mill People," p. 260.

45. *Dallas Morning News,* Sept. 12, Sept. 13, Sept. 14, Sept. 15, Sept. 18, 1903.

46. C. W. Woodman to Ben Owens, Apr. 22, 1940, Gower Letters; *Dallas Morning News,* Sept. 13, Sept. 17, Sept. 18, 1903.

47. Woodman to Owens, Apr. 22, 1940, Gower Letters; *Dallas Morning News,* Sept. 20, 1903.

48. Report to Delegates of the Sixth Annual Convention of District 21, Hanraty Papers; *Dallas Morning News,* Sept. 27, 1903; the *United Mine Workers' Journal,* Oct. 1, 1903; Texas & Pacific Coal Company Payroll Records, Nov., 1903, Texas and Pacific Coal Company Records; copy of Agreement between Miners and Operators in the Bituminous Mines of Texas, Sept. 26, 1903, William K. Gordon, Jr. Papers. Gordon's copy of the 1903 agreement includes a 15–17 percent tonnage rate increase for Thurber rather than the 35 percent described in some accounts. The miners originally demanded a 35 percent increase. Gower claims the increase was from $1.00 to $1.32 per ton. The agreement also provided for an eight-hour day for day labor.

49. Woodman to Owens, Apr. 22, Nov. 12, 1940, Gower Letters; Gentry, "Thurber," p. 110; John S. Spratt, Sr., *Thurber, Texas: The Life and Death of a Company Coal Town,* ed. Harwood P. Hinton, pp. 6–7.

50. Gentry, "Thurber," p. 100; see Allen, *Chapters in the History of Organized Labor,* for a full description of militant labor activity in late nineteenth-century Texas; *Sixteenth Annual Report of the Commissioner of Labor, 1901,* "Strikes and Lockouts," pp. 108, 252, 348; Texas State Federation of Labor, *Proceedings,* 1904, p. 17, Gower Letters; *Union Banner,* Apr. 10, 1909.

51. Gower to Owens, Apr. 12, 1940, Gower Letters; Gower to Gentry, Jan. 18, 1945, in Gentry, "Thurber," p. 235; Maroney, "The Unionization of Thurber, 1903," p. 2; idem, "Organized Labor in Texas, 1900–1929," pp. 52, 59, 62, 65, 121; Allen, *Chapters in the History of Organized Labor in Texas,* pp. 98, 131–34, 137; Woodman to Owens, Apr. 22, 1940, Gower Letters.

V. BOOM TO BUST IN UNIONIZED THURBER

1. Data submitted by W. K. Gordon, pp. 29–30; Department of the Interior, United States Geological Survey, *Mineral Resources of the United States, 1904,* p. 394, *1907,* p. 13; *1913,* part 2, Nonmetals, pp. 906–907; Gordon, Jr., Biographical Data Information Sheet.

2. Data submitted by W. K. Gordon, pp. 6–7, 22–24; Sanborn Fire Insurance Map, Thurber, Texas, 1905 and 1911, Sanborn Fire Insurance Map Collection; J. W. Downs to Mrs. J. R. Williamson, Feb. 3, 1937, Eugenia Smith to Willie Floyd, Dec. 29,

1938, Mrs. J. B. Dodson to Willie Floyd, undated, all in Floyd Papers. The mine cashier in Thurber recorded rent payments on meeting space for 1904-1906 from the Good Templar Lodge, Order of Red Men, IOOF, Knights of Pythias, Masonic Lodge, Italian Masons, Rathbone Sisters, Rebekah Lodge, and Star of Italy (Accounts Receivable, Mine Cashier, 1904-1906, Texas & Pacific Coal Company, Financial Material, Texas and Pacific Coal Company Records).

3. Thirteenth Census, 1901, MS; computer analysis of data base, Thurber, Texas, 1910; Twelfth Census, 1900, MS; computer analysis of data base, Thurber, Texas, 1900. The poor quality of the first reproduction of the 1910 census limited my effort to glean accurately all the data included for each person. The copy is simply unreadable at certain points. Hence, some statistics are imprecise. Considering, however, that I did not randomly sample the data but rather analyzed all that was given and readable for the 3,805 persons listed in the census, I would expect a very small margin of error.

4. Thirteenth Census, 1910, MS; computer analysis of data base, Thurber, Texas, 1910; Twelfth Census, 1900, MS; computer analysis of data base, Thurber, Texas, 1900; *Immigrants in Industries,* "The Bituminous Coal Mining Industry in the Southwest," p. 125.

5. Dodson to Floyd, Downs to Williamson, Feb. 3, 1937, "Thurber Wesley House" (no author), all in Floyd Papers; Twelfth Census, 1900, MS; Thirteenth Census, 1910, MS; computer analysis of data base, Thurber, Texas, 1900 and 1910; the *Abilene Reporter-News,* Sept. 4, 1966; *Report of the United States Coal Commission,* "Bituminous Coal," p. 1416 (see pp. 1414-19 for a description of bituminous coal miners nationally).

6. Thirteenth Census, 1910, MS; computer analysis of data base, Thurber, Texas, 1910; Franks interview, Thurber Collection; Grace Pinkston Strickland, Brown, Biographical Data Information Sheets.

7. Twelfth Census, 1900, MS; Thirteenth Census, 1910, MS; computer analysis of data base, Thurber, Texas, 1900 and 1910; Santi, Franks, Solignani interviews, Thurber Collection. Geno Solignani stated that the Italian local had a black president at one time.

8. Thirteenth Census, 1910, MS; Meislohn, Brown, B. Havins, Biographical Data Information Sheets.

9. Jordan, Lorene Smith Dobson, Biographical Data Information Sheets; Minutes, Texas & Pacific Coal Company, Apr. 17, 1918, Texas and Pacific Coal Company Records; Map, Strawn East Quadrangle Texas, Provisional Edition, 1984, shows New York Hill to the southeast of Italian and Stump hills and just west of Thurber Lake; Gentry, "Thurber," p. 139; Brown, Costa, B. Havins, Meislohn, Gordon, Jr., Sherrill, George Stoddard, Biographical Data Information Sheets; Dodson to Floyd, By-Laws of the R. D. Hunter Fishing and Boating Club (subsequently called the Thurber Athletic Club), both in Floyd Papers; the *Abilene Reporter-News,* Sept. 4, 1966.

10. Dodson to Floyd, Floyd Papers; Jordan, Biographical Data Information Sheet.

11. Twelfth Census, 1900, MS; Thirteenth Census; 1910, MS; computer analysis of data base, Thurber, Texas, 1900 and 1910; *Immigrants in Industries,* "The Bituminous Coal Mining Industry in the Southwest," p. 79.

12. The *Stephenville Empire,* Oct. 8, 1915; Dealy Briley Hilburn, P. Havins, Biographical Data Information Sheets.

13. The *Stephenville Empire (Tribune),* Feb. 9, Feb. 16, Feb.23, Mar. 8, Mar. 15,

Apr. 5, May 10, Aug. 23, Nov. 29, 1912, Dec. 3, Dec. 5, 1915, Mar. 3, May 19, 1916, Nov. 16, 1923; Oddis Patton, Annie Southern Simmans, Biographical Data Information Sheets; Franks interview, Thurber Collection.

14. Gentry, "Thurber," pp. 128–30. The company's effort to keep the county wet is discussed in W. K. Gordon to Edgar L. Marston, Aug. 8, Aug. 27, 1911, W. K. Gordon, Jr. Papers. The mercantile purchased almost sixty thousand dollars' worth of beer in 1910, and nearly seventy thousand dollars' worth in 1912 to stock the saloon for Thurber's residents (Research Notes, Literary Productions, Floyd Papers. See also prohibition elections in Erath County Election returns).

15. John B. Gillon to Gen. Thomas D. Barton, Oct. 14, 1922, General Correspondence, Adjutant General Records; the *Stephenville Empire (Tribune)*, Jan. 24, 1913, Oct. 19, 1917, Nov. 11, 1921, Mar. 30, 1923; Dobson, Costa, Meislohn, B. Havins, Sherrill, Biographical Data Information Sheets; Solignani interview, Thurber Collection.

16. Mathews, "An Immigrant Community in Indian Territory," p. 391; Weitz, "Class Formation and Labor Protest in the Mining Communities of Southern Illinois and the Ruhr, 1890–1925," p. 93; James R. Green, *Grass-Roots Socialism: Radical Movements in the Southwest, 1895–1943*, p. 203; Santi interview, Thurber Collection; United Mine Workers, *Proceedings of the Inter-State Convention of the United Mine Workers, Districts No. 14, 21, and 25*, Hanraty Papers, lists one Thurber local (2538); United Mine Workers, *Proceedings of the Twenty-Third Annual Convention of the United Mine Workers of America*, pp. 94A, 96A, lists 894 members in Local 2538 and 580 in Local 2763. Unfortunately, no researcher, to my knowledge, has uncovered any local union records for Thurber's miners' unions. Fire destroyed the bulk of District 21's records.

17. John H. M. Laslett, *Labor and the Left: A Study of Socialist and Radical Influences in the American Labor Movement, 1881–1924*, pp. 203–204.

18. W. K. Gordon to Edgar L. Marston, Mar. 1, 1908, Dec. 10, 1906, W. K. Gordon, Jr. Papers.

19. Gordon to Marston, Dec. 10, 1906, W. K. Gordon, Jr. Papers.

20. Rent Book, 1907; Franks interview, Thurber Collection; Laslett, *Labor and the Left*, p. 210; Thurber Election Returns, General Elections, 1904–24, Erath County Election Returns; Green, *Grass-Roots Socialism*, pp. 193–204.

21. Gordon to Marston, Dec. 10, 1906, W. K. Gordon, Jr. Papers.

22. Telegram, W. K. Gordon to Edgar L. Marston, Mar. 27, 1908, Apr. 2, 1908, W. K. Gordon, Jr. Papers.

23. Maroney, "The Unionization of Thurber, 1903," p. 32; Edgar L. Marston to John Mitchell, Feb. 16, 1906, Mar. 6, Apr. 3, 1908, May 10, May 11, June 29, 1909, Feb. 27, 1912, John Mitchell to Edgar L. Marston, June 30, 1909, Sept. 22, Dec. 5, 1910, John Mitchell to Hunter S. Marston, Dec. 23, 1903, all in John Mitchell Papers (Catholic University of America, Washington, D.C.), hereafter referred to as Mitchell Papers. James C. Maroney generously shared with me copies of material he found in the Mitchell Papers that related to Edgar Marston and Texas.

24. Edgar L. Marston to John Mitchell, Mar. 2, 1910, May 15, 1913, Mitchell Papers.

25. Laslett, *Labor and the Left*, pp. 214–15; John Mitchell to Edgar L. Marston, Mar. 3, 1910, May 17, 1913, Mitchell Papers; Spratt, *Thurber, Texas*, p. 7.

26. W. K. Gordon to P. R. Stewart, Oct. 4, Nov. 1, 1910, W. K. Gordon to John W.

Ward, Oct. 31, 1910, W. K. Gordon to T. L. Lewis, Nov. 1, 1910, all in Mitchell Papers.

27. Discussion of Matter of Laying All Mines Idle November 1st, by Miners, Account Train Being Late on Previous Day in Committee Meeting, Nov. 28, 1910, Thurber, Texas, Decision—Train, Thurber, John Mitchell to P. R. Stewart and W. K. Gordon, June 29, 1911, both in Mitchell Papers.

28. Decision on Screens, June 29, 1911, John Mitchell to W. K. Gordon and P. R. Stewart, Decision on Engineers, John Mitchell to P. R. Stewart and W. K. Gordon, June 29, 1911, W. K. Gordon to John Mitchell, July 5, 1911, telegram, Ed Cunningham, W. K. Gordon to John Mitchell, July 25, July 26, 1912, John Mitchell to Cunningham and Gordon, July 26, July 27, 1912, all in Mitchell Papers.

29. W. K. Gordon to Edgar L. Marston, Aug. 27, 1911, W. K. Gordon, Jr. Papers; Mine Payrolls, 1904–21. A 1901 Texas law prohibited payment of wages in scrip but not its use between paydays for "advances" on the employees' request (*Bulletin of the Department of Labor,* no. 43 [Nov., 1902]: 1318).

30. Copy, Department of State, State of Texas, H.B. 15, "An Act Providing for the health and safety of persons in and around mines and for creating a state Mining Board and the office of State Mining Inspector and defining the duties of such inspector (enacted 30th Legislature, Jan. 8, 1907–Apr. 12, 1907), W. K. Gordon, Jr. Papers; *Twenty-Second Annual Report of the Commissioner of Labor, 1907,* "Labor Laws of the United States," pp. 1290, 1299–1302; Bureau of Labor Statistics of the State of Texas, *Second Biennial Report, 1911–1912,* pp. 221–30; *Haney* v. *Texas & Pacific Coal Co.* (no. 8929), *Southwestern Reporter* 207 (1918): 375–82; *Texas & Pacific Coal Co.* v. *Davies et al., Southwestern Reporter* 92 (1906): 275; *Texas & Pacific Coal Co.* v. *Choate, Southwestern Reporter* 159 (1913): 1058–59; *Texas & Pacific Coal Co.* v. *Beall et al., Southwestern Reporter* 144 (1912): 363–64; *Texas & Pacific Coal Co.* v. *Kowsikowski, Southwestern Reporter* 118 (1909): 829–31; *Texas & Pacific Coal Co.* v. *Gibson* (no. 8256), *Southwestern Reporter* 180 (1915): 1134–38; *Texas & Pacific Coal Co.* v. *Sherbly* (no. 938), *Southwestern Reporter* 212 (1919): 758–61; W. K. Gordon to Edgar L. Marston, June 24, 1916, W. K. Gordon, Jr. Papers. The *Second Biennial Report* of the Bureau of Labor Statistics listed injuries or deaths in Texas coal mines in the period 1911–12 from two gas explosions, two premature blasts, five roof collapses (falling rock), one fall down an elevator shaft, and one underground pit car accident.

31. *Stephenville Empire (Tribune),* Mar. 15, Apr. 5, 1912, Aug. 23, Nov. 29, Dec. 3, 1915, Aug. 30, 1918, Nov. 16, 1923; John Zinanni, Biographical Data Information Sheet; *First Biennial Report of the Bureau of Labor Statistics of the State of Texas, 1909–1910,* p. 136, reported $3,600 in sick benefits paid by United Mine Workers' Local 2763 (reporting 479 members) and $110 in funeral benefits during 1909; United States Department of Labor, Bureau of Labor Statistics, *Monthly Review* (Feb., 1917): 266–67, lists a worker's compensation act in Texas that became operative Sept. 1, 1913. The law did not require employers to adhere to the act, but those who did were required to report all accidents. See footnote 30 for court cases involving damage payments.

32. The *Stephenville Empire (Tribune),* Sept. 8, Oct. 6, 1916; USGS, *Mineral Resources of the United States, 1904,* p. 552, *1905,* p. 678, *1906,* pp. 602, 726, *1907,* p. 49, *1908,* part 2, Nonmetallic Products, p. 177, *1909,* part 2, Nonmetals, pp. 39, 179, *1910,* part 2, Nonmetals, pp. 46, 201, *1911,* part 2, Nonmetals, p. 51, *1912,* part 2, Nonmetals, pp. 52–53, 206, *1913,* pp. 757–58, 905, *1914,* part 2, Nonmetals, pp.

620, 726–27, *1915*, part 2, Nonmetals, p. 366, *1916*, part 2, Nonmetals, pp. 916, 980, *1917*, part 2, Nonmetals, p. 937, *1918*, part 2, Nonmetals, p. 723; Bruce Gentry, "Texas," *Coal Age* 13 (Jan. 19, 1918): 99; idem, "Texas," *Coal Age* 15 (Jan. 16, 1919): 91.

33. USGS, *Mineral Resources of the United States, 1914*, p. 726.

34. Edgar L. Marston to W. K. Gordon, May 22, 1915, W. K. Gordon, Jr. Papers; the *Stephenville Empire (Tribune)*, Nov. 30, 1917; Minutes, Texas & Pacific Coal Company, Apr. 17, 1918, Texas and Pacific Coal Company Records. Net profits for the Texas Pacific Mercantile & Manufacturing Company between 1915 and 1923 were 1915, $94,844.25; 1916, $99,294.98; 1917, $125,633.06; 1918, $151,253.71; 1919, $197,600.63; 1920, $183,060.00; 1921, $64,796.40; 1922, $16,523.81; 1923, $43,884.26. Until 1921, the mercantile made a considerable profit off of the residents, although coal production had declined (Research Notes, Literary Productions, Floyd Papers).

35. USGS, *Mineral Resources of the United States, 1904*, pp. 552–53, *1905*, pp. 678–79, *1906*, pp. 725–26, *1907*, pp. 186–87, *1908*, pp. 176–78, *1909*, pp. 178–79, *1910*, pp. 201–202, *1912*, pp. 205–207, *1913*, pp. 904–907, *1914*, pp. 726–28, *1915*, pp. 423–24, *1916*, pp. 980–81, *1917*, pp. 1034–36, *1918*, pp. 799–800, *1921*, part 2, Nonmetals, pp. 644–46, *1922*, part 2, Nonmetals, pp. 655–56, *1923*, part 2, Nonmetals, pp. 534, 561–66, 570–71, 731–33; Gordon to Marston, Apr. 8, Apr. 11, 1908, W. K. Gordon, Jr. Papers; *First Biennial Report of the Bureau of Labor Statistics of the State of Texas*, p. 145; Agreement and Scale of Wages between the Texas & Pacific Coal Company, the Strawn Coal Mining Company, Mt. Marion Coal Mining Company, and the Bridgeport Coal Company and the United Mine Workers of America, District 21, June 1, 1910, to Mar. 31, 1912, p. 21, Miscellaneous File, Texas and Pacific Coal Company Records; Minutes, Joint Conference between Texas Miners and Operators, Thurber, Texas, May 28–29, 1910, W. K. Gordon, Jr. Papers; Agreement and Scale of Wages between the Texas & Pacific Coal Company, Strawn Coal Company, Belknap Coal Company, Bridgeport Coal Company, Wise County Coal Company, Sally Alice Coal Company, and United Mine Workers of America, District 21, Aug. 1, 1914, to Sept. 1, 1916, p. 18, Hanraty Papers; "Texas Tonnage Rate So High That Increase Is Forty Cents per Ton," *Coal Age* 18 (May 6, 1920): 953; "Despite Steady Work Texas Mine Workers Ask for Increased Pay," *Coal Age* 18 (Sept. 30, 1920): 696; "Texas Miners Get Raise in Tonnage Rate," *Coal Age* 18 (Oct. 28, 1920): 896; Bruce Gentry, "Texas." *Coal Age* 11 (Jan. 13, 1917): 61; Mine Payrolls, 1904–26.

36. Financial Statement, Aug. 15, 1896, "Special Deposits, Miners ($15,876.86)," W. K. Gordon, Jr. Papers; Minutes, Meeting of Board of Directors, July 25, 1902, Texas and Pacific Coal Company Records (mentions miners' deposits invested by Marston); Dodson to Floyd, Floyd Papers; Claude Joe Marchioni interview, Thurber Collection.

37. Verbatim Minutes, Meeting, Texas Committee on Coal Production, Council of National Defense, Hotel Worth, Fort Worth, Texas, Aug. 20, 1917, pp. 2–3, W. K. Gordon, Jr. Papers; Laslett, *Labor and the Left*, p. 223.

38. *Report of the United States Coal Commission*, "Bituminous Coal," p. 1340; "Texas Tonnage Rate So High That Increase Is Forty Cents per Ton," p. 953; "Despite Steady Work Texas Mine Workers Ask for Increased Pay," p. 696; "Texas Miners Get Raise in Tonnage Rate," p. 896; USGS, *Mineral Resources of the United States, 1922*, p. 443; Bruce Gentry, "Texas," *Coal Age* 17 (Jan. 15, 1920): 130.

39. The *Stephenville Empire (Tribune)*, Sept. 16, 1921; "No Wage Reduction in

Texas—And No Work," *Coal Age* 20 (Aug. 18, 1921): 270; *Report of the United States Coal Commission,* "Bituminous Coal," p. 1341; "Fight for Open Shop Started in Texas Mines," *Coal Age* 20 (Oct. 13, 1921): 615; Lawrence Santi, interview with George N. Green.

40. Poster, "Important Notice" (Sept. 19, 1921), W. K. Gordon, Jr. Papers; Sydney A. Hale, "Miners' Union Is Disintegrating in Southwest, Thanks to Policy of 'No Backward Step,'" *Coal Age* 28 (Oct. 29, 1925): 596; McCorkle, Santi interviews, Thurber Collection; William K. Gordon, Jr., interview, June 9, 1985.

41. W. K. Gordon to Edgar L. Marston, Mar. 1, 1917, W. K. Gordon Papers, 1911–21, and Undated (Southwest Collection, Texas Tech University, Lubbock, Texas), hereafter referred to as Gordon Papers. As Gordon's correspondence with Marston reveals, Ruth Allen erroneously described Gordon as having "no profound personal objection to labor organization" in *Chapters in the History of Organized Labor in Texas* (see p. 97). Gordon's negotiating ability is recorded in minutes of the Joint Conference between Texas Miners and Operators, Thurber, Texas, May 28–29, 1910, and Report of Joint Conference, Texas Mines and Operators, Fort Worth, Texas, Mar. 3, 1914, W. K. Gordon, Jr. Papers; Woodman to Owens, Apr. 22, 1940, Gower to Owens, Apr. 12, 1940, Gower Letters; Gower to Gentry, Aug. 14, 1944, in Gentry, "Thurber," p. 234; Brown, Biographical Data Information Sheet; Franks, Solignani interviews, Thurber Collection.

42. "A Brief History of the Bituminous Coal Mining Industry of Texas" (1921), W. K. Gordon, Jr. Papers; Marston quoted in Richard Mason, "Ranger and the First West Texas Drilling Boom," *West Texas Historical Association Year Book* 58 (1982): 56.

43. *Fort Worth Star Telegram,* Dec. 16, 1973; John Stricklin Spratt, *The Road to Spindletop: Economic Change in Texas, 1875–1901,* p. 262.

44. "Texas Unaffected by Strike Developments; Large Mines Operate Open-Shop," *Coal Age* 22 (Sept. 14, 1922): 417; "Strike Is Practically Complete in Union Fields," *Coal Age* 21 (Apr. 6, 1922): 589; "Coal Production in Texas and Wyoming in 1925," *Coal Age* 31 (Jan. 20, 1927): 98; USGS, *Mineral Resources of the United States, 1922,* p. 441; Mine Payrolls, 1921–26.

45. Texas Pacific Coal and Oil Company, Annual Reports, 1919, 1921, 1922, 1923, 1927, 1928, 1937, "The Story of Texas Pacific Coal and Oil Company, 1888–1955," Miscellaneous File, Texas and Pacific Coal Company Records; Santi, interview with Green.

46. Bruce Gentry, "Texas" (Jan. 15, 1920), p. 131; Solignani, Franks interviews, Thurber Collection; Zinanni, Biographical Data Information Sheet; Mary Jane Gentry, "Thurber," pp. 201–203.

47. Annie Cathcart, Biographical Data Information Sheet.

48. Lawrence Santi quoted in *Forth Worth Star Telegram,* Dec. 16, 1973.

CONCLUSION

1. *Report of the United States Coal Commission; Reports of the Immigration Commission: Immigrants in Industries;* USGS, *Mineral Resources of the United States, 1882–1926.* See also George Stanley McGovern, "The Colorado Coal Strike, 1913–1914"; Allan Kent Powell, "The 'Foreign Element' and the 1903–4 Carbon County Coal Miners' Strike," *Utah Historical Quarterly* 43 (Spring, 1975): 125–54; Powell, *The Next*

Time We Strike; David Alan Corbin, *Life, Work, and Rebellion in the Coal Fields: The Southern West Virginia Miners, 1880–1922;* Miller and Sharpless, *The Kingdom of Coal;* Mathews, "An Immigrant Community in Indian Territory"; McCormick, "A Comparative Study of Coal Mining Communities in Southern Illinois and Southeastern Ohio in the Late Nineteenth Century."

2. Telegram, Marston to Mitchell, Dec. 16, 1903, Mitchell Papers.

3. The tragic militia attack on striking tent city occupants at Ludlow left two strikers and a boy killed in the initial confrontation and two women and eleven children dead in the aftermath of that incident when the troops torched the camp. A furiously violent response against mine guard camps and the hated state militia resulted. Such events occurred in the midst of a decade-long effort by southern Colorado coal miners to win recognition of the United Mine Workers' Union and concessions from the Rockefeller-owned Colorado Fuel and Iron Company. The presence of the detested Baldwin-Felts detective agency, the company's complete intransigence, the imposition of martial law by a governor unsympathetic to the workers' deep-felt grievances and difficult condition, and the deportation, arrest, and brutalization of striking workers set the stage for a violent encounter that shocked the nation but won no immediate success for coal miners seeking union recognition. For a complete account, see McGovern, "The Colorado Coal Strike, 1913–1914."

4. Gower to Owens, Jan. 28, 1941, Gower Letters.

5. Gordon to Marston, Dec. 24, 1906, W. K. Gordon, Jr. Papers; Data submitted by W. K. Gordon, 28; Gentry, "Thurber," p. 102.

6. Gower to Gentry, Aug. 14, 1944, in Gentry, "Thurber," p. 227.

Bibliography

MANUSCRIPT SOURCES

Floyd, Willie M. Papers. Southwest Collection, Texas Tech University, Lubbock, Texas.

Gordon, William K., Jr. Papers. William K. Gordon, Jr., Fort Worth, Texas.

Gordon, W. K. Papers. Southwest Collection, Texas Tech University, Lubbock, Texas.

Hanraty, Peter. Papers. Archives and Manuscripts Division, Oklahoma Historical Society, Oklahoma City.

Hart, Miles B. Papers. Nita Stewart Haley Memorial Library, Midland, Texas.

Indian/Pioneer History Collection. Archives and Manuscripts Division, Oklahoma Historical Society, Oklahoma City.

Johnson, William Whipple. Papers. Southwest Collection, Texas Tech University, Lubbock, Texas.

Labor Movement in Texas Collection, 1845–1943. Barker Texas History Center, University of Texas at Austin.

Mitchell, John. Papers. Catholic University of America, Washington, D.C.

Sanborn Fire Insurance Map Collection. Barker Texas History Center, University of Texas at Austin.

Texas and Pacific Coal Company Records. Southwest Collection, Texas Tech University, Lubbock, Texas.

Thurber Collection. Texas Labor Archives, Special Collections, University of Texas at Arlington.

Thurber, Texas Collection. Southwest Collection, Texas Tech University, Lubbock, Texas.

Webb, Walter Prescott. Papers. Barker Texas History Center, University of Texas at Austin.

Woodman, C. W. Papers. Texas Labor Archives, Special Collections, University of Texas at Arlington.

INTERVIEWS

Conn, Daisy, Interview by Ann Clark. Fort Worth, Texas, August 7, 1967. Thurber, Texas Collection, Southwest Collection, Texas Tech University.

Franks, Johnnie. Interview by Charles Townsend. April 1, 1967. Thurber, Texas Collection, Southwest Collection, Texas Tech University.

Gordon, William K., Jr. Interview by James C. Maroney, Jan Hart, and Marilyn Rhinehart. Fort Worth, Texas, June 9, 1985.

Kostiha, Walter. Interview by Richard Mason. Strawn, Texas, March 5, 1980. Thurber, Texas Collection, Southwest Collection, Texas Tech University.

Lishman, Nell Turbow. Interview by Lou Scoggins. N.p., May 10, 1967. Thurber, Texas Collection, Southwest Collection, Texas Tech University.

McCorkle, John. Interview by Mr. and Mrs. Spoede. Strawn, Texas, August 10, 1967. Thurber, Texas Collection, Southwest Collection, Texas Tech University.

Santi, Lawrence. Interview. Mingus, Texas, n.d. Thurber, Texas Collection, Southwest Collection, Texas Tech University.

Santi, Lawrence. Interview by George N. Green. Mingus, Texas, February 15, 1974. Oral History Interviews, Texas Labor Archives, Special Collections, University of Texas at Arlington.

Solignani, Geno. Interview by Richard Mason. Strawn, Texas, March 5, 1980. Thurber, Texas Collection, Southwest Collection, Texas Tech University.

Studdard, George B. Interview by Richard Mason. Fort Worth, Texas, February 13, 1981. Thurber, Texas Collection, Southwest Collection, Texas Tech University.

LOCAL, STATE, AND NATIONAL GOVERNMENT RECORDS: UNPUBLISHED

Adjutant General Records. State Archives, Texas State Library, Austin.

Commons, John R., United States Commission of Industrial Relations, material related to U.S. Senate, *Industrial Relations; Final Report and Testimony Submitted to Congress by the Commission on Industrial Relations Created by the Act of August 23, 1912.* 64th Cong., 1st Sess. 1916, Document no. 415. State Historical Society of Wisconsin, Madison, Wisconsin. Microfilm set. University of Houston, Houston, Texas.

Computer-Assisted Statistical Analysis of Data Base, Thurber, Texas, 1910 (based on Thirteenth Census, Population Schedule, manuscript copy). Rhinehart Collection, Houston, Texas.

Computer-Assisted Statistical Analysis of Data Base, Thurber, Texas, 1900 (based on Twelfth Census, Population Schedule, manuscript copy). Rhinehart Collection, Houston, Texas.

County Superintendent's School Record, 1890–1937. Local Records Division, Texas State Library, Depository, Tarleton State University, Stephenville, Texas.

General School Fund, 1884–96. Local Records Division, Texas State Library, Depository, Tarleton State University, Stephenville, Texas.

J. W. Connaughton v. *Texas & Pacific Coal Company.* Case no. 3161 (1899), Court of Civil Appeals, Second Supreme Judicial District of Texas (Fort Worth). Trial transcript. Clerk's Office, Texas Court of Civil Appeals, 2d District, Fort Worth, Texas.

Naturalization Records, 1886–1910, 1905. District Clerk's Office, Erath County Courthouse, Stephenville, Texas. Microfilm. Tarleton State University, Stephenville.

Record Declarations of Citizenship, 1894–1906. Districk Clerk's Office, Erath County Courthouse, Stephenville, Texas. Microfilm. Tarleton State University, Stephenville.

Records of Naturalization, 1892–1905. District Clerk's Office, Erath County Courthouse, Stephenville, Texas. Microfilm. Tarleton State University, Stephenville.

Texas & Pacific Coal Company v. *Thomas Lawson.* Case no. 346, Supreme Court of Texas Records, 1838–1945. Trial transcript. State Archives, Texas State Library, Austin.

Texas Election Returns, Erath County, Record of Elections, 1886–1924. Local Records Division, Texas State Library, Depository, Tarleton State University, Stephenville, Texas.

Thirteenth Census of the United States, 1910, Population Schedule, Thurber, Erath County, Texas. Microfilm of manuscript copy. Library of Congress, Washington, D.C.

Twelfth Census of the United States, 1900, Population Schedule, Thurber, Erath County, Texas. Microfilm of manuscript copy. Library of Congress, Washington, D.C.

GOVERNMENT PUBLICATIONS

Bureau of Labor Statistics of the State of Texas. *Fifth Biennial Report 1917–1918.* Austin: Von Boeckmann-Jones Co., 1919.

———. *Fourth Biennial Report 1915–1916.* Austin: Von Boeckmann-Jones Co., 1917.

———. *Second Biennial Report 1911–1912.* Austin: Von Boeckmann-Jones Co., 1912.

———. *Third Biennial Report 1913–1914.* Austin: Von Boeckmann-Jones Co., 1915.

"Coal Mine Fatalities in the United States, 1915, and during the period 1870 to 1914." *Monthly Review of the United States Bureau of Labor Statistics* 3 (August, 1916): 233–44.

Dublin, Louis I. *Causes of Death by Occupation.* U.S. Department of Labor, Bureau of Labor Statistics, no. 207. Washington, D.C.: Government Printing Office, 1917.

First Biennial Report of the Bureau of Labor Statistics of the State of Texas 1909–1910. Austin: Von Boeckmann-Jones Co., 1910.

General Land Office. State of Texas. Austin, Texas. "Erath County, Texas" (1879). Map. Geography and Map Division, Library of Congress, Washington, D.C.

———. State of Texas. Austin, Texas. "Map of Erath County" (1896). Geography and Map Division, Library of Congress, Washington, D.C.

Hall, Clarence, and Walter O. Snelling. *Coal Mine Accidents: Their Causes and Prevention.* Department of the Interior, United States Geological Survey Bulletin no. 333. Washington, D.C.: Government Printing Office, 1907.

Haney v. Texas & Pacific Coal Co. (no. 8929). *Southwestern Reporter* 207 (1918): 375–82.

"Labor Laws, Acts of 1901." *Bulletin of the Department of Labor,* No. 43. Washington, D.C.: Government Printing Office, 1902.

"Laws Relating to Employment of Children." *Bulletin of the Bureau of Labor,* no. 62. Washington, D.C.: Government Printing Office, 1906.

Magnusson, Leifur. "Company Housing in the Bituminous Coal Fields." *Monthly Labor Review* 10 (April, 1920): 1045–52.

———. "Employers' Housing in the United States," *Monthly Labor Review* 5 (November, 1917): 869–94.

———. "Sanitary Aspects of Company Housing." *Monthly Labor Review* 8 (January, 1919): 289–99.

———. United States Department of Labor, Bureau of Labor Statistics. *Housing by Employers in the United States.* Washington, D.C.: Government Printing Office, 1920.

Nineteenth Annual Report of the United States Geological Survey, 1897–1898. Part 4, *Mineral Resources of the United States, 1897, Metallic Products, Coal, and Coke.* Washington, D.C.: Government Printing Office, 1898.

Report of the Adjutant General of the State of Texas for 1889–1890. Austin: Henry Hutchings, State Printer, 1890.

Report of the United States Coal Commission. 5 parts. 68th Cong. 2d Sess., Senate Document no. 195. Serial Sets 8402–8403. Washington, D.C.: Government Printing Office, 1925

Reports of the Immigration Commission: Immigrants in Industries. 42 vols., 25 parts. 61st Cong. 2d Sess., Senate Document no. 633. Serial Sets 5667–5684. Washington, D.C.: Government Printing Office, 1911.

Seventeenth Annual Report of the United States Geological Survey, 1895–1896. Part 3, *Mineral Resources of the United States, 1895, Metallic Products and Coal.* Washington, D.C.: Government Printing Office, 1896.

Sewall, Hannah R. "Child Labor in the United States." *Bulletin of the Bureau of Labor* 52 (May, 1904): 485–637.

Sixteenth Annual Report of the Commissioner of Labor, 1901. "Strikes and Lockouts." Washington, D.C.: Government Printing Office, 1901.

Sixteenth Annual Report of the United States Geological Survey. Part 4, *Mineral Resources of the United States, 1894, Nonmetallic Products.* Washington, D.C.: Government Printing Office, 1895.

Sixth Biennial Report of the Bureau of Labor Statistics of the State of Texas 1919–1920. Austin: Von Boeckmann-Jones, 1921.

Smith, Larry Lane (comp. for Railroad Commission of Texas Surface Mining and Reclamation Division). *Historical Coal Mines in Texas, an Annotated Bibliography.* Austin: N.p., © 1979.

Stoddard, C. F. "The Bituminous Coal Strike." *Monthly Labor Review* 9 (December, 1919): 61–78.

Tenth Annual Report of the Commissioner of Labor, 1894. "Strikes and Lockouts." 2 vols. Washington, D.C.: Government Printing Office, 1896.

"Texas." *Monthly Review of the U.S. Bureau of Labor Statistics* 4 (February, 1917): 266–67.

Texas & Pacific Coal Co. v. Beall et al. Southwestern Reporter 144 (1912): 363–64.

Texas & Pacific Coal Co. v. Choate. Southwestern Reporter 159 (1913): 1058–59.

Texas & Pacific Coal Co. v. Davies et al. Southwestern Reporter 92 (1906): 275.

Texas & Pacific Coal Co. v. Gibson (no. 8256). *Southwestern Reporter* 180 (1915): 1134–38.

Texas & Pacific Coal Co. v. Kowsikowsiki. Southwestern Reporter 118 (1909): 829–31.

Texas & Pacific Coal Co. v. Sherbly (no. 938). *Southwestern Reporter* 212 (1919): 758–61.

The Texas Civil Appeals Reports: Cases Argued and Adjudged in the Courts of Civil Appeals of the State of Texas during the Months of December, 1898, and January, February and March, 1899 20 (1900): 642–46.

Third Annual Report of the Commission of Labor, 1887. "Strikes and Lockouts." Washington, D.C.: Government Printing Office, 1888.

Twentieth Annual Report of the United States Geological Survey, 1898–99. Part 6, *Mineral Resources of the United States, 1898, Metallic Products, Coal, and Coke.* Washington, D.C.: Government Printing Office, 1899.

Twenty-first Annual Report of the Commissioner of Labor, 1906. "Strikes and Lockouts." Washington, D.C.: Government Printing Office, 1907.

Twenty-first Annual Report of the United States Geological Survey, 1899–1900. Part 6, *Mineral Resources of the United States, 1899, Metallic Products, Coal, and Coke.* Washington, D.C.: Government Printing Office, 1901.

Twenty-second Annual Report of the Commissioner of Labor, 1907. "Labor Laws of the United States." Washington, D.C.: Government Printing Office, 1908.

Twenty-second Annual Report of the United States Geological Survey, 1900–1901. Part 3, *Coal, Oil, Cement.* Washington, D.C.: Government Printing Office, 1902.

Twenty-third Annual Report of the Commissioner of Labor, 1908. "Workmen's Insurance and Benefit Funds in the United States." Washington, D.C.: Government Printing Office, 1909.

United States Department of Commerce. Bureau of the Census. *Census of Manufactures, 1914.* Washington, D.C.: Government Printing Office, 1918.

———. *Fifteenth Census of the United States: Manufactures: 1929.* Washington, D.C.: Government Printing Office, 1933.

———. *Fifteenth Census of the United States: 1930, Population.* Washington, D.C.: Government Printing Office, 1932.

———. *Fourteenth Census of the United States Taken in the Year 1920, Manufactures: 1919.* Washington, D.C.: Government Printing Office, 1923.

———. *Fourteenth Census of the United States Taken in the Year 1920, Population: 1920.* Washington, D.C.: Government Printing Office, 1922.

———. *Thirteenth Census of the United States Taken in the Year 1910, Manufactures: 1909.* Washington, D.C.: Government Printing Office, 1912.

———. *Thirteenth Census of the United States Taken in the Year 1910, Population: 1910.* Washington, D.C.: Government Printing Office, 1913.

United States Department of Labor. Bulletin no. 604, *History of Wages in the United States from Colonial Times to 1928.* Washington, D.C.: Government Printing Office, 1934.

———. Bulletin no. 186, *Review of Labor Legislation of 1915.* Washington, D.C.: Government Printing Office, 1915.

———. Bureau of Labor Statistics, no. 207, *Causes of Death by Occupation.* Washington, D.C.: Government Printing Office, 1917.

United States Department of the Interior. Census Office. *Compendium of the Eleventh Census, Population: 1890.* Washington, D.C.: Government Printing Office, 1892.

———. Census Office. *Twelfth Census of the United States Taken in the Year 1900, Manufactures.* Washington, D.C.: Government Printing Office, 1902.

———. Census Office. *Twelfth Census of the United States Taken in the Year 1900, Population.* Washington, D.C.: Government Printing Office, 1901.

———. Geological Survey. Map, Strawn East, Texas Provisional Edition, 1984.

———. United States Geological Survey. *Coal-Mine Accidents: Their Causes and Prevention.* Washington, D.C.: Government Printing Office, 1907.

———. United States Geological Survey. *Mineral Resources of the United States,* 1882–1926. Washington, D.C.: Government Printing Office, various years.

Warne, Frank Julian, "The Union Movement among Coal-Mine Workers." *Bulletin of the Bureau of Labor* 51 (March, 1904): 380–414.

NEWSPAPERS

Abilene Reporter-News, September 4, 1966.
Dallas Morning News, December, 1888, June, 1894, September, 1903.
Fort Worth (Daily) Gazette, December, 1888–January, 1889 (State Archives, Texas State Library, Austin).
Fort Worth Star Telegram, December 16, 1973.
Fort Worth Telegram, September 20, 1903 (State Archives, Texas State Library, Austin).
Houston Labor Journal, June 4, 1910 (Labor Movement in Texas Collection, Barker Texas History Center, University of Texas at Austin).
Journal of United Labor, March, 1887–October, 1889.
National Labor Tribune, January, 1887–March, 1889.
Stephenville Empire (Tribune), 1888–1922 (Secured Collections, Tarleton State University, Stephenville, Texas).
Texas Miner, 1894–97 (Secured Collections, Tarleton State University, Stephenville, Texas).
Texas Mining and Trade Journal, 1898–1900 (Secured Collections, Tarleton State University, Stephenville, Texas).
Union Banner, April, 1909 (Labor Movement in Texas Collection, Barker Texas History Center, University of Texas at Austin).
United Mine Workers' Journal, September–October, 1903 (Labor Movement in Texas Collection, Barker Texas History Center, University of Texas at Austin).

BOOKS, THESES, DISSERTATIONS, AND
PUBLISHED PROCEEDINGS

Acker, Eva. "The Development of the Mineral Resources of Texas." Master's thesis, East Texas State Teachers' College, 1939.
Aldrich, Gene. "A History of the Coal Industry in Oklahoma to 1907." Ph.D. diss., University of Oklahoma, 1952.
Allen, James B. *The Company Town in the American West.* Norman: University of Oklahoma Press, 1966.
Allen, Ruth A. *Chapters in the History of Organized Labor in Texas.* Austin: University of Texas, 1941.
Aurand, Harold W. *From the Molly Maguires to the United Mine Workers: The Social Ecology of an Industrial Union, 1869–1897.* Philadelphia: Temple University Press, 1971.
———. *Population Change and Social Continuity: Ten Years in a Coal Town.* Selinsgrove, Pa.: Susquehanna University Press, 1986.

Baker, T. Lindsay, *The First Polish Americans: Silesian Settlements in Texas.* College Station: Texas A&M University Press, 1979.

Belfiglio, Cav. Valentine J. *The Italian Experience in Texas.* Austin: Eakin Press, 1983.

Berthoff, Rowland T. *British Immigrants in Industrial America.* Cambridge: Harvard University Press, 1953.

Bodnar, John. *The Transplanted: A History of Immigrants in Urban America.* Bloomington: Indiana University Press, 1985.

Boothe, Stephanie Elise. "The Relationship between Radicalism and Ethnicity in Southern Illinois Coal Fields, 1870–1940." Ph.D. diss., Illinois State University, 1983.

Brandes, Stuart. *American Welfare Capitalism, 1880–1940.* Chicago: University of Chicago Press, 1970.

Brody, David. *Steelworkers in America: The Nonunion Era.* Cambridge: Harvard University Press, 1960.

———. *Workers in Industrial America: Essays on the Twentieth Century Struggle.* New York: Oxford University Press, 1980.

Brown, Ronald C. *Hard Rock Miners: The Intermountain West, 1860–1920.* College Station: Texas A&M University Press, 1979.

Cantor, Milton, ed. *American Working Class Culture: Explorations in American Labor and Social History.* Westport, Conn.: Greenwood Press, 1979.

Caroli, Betty Boyd. *Italian Repatriation from the United States, 1900–1914.* New York: Center for Migration Studies, 1973.

Cawyer, Shirley Brittain, and Weldon I. Hudson, comps. *Erath County, Texas Cemetery Inscriptions.* 3 vols. 1973. Reprint. N.p.: 1983.

Corbin, David Alan. *Life, Work and Rebellion in the Coal Fields: The Southern West Virginia Miners, 1880–1922.* Urbana: University of Illinois Press, 1981.

Cumbler, John T. *Working Class Community in Industrial America: Work, Leisure, and Struggle in Two Industrial Cities, 1880–1930.* Westport, Conn.: Greenwood Press, 1979.

Ehrlich, Richard L., ed. *Immigrants in Industrial America, 1850–1920.* Charlottesville: University Press of Virginia, 1977.

Eller, Ronald D. *Miners, Millhands, and Mountaineers: Industrialization of the Appalachian South, 1880–1930.* Knoxville: University of Tennessee Press, 1982.

Erickson, Charlotte. *American Industry and the European Immigrant, 1861–1885.* New York: Russell and Russell, 1957.

Evans, Chris. *History of United Mine Workers of America from the Year 1860 to 1890.* 2 vols. Indianapolis: N.p., n.d.

Fenton, Edwin. *Immigrants and Unions, a Case Study: Italians and American Labor, 1870–1920.* New York: Arno Press, 1975.

Floyd, Willie M. "Thurber, Texas: An Abandoned Coal Field Town." Master's thesis, Southern Methodist University, 1939.

Foerster, Robert F. *The Italian Emigration of Our Times.* Cambridge: Harvard University Press, 1924.

Frisch, Michael F., and Daniel J. Walkowitz, eds. *Working Class America: Essays on Labor, Community, and American Society.* Urbana: University of Illinois Press, 1983.

Garlock, Jonathan, comp. *Guide to the Local Assemblies of the Knights of Labor.* Westport, Conn.: Greenwood Press, 1982.

Garner, John S. *The Model Company Town: Urban Design through Private Enterprise in Nineteenth Century New England.* Amherst: University of Massachusetts Press, 1984.

Gentry, Mary Jane. " Thurber: The Life and Death of a Texas Town." Master's thesis, University of Texas at Austin, 1946.

Gibson, Charles Mac. "Organized Labor in Texas from 1890–1900." Master's thesis, Texas Tech University, 1973.

Goodrich, Carter. *The Miner's Freedom: A Study of the Working Life in a Changing Industry.* Boston: Marshall Jones Co., 1925.

Green, James R. *Grass-Roots Socialism: Radical Movements in the Southwest, 1895–1943.* Baton Rouge: Louisiana State University Press, 1978.

————. *The World of the Worker: Labor in Twentieth-Century America.* New York: Hill and Wang, 1980.

Greene, Homer. *Coal and the Coal Mines.* New York: Houghton Mifflin, 1917.

Greene, Victor. *The Slavic Community on Strike: Immigrant Labor in Pennsylvania Anthracite.* Notre Dame, Ind.: University of Notre Dame Press, 1968.

Gutman, Herbert. *Work, Culture, and Society in Industrializing America: Essays in American Working-Class and Social History.* New York: Alfred A. Knopf, 1977.

Hale, Duane Kendall. "Prospecting and Mining on the Texas Frontier." Ph.D. diss., Oklahoma State University, 1977.

Hamilton, Walton H., and Helen R. Wright. *The Case of Bituminous Coal.* New York: Macmillan, 1926.

Hardman, Weldon B. *Fire in a Hole!* Gordon, Tex.: Thurber Historical Association, 1975.

Hareven, Tamara K. *Family Time and Industrial Time: The Relationship between the Family and Work in a New England Industrial Community.* Cambridge: Cambridge University Press, 1982.

Hewitt, William Phillip. "The Czechs in Texas: A Study of the Immigration and the Development of Czech Ethnicity, 1850–1920." Ph.D. diss., University of Texas, 1978.

Hobsbawm, Eric. *Primitive Rebels and Social Bandits*. Manchester, England: Norton, 1959.

Hunt, Edward Eyre; F. G. Tryon; and Joseph H. Willits, eds. *What the Coal Commission Found*. Baltimore: The Williams and Wilkins Co., 1925.

Kleinig, John. *Paternalism*. Totowa, N.J.: Rowman and Allenheld, 1984.

Knights of Labor. *Proceedings of the General Assembly of the Knights of Labor of America Thirteenth Regular Session, November 12–20, 1889*. Philadelphia: Journal of United Labor, 1890.

Koch, Carl, Jr. "A Historical Review of Compulsory School Attendance Laws and Child Labor Laws." Ed.D. diss., University of Wyoming, 1972.

Korson, George. *Coal Dust on the Fiddle: Songs and Stories of the Bituminous Industry*. Philadelphia: University of Pennsylvania Press, 1943.

Lantz, Herman R. *People of Coal Town*. New York: Columbia University Press, 1958.

Laslett, John H. M. *Labor and the Left: A Study of Socialist and Radical Influences in the American Labor Movement, 1881–1924*. New York: Basic Books, 1970.

Lord, Eliot; John J. D. Trenor; Samuel J. Barrows. *The Italian in America*. 1905. Reprint. Freeport, N.J.: Books for Libraries Press, 1970.

McCormick, Michael Ray. "A Comparative Study of Coal Mining Communities in Southern Illinois and Southeastern Ohio in the Late Nineteenth Century." Ph.D. diss., Ohio State University, 1978.

McCoy, Joseph G. *Historic Sketches of the Cattle Trade of the West and Southwest*. 1874. Reprint. Kansas City, Mo.: Ramsey, Millett and Hudson, 1951.

McGovern, George Stanley. "The Colorado Coal Strike, 1913–1914." Ph.D. diss., Northwestern University, 1953.

Machann, Clinton, and James W. Mendl. *Krasna Amerika: A Study of the Texas Czechs, 1851–1939*. Austin: Eakin Press, 1983.

McLaurin, Melton Alonzo. *Paternalism and Protest: Southern Cotton Mill Workers and Organized Labor, 1875–1905*. Westport, Conn.: Greenwood, 1971.

Maroney, James C. "Organized Labor in Texas, 1900–1929." Ph.D. diss., University of Houston, 1975.

Martin, Roscoe C. *The People's Party in Texas: A Study in Third-Party Politics*. 1933. Reprint. Austin: University of Texas Press, 1970.

Miller, Donald L., and Richard E. Sharpless. *The Kingdom of Coal: Work, Enterprise, and Ethnic Communities in the Mine Fields*. Philadelphia: University of Pennsylvania Press, 1985.

Montgomery, David. *Workers' Control in America: Studies in the History of Work, Technology and Labor Struggles*. New York: Cambridge University Press, 1979.

Morris, Homer Lawrence. *The Plight of the Bituminous Coal Miner.* Philadelphia: University of Pennsylvania Press, 1934.

Powell, Allan Kent. *The Next Time We Strike: Labor in Utah's Coal Fields, 1900–1903.* Logan: Utah State University Press, 1985.

Reese, James V. "The Worker in Texas, 1821–1876." Ph.D. diss., University of Texas, 1964.

Rikard, Marlene Hunt. "An Experiment in Welfare Capitalism: The Health Care Services of the Tennessee Coal, Iron and Railroad Company." Ph.D. diss., University of Alabama, 1983.

Rosenblum, Gerald. *Immigrant Workers: Their Impact on American Radicalism.* New York: Basic Books, 1973.

Rosenzweig, Roy. *Eight Hours for What We Will: Workers and Leisure in an Industrial City, 1870–1920.* Cambridge: Cambridge University Press, 1983.

Ryan, Frederick Lynne. *The Rehabilitation of Oklahoma Coal Mining Communities.* Norman: University of Oklahoma Press, 1935.

Spoede, Robert William. "William Whipple Johnson: An Enterprising Man." Master's thesis, Hardin-Simmons University, 1968.

Spratt, John S., Sr. *Thurber, Texas: The Life and Death of a Company Coal Town.* Edited by Harwood P. Hinton. Austin: University of Texas Press, 1986.

Spratt, John Stricklin. *The Road to Spindletop: Economic Change in Texas, 1875–1901.* Austin: University of Texas Press, 1970.

Suffern, Arthur. *The Coal Miners' Struggle for Industrial Status: A Study of the Evolution of Organized Relations and Industrial Principles in the Coal Industry.* New York: Macmillan, 1926.

———. *Conciliation and Arbitration in the Coal Industry of America.* New York: Houghton Mifflin, 1915.

Sullivan, W. J. L. *Twelve Years in the Saddle for Law and Order on the Frontiers of Texas.* 1909. Reprint. New York: Buffalo-Head Press, 1966.

Sutter, Ruth E. *The Next Place You Come To: A Historical Introduction to Communities in North America.* Englewood Cliffs, N.J.: Prentice-Hall, 1967.

Thompson, Eric P. *The Making of the English Working Class.* London: Random House, 1963.

United Mine Workers. *Proceedings of the Inter-State Convention of the United Mine Workers, Districts No. 14, 21, and 25, 1904.* N.p., n.d.

———. *Proceedings of the Twenty-Third Annual Convention of the United Mine Workers of America, 1912.* Indianapolis: Cheltenham-Aetna Press, 1912.

Walkowitz, Daniel J. *Worker City, Company Town: Iron and Cotton-Worker Protest in Troy and Cohoes, New York, 1855–84.* Urbana: University of Illinois Press. 1978.

Warne, Frank Julian. *The Coal Mine Workers: A Study in Labor Organization.* New York: Longmans, Green, and Co., 1905.

Weiss, Harold J., Jr. "'Yours to Command': Captain William J. McDonald and the Panhandle Rangers of Texas." Ph.D. diss., Indiana University, 1980.

Wilkins, Charles S. "Thurber: A Sociological Study of a Company-Owned Town." Master's thesis, University of Texas, 1929.

Winkler, Ernest William, ed. *Platforms of Political Parties in Texas.* Austin: University of Texas Press, 1916.

Wynn, David Robert. "Trade Unions and the 'New' Immigration: A Study of the United Mine Workers of America, 1890–1920." Ph.D. diss., University of London, 1976.

Yans-McLaughlin, Virginia. *Family and Community: Italian Immigrants in Buffalo, 1880–1930.* Ithaca, N.Y.: Cornell University Press, 1977.

Yearley, Clifton K., Jr. *Britons in American Labor: A History of the Influence of the United Kingdom Immigrants on American Labor, 1820–1914.* Baltimore: Johns Hopkins Press, 1957.

ARTICLES

Allen, James B. "The Company Town: A Passing Phase of Utah's Industrial Development." *Utah Historical Quarterly* 34 (1966): 138–60.

Barnhill, John. "Triumph of Will: The Coal Strike of 1899–1903." *The Chronicles of Oklahoma* 61 (Spring, 1983): 80–95.

Bauman, John F. "Ethnic Adaptation in a Southwestern Pennsylvania Coal Patch, 1910–1940." *Journal of Ethnic Studies* 7 (Fall, 1979): 1–23.

Bielinski, Leo S. "Beer, Booze, Bootlegging and Bocci Ball in Thurber-Mingus." *West Texas Historical Association Year Book* 59 (1983): 75–89.

Brody, David. "The Old Labor History and the New: In Search of an American Working Class." *Labor History* 20 (Winter, 1979): 111–26.

Brown, Kenny L. "Peaceful Progress: The Italians of Krebs." *The Chronicles of Oklahoma* 53 (Fall, 1975): 332–52.

Browning, David. "The Price of Progress: The Story of Thurber's Fate." *Texas Historian* 31 (September, 1970): 24–29.

Cinel, Dino. "The Seasonal Emigration of Italians in the Nineteenth Century: From Internal to International Destinations." *Journal of Ethnic Studies* 10 (Spring, 1982): 43–68.

"Coal Production in Texas and Wyoming in 1925." *Coal Age* 31 (January 20, 1927): 98.

Corn, Jacqueline Karnell. "'Dark as a Dungeon': Environment and Coal Miners' Health and Safety." *Environmental Review* 7 (1983): 257–68.

Cravens, John N. "Two Miners and Their Families in the Thurber-Strawn Coal

Mines, 1905–1918." *West Texas Historical Association Year Book* 45 (1969): 115–26.

Cybriwski, Roman A., and Charles Hardy III. "The Stetson Company and Benevolent Feudalism." *Pennsylvania Heritage* (Spring, 1981): 14–19.

Davis, Horace B. "Company Towns." *Encyclopedia of the Social Sciences,* vol. 4, pp. 119–23. New York: Macmillan, 1931.

"Despite Steady Work Texas Mine Workers Ask for Increased Pay." *Coal Age* 18 (September 30, 1920): 696.

Emmons, David M. "Immigrant Workers and Industrial Hazards: The Irish Miners of Butte, 1880–1919." *Journal of American Ethnic History* 5 (Fall, 1985): 41–64.

Fenton, Edwin. "Italians in the Labor Movement." *Pennsylvania History* 26 (April, 1959): 133–48.

"Fight for Open Shop Started in Texas Mines." *Coal Age* 20 (October 13, 1921): 615.

Floyd, Willie M. "Thurber, Texas, an Abandoned Coal Field Town." *Texas Geographic Magazine* 3 (Autumn, 1939): 1–21.

Friedberger, Mark, and Janice Reiff Webster. "Social Structure and State and Local History." *Western Historical Quarterly* 9 (July, 1978): 297–314.

Gentry, Bruce S. "Texas." *Coal Age* 11 (January 13, 1917): 61.

———. "Texas." *Coal Age* 13 (January 19, 1918): 99.

———. "Texas." *Coal Age* 15 (January 16, 1919): 91.

———. "Texas." *Coal Age* 17 (January 15, 1920): 130.

Glass, Brent D. "The Miner's World: Life and Labor at Gold Hill." *North Carolina Historical Review* 62 (October, 1985): 420–47.

Goldman, Robert, and John Wilson. "The Rationalization of Leisure." *Politics and Society* 7 (1977): 157–87.

Green, Jim. "Culture, Politics and Workers' Response to Industrialization in the US." *Radical America* 16 (1982): 101–28.

Hale, Douglas. "European Immigrants in Oklahoma." *The Chronicles of Oklahoma* 53 (Summer, 1975): 179–203.

Hale, Sydney A. "Miners' Union Is Disintegrating in Southwest, Thanks to Policy of 'No Backward Step,'" *Coal Age* 28 (October 29, 1925): 596.

Hall, Jacqueline Dowd; Robert Korstad; and James Leloudis. "Cotton Mill People: Work, Community, and Protest in the Textile South, 1880–1940." *American Historical Review* 91 (April, 1986): 245–86.

Hareven, Tamara K. "Family Time and Industrial Time: Family and Work in a Planned Corporation Town, 1900–1924," *Journal of Urban History* 1 (May, 1975): 365–89.

———. "Family and Work Patterns of Immigrant Laborers in a Planned Industrial Town, 1900–1930," In *Immigrants in Industrial America, 1850–1920,* edited by Richard L. Ehrlich, pp. 56–64. Charlottesville: University Press of Virginia, 1977.

Henderson, Dwight F. "The Texas Coal Mining Industry." *Southwestern Historical Quarterly* 68 (October, 1964): 207–19.

Hooks, Michael Q. "Thurber: A Unique Texas Community." *Panhandle-Plains Historical Review* 56 (1983): 1–17.

Kalisch, Philip A. "Ordeal of the Oklahoma Coal Miners." *The Chronicles of Oklahoma* 48 (Autumn, 1970): 331–40.

McAllister, S. B. "Building the Texas and Pacific Railroad West of Fort Worth." *West Texas Historical Association Year Book* 4 (June, 1928): 50–57.

Maroney, James C. "The Unionization of Thurber, 1903." *Red River Valley Historical Review* 4 (Spring, 1979): 27–32.

Mason, Richard. "Ranger and the First West Texas Drilling Boom." *West Texas Historical Association Year Book* 58 (1982): 49–66.

Mathews, Glenna. "An Immigrant Community in Indian Territory." *Labor History* 23 (Summer, 1982): 374–94.

Melish, John Howard. "The Church and the Company Town." *The Survey* 33 (December 5, 1914): 263.

Montgomery, David. "Gutman's Nineteenth Century America." *Labor History* 19 (Summer, 1978): 416–29.

———. "To Study the People: The American Working Class." *Labor History* 21 (Fall, 1980): 485–512.

Munn, Robert F. "The Development of Model Towns in the Bituminous Coal Fields." *West Virginia History* 40 (1979): 243–53.

"No Wage Reduction in Texas—And No Work." *Coal Age* 20 (August 18, 1921): 270.

Northrup, Herbert R. "The Negro and the United Mine Workers of America." *Southern Economic Journal* 9 (April, 1943): 313–26.

Notarianni, Philip F. "Italian Fraternal Organizations in Utah, 1897–1934." *Utah Historical Quarterly* 43 (Spring, 1975): 172–87.

Ozanne, Robert. "Trends in American Labor History." *Labor History* 21 (Fall, 1980: 513–21.

Padgitt, James T. "Captain Joseph C. Lea, the Father of Roswell." *West Texas Historical Association Year Book* 35 (October, 1959): 50–65.

Powell, Allan Kent. "The 'Foreign Element' and the 1903–4 Carbon County Coal Miners' Strike." *Utah Historical Quarterly* 43 (Spring, 1975): 125–54.

Powell, William E. "European Settlement in the Cherokee-Crawford Coal Field of Southeastern Kansas." *Kansas Historical Quarterly* 41 (Summer, 1975): 150–65.

Reese, James V. "Early History of Labor Organizations in Texas, 1838–1876." *Southwestern Historical Quarterly* 72 (July, 1968): 1–20.

Rhinehart, Marilyn, "'Underground Patriots': Thurber Coal Miners and the

Struggle for Individual Freedom, 1888–1903," *Southwestern Historical Quarterly* 92 (April, 1989): 509–42.

Ristow, Walter W. "U.S. Fire Insurance Maps, 1852–1968." *Surveying and Mapping* 30 (March, 1970): 19–41.

Ryan, Frederick L. "The Development of Coal Operators' Associations in the Southwest." *Southwestern Social Sciences Quarterly* 14 (June, 1933): 133–44.

Schatz, Ronald W. "Review Essay/Labor Historians, Labor Economics, and the Question of Synthesis." *Journal of American History* 71 (June, 1984): 93–100.

Senter, E. G. "A Pioneer Texas Industry." *Texas Farm and Ranch* 17 (January 22, 1898): 1–2.

Skaggs, Jimmy M. "To Build a Barony: Colonel Robert D. Hunter." *Arizona and the West* 15 (Autumn, 1973): 245–56.

Spoede, Robert William. "W. W. Johnson and the Beginnings of Coal Mining in the Strawn-Thurber Vicinity, 1880–1888." *West Texas Historical Association Year Book* 44 (October, 1968): 48–59.

"Strike Is Practically Complete in Union Fields." *Coal Age* 21 (April 6, 1922): 589.

"Texas Miners Get Raise in Tonnage Rate." *Coal Age* 18 (October 28, 1920): 896.

"Texas Tonnage Rate So High That Increase Is Forty Cents per Ton." *Coal Age* 18 (May 6, 1920): 953.

"Texas Unaffected by Strike Developments; Large Mines Operate Open-Shop." *Coal Age* 22 (September 14, 1922): 417.

"United Mine Workers' Convention." *Coal Age* 1 (February 3, 1912): 550.

Weitz, Eric D. "Class Formation and Labor Protest in the Mining Communities of Southern Illinois and the Ruhr, 1890–1925." *Labor History* 27 (Winter, 1985–86): 85–105.

"William Knox Gordon." In *Fort Worth and the Texas Northwest*, pp. 155–56. New York: Lewis Publishing Co., 1922.

Wolfle, Lee M. "Historical Reconstruction of Socialist Voting among Coal Miners, 1900–1940." *Historical Methods* 12 (Summer, 1979): 111–21.

Zeiger, Robert. "Workers and Scholars: Recent Trends in American Labor Historiography." *Labor History* 13 (Spring, 1972): 245–66.

Index

fire, 27, 34–35; and union records,
140n.16
firefighters, 22
folklore, mining, 26, 35
foremen, 22
Fort Worth (Tex.), 74
Freeman, T. W., quoted, 130n.28
French, 13
funerals, 61–62; expenses of, 35, 58,
141n.31

gambling, 65, 101
gas: natural, 115, 118; and underground
explosions, 33
gender, and education, 60
Germans, 13
Good Templar Society, 100
Goodwin, Frank, 34
Gordon, William K., 81, 92, 134n.77,
143n.41; arrested, 50–51; management
style of, 71–72, 114, 116; quoted, 23,
28, 52, 61, 84–85, 102–103, 109–10
Gordon (Tex.), 4–6, 72
Gould, Jay, 4, 72
Gower, Gomer, 25–26, 71, 80; quoted,
xvi, 8, 10, 42, 46, 59, 73, 77, 82, 91, 116
Gower, Thomas, xvi, 42
Green, R., *The World of the Worker,* 40
group consciousness, development of,
16–17. *See also* community, occupational
Gutman, Herbert, xv

Hall, Covington A., quoted, 77
Hamilton, Clint, 33
Hanraty, Peter, 87, 89, 117; quoted, 85–
86, 88
Hartford (Tex.), 86
hazards: and occupational community,
33, 35; underground, 20, 27, 34, 105,
118, 128n.51
health, of miners, 21
health care, 115, 141n.31; changes in, 90;
deductions for, 32, 35, 58–59
historians: economic, 110; labor, xv,
120n.3
history, labor, xv, 120n.3
Hogg, James S., 77, 82
holidays: public, 62–63, 86–87; self-
awarded, 28
Holland, James J., 79–80

hospital facilities, company, 32, 35, 58
Hotel Knox, 43
Household of Ruth, 64
household structure, 99; Italian, 43–44;
of miners, 16–17, 55–56
housing: company, 41–45, 95, 98–100,
128n.7, 129n.9; private, 42
Hughes, Tom, 33
Hulen, John A., 86
Hungarians, 13
Hunter, Robert Dickey: and Johnson
takeover, 6–11, 45, 122n.10; and labor
movement, 73–82; and local politics,
52–53; power of, 42, 46–49, 51, 76, 78;
quoted, 42, 45–46, 48, 73; retirement
of, 84; and wages, 25, 29; and welfare
capitalism, 57
Hunter Concert Band, 64
Hunter, Evans & Company, 7
Hunter Fishing and Boating Club, 63
Hunter Morning Star Church, 61,
130n.15
Hunter Rifles, 49
Hunter School, 59

Illinois, 73, 113
immigrants: and local politics, 54–55; as
miners, 12–16, 18, 55–56; numbers of,
xvi; occupations of, 93–97; and unionization, 85–86, 88, 117. *See also* nationalities
Immigration Commission, and coal industry, 47
Independence Day, celebration of, 62–
63
Independent Order of Foresters, 63
Independent Order of Good Templars,
63–64
Indiana, 73; mining in, 30
Indian Territory, 4, 84, 88
industrialization, and coal industry, 3–4
industrial workers: and legislation, 91;
and unionization, 88
Industrial Workers of the World, 102, 115
injuries, 33–35, 105, 141n.30
integration, racial, 45
Irish, 13–14, 18, 44, 71
Italian Hill, 44–46, 99, 129n.14
Italians, 13, 64, 93, 95; autonomy of,
101–103, 115; households of, 43–44, 99

A Way of Work and a Way of Life was composed into type on a Compu-graphic digital phototypesetter in eleven point Garamond with two points of spacing between the lines. Garamond was also selected for dis-play. The book was designed by Jim Billingsley, typeset by Metricomp, Inc., printed offset by Thomson-Shore, Inc., and bound by John H. Dek-ker & Sons, Inc. The paper on which this book is printed carries acid-free characteristics for an effective life of at least three hundred years.

TEXAS A&M UNIVERSITY PRESS : COLLEGE STATION